THE CASSELL
DICTIONARY OF
WORD AND
PHRASE ORIGINS

THE CASSELL
DICTIONARY OF
WORD AND PHRASE
ORIGINS

NIGEL REES

CASSELL

Cassell
Villiers House, 41/47 Strand
London WC2N 5JE

(©) Nigel Rees Productions Ltd 1987

First published 1987 as *Why Do We Say...?* by
Blandford Press Limited
Paperback edition published 1988
Cassell edition first published 1992

British Library Cataloguing-in-Publication Data
A catalogue entry for this book is
available from the British Library.

ISBN 0-304-32050-1

Printed and bound in Great Britain by
Biddles Ltd, Guildford and King's Lynn

PREFACE

'Why do we say . . .?' is the question behind every entry in *The Cassell Dictionary of Word and Phrase Origins*. Why do we say a person makes money 'hand over fist' or is the 'spitting image' of someone else? Why do we say 'take a rain-check' or 'don't teach your grandmother to suck eggs'?

These are the sort of questions that normal dictionaries duck out of by saying 'orig.obsc.' or 'orig.uncert.' or 'orig.unknown'. On the other hand, books which specialize in word and phrase origins often seem to assert that one explanation (and one explanation only) can be provided.

The purpose of *The Cassell Dictionary of Word and Phrase Origins* is to compare the many explanations on offer and to test them, even if in the end it serves to emphasize that in this field hard-and-fast conclusions are difficult to come by.

The especial need for this approach derives from the fact that a good deal of amateur etymological folklore has been established. It is now very difficult, for example, to convince people that the word 'posh' is not derived from the request for cabins positioned 'Port Out, Starboard Home' on ships going to and from India. Or that the word 'crap' had in fact existed for centuries before Thomas Crapper, the Victorian sanitary engineer, came along.

In addition, a number of quizzes and newspaper strips have arisen recently which claim to explain the origins of well-known words and phrases with difficult and/or colourful roots. Frequently, however, these merely pass on old myths and legends, unsubstantiated by evidence.

This book tries to sift through the lore and disentangle the misconceptions. Sometimes it exposes an imposter, sometimes it throws up its hands and offers no solution of its own.

In one or two cases I examine words and phrases which seem to have been neglected entirely by the substantial number of reference books I have consulted. In these cases, as in others, I hope that I have not created any new misconceptions.

The choice of words and phrases examined may at times seem eccentric. It ranges from those that have entered the language within the past decade to venerable examples that are still a puzzle. The book is certainly not intended to be comprehensive — how could it be? — and where I have included a word or phrase, the usual criterion has been that there is something interesting or new to say about it.

As I have found previously when tracing quotations, once you get drawn into an area of linguistic research like this, it becomes addictive. James Boswell in his *Life of Johnson* talked of being obliged to 'run half over London in order to fix a date correctly'. Something of that obsessive urge has gone into this book and I should like to thank everyone who has responded to my queries.

At this point, word and phrase detectives are invited to join with me in the hunt, magnifying glasses at the ready. So read on, asking, 'Why do we say . . .?'

Nigel Rees
London 1992

ABBREVIATIONS USED TO IDENTIFY BOOKS CONSULTED

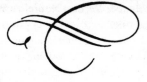

Brewer	*Brewer's Dictionary of Phrase and Fable*, 1975
Burnam	Tom Burnam, *The Dictionary of Misinformation*, 1975
Burnam 2	Tom Burnam, *More Misinformation*, 1980
CODP	*The Concise Oxford Dictionary of Proverbs*, 1982
DOAS	*Dictionary of American Slang* (2nd Supplemented edition), 1975
Ewart	Neil Ewart, *Everyday Phrases*, 1983
Flexner	Stuart Berg Flexner, *I Hear America Talking*, 1976
Flexner 2	Stuart Berg Flexner, *Listening to America*, 1982
Fowler	H.W. Fowler, *A Dictionary of Modern English Usage* (2nd edition), 1968
Longman	*Longman Dictionary of English Idioms*, 1979
Macquarie	*The Macquarie Dictionary*, 1981
Morris	Desmond Morris, *Catwatching*, 1986
Morrises	William and Mary Morris, *Morris Dictionary of Word and Phrase Origins*, 1977
ODCIE	*Oxford Dictionary of Contemporary Idiomatic English* (2 vols.), 1975/83
OED Supp.	*A Supplement to the Oxford English Dictionary* (4 vols.), 1972/86
Partridge	Eric Partridge, *A Dictionary of Slang and Unconventional English*, (8th edition, edited by Paul Beale), 1984
Radford	Edwin Radford, *To Coin a Phrase* (edited and revised by Alan Smith), 1974
Room	Adrian Room, *Dictionary of Trade Name Origins*, 1982

Safire	William Safire, *Safire's Political Dictionary*, 1978
Shook	Robert L. Shook, *The Book of Why*, 1983
SOED	*The Shorter Oxford English Dictionary*, 1933 (1967 revision)
SOTC	Nigel Rees, *Sayings of the Century*, 1984
WWNN	Nigel Rees & Vernon Noble, *A Who's Who of Nicknames*, 1985

'...ABANDON HOPE, ALL YE WHO ENTER HERE'?
Because everyone makes the same mistake.

This is the popular translation of the words written over the entrance to Hell in Dante's *The Divine Comedy*. It trips off the tongue more easily than 'All hope abandon, ye who enter here,' which would be a more accurate translation of the Italian, *lasciate ogni speranza voi ch'entrate*.

...SOMETHING OR SOMEONE IS AN *ABOMINABLE SNOWMAN*?
– meaning, indescribable and unpleasant. In Tibetan, *meetoh kangmi* ('abominable snowmen') or *yeti* are unidentified creatures of the Himalayas about which there are many legends. They are said to raid mountain villages and to be tall, powerful and bear-like, with near-human faces. The name became known to European mountaineers attempting to climb Everest in the 1920s. Since the mid-1950s special expeditions have been mounted to search for them but have only succeeded in photographing footprints which seemed to be those of an animal such as a bear (*WWNN*).

...SOMETHING IS *ACCORDING TO HOYLE*?
A now somewhat-dated way of saying 'exactly', 'correctly', 'according to the recognised rules of the game' or 'according to the highest authority'. It derives from the name of the one-time standard authority on the game of whist (and other card games), Edmond Hoyle (1672–1769). He was the author of *A Short Treatise*

9

on the Game of Whist, first published in 1742, as well as several
other books on card games.

... THERE'S AN *ACE IN THE HOLE*?
This American expression was made more familiar elsewhere
when it was used as the title of a Billy Wilder film in 1951. The
film is literally about a hole. For his own sensation-seeking pur-
poses, a journalist delays the rescue of a man stuck in a cave.

'Ace in the hole' meaning 'hidden advantage' or 'secret source
of power' comes from the game of stud poker. A 'hole' card is one
that is not revealed until the betting has taken place. If it is an ace,
so much the better. *DOAS* dates the use of this expression, in a
poker context, from the 1920s.

In British English, the nearest equivalent would be to talk of an
'ace up one's sleeve'.

... *AEROBICS*?
The adjective 'aerobic' means living on the oxygen of the air and
comes from the Greek words for 'air' and 'life'.

'Aerobics' is the name of the physical fitness programme created by Dr Kenneth Cooper, a former USAF flight surgeon, who
coined the phrase for a book called *Aerobics*, first published in
March 1968.

... GO UP THE *AISLE*?
See *go*.

... AN *ALICE BLUE GOWN*?
Celebrated in song, the 'Alice Blue Gown' takes its colour from a
particular Alice – Alice Roosevelt Longworth, daughter of President Theodore Roosevelt. 'Alice Blue' is a light-greenish blue.
The song was written for her by Harry Tierney when she was
sixteen. Later famed for her acid tongue, she died aged 96 in 1980.

'... *ALL GOOD THINGS MUST COME TO AN END*'?
What are the origins of this proverbial expression meaning 'pleasure cannot go on for ever'? Michael Watts in the *Sunday Express*
(8 August 1981) passed on the view that it might be a corruption
of the *Book of Common Prayer* version of Psalm 119, verse 96: 'I see

that all things come to an end: but thy commandment is exceeding broad.'

CODP confirms that the addition of 'good' is a more recent development. Otherwise there are versions going back to 1440 and, as 'Everything has an end', the idea occurs in Chaucer's *Troilus and Criseyde* (1385).

. . . ALL MY EYE AND BETTY MARTIN?

– meaning that something is nonsense, this curious phrase dates back at least as far as 1781. According to the *OED Supp.*, a letter written by one S. Crispe in that year states, 'Physic, to old, crazy Frames, like ours, is all my eye and Betty Martin – (a sea phrase that Admiral Jemm frequently makes use of)'.

The expression frequently appears in the truncated forms, 'All my eye' or 'My eye!' – both of which almost certainly pre-date the longer version.

As to how it originated, Radford repeats the suggestion that it was a British sailor's garbled version of words heard in an Italian church, *O, mihi, beate Martine*, meaning 'Oh, grant me, blessed St Martin . . . ' But this sounds too ingenious.

I suspect there *was* a Betty Martin of renown in the late eighteenth century (Partridge found mention of an actress with the name whose favourite expression is supposed to have been 'My eye!') and that her name was co-opted for popular use (like Gordon Bennett, q.v., a century later).

Still, I wonder if there is not another reason why it caught on – could 'Betty Martin' have been rhyming slang for 'fartin' '?

' . . . AN' HOTEL?

Yes, why *do* people say 'an hotel' when it is perfectly all right to say simply 'a hotel'? Presumably, because they think there is some rule of grammar saying they should. But there is not.

As Fowler explains:

An was formerly usual before an unaccented syllable beginning with h (*an historian, an habitual offender* . . .) But now that the h in such words is pronounced the distinction has become anomalous and will no doubt disappear in time. Meantime speakers who like to say *an* should not try to have it both ways by aspirating the h.

Yes, people should surely stop saying 'an hour' while aspirating the h . . .

11

'... *ANGEL*' TO DESCRIBE A BACKER?

The use of this phrase for investors in theatrical productions
seems to have started in the US but, whatever is being backed, it is
a fairly obvious extension of 'guardian angel'. Perhaps the most
far-fetched version of the phrase's origin is that one Luis de
Santangel was the backer who put up the money for Christopher
Columbus's voyage to America. The use of the word 'angel' in this
context seems not to date from much before the turn of the
century, however.

... AN *ANTIMACASSAR* PROTECTS FURNITURE?

Antimacassars were coverings thrown over chairs and sofas in
Victorian times to protect them from hair-oil stains. But why such
an impressive-sounding name?

Quite simple, really. 'Macassar' was the proprietory name of a
hair oil and so they acted 'anti' (or against) it.

The coverings really did exist – which is more than can be said
for the legendary coverings said to have been put over too-
shocking piano legs in Victorian times.

'... *ANYTHING YOU SAY MAY BE TAKEN DOWN AND USED IN EVIDENCE*'?

The police caution in the UK does not have a fixed form. The
version that one might expect from reading fiction would be
something like: 'You are not obliged to say anything unless you
wish to do so but, I must warn you, whatever you do say will be
taken down and may be given in evidence against you.'

But this is wrong. British police are advised that care should be
taken to avoid any suggestion that evidence might only be used
against a person, as this could prevent an innocent person making
a statement which might help clear him of a charge.

In the US, on the other hand, things can be different. In *Will*,
G. Gordon Liddy describes a raid on Dr Timothy Leary's house in
connection with drugs charges (in March 1966):

'Doctor, my name is G. Gordon Liddy and I'm assistant district attorney of
Dutchess County. I want to question you about what's been going on here, but
first I want you to understand that you don't have to make any statement, and
any statement you do make may be used *against*[1] you in a court of law. You also
have the right to a lawyer. You understand?'

[1] *My italics*

12

The law of the state of New York did not then require that these warnings be given prior to interrogation. They were, however, the standard prelude to questioning by special agents of the FBI. As a former FBI agent, I gave them as a matter of routine and had advised the sheriff's officers to do the same.

... *A-OKAY*?

Another way of saying 'OK' or 'All systems working', this was devised by NASA engineers in the early days of the American space programme, '... who used to say it during radio transmission tests because the sharper sound of *A* cut through the static better than *O*,' (Tom Wolfe, *The Right Stuff*, 1979).

It was made known to a wider public by Shorty Powers – 'This is Mercury Control ...' – who reported the astronauts' progress during missions. He said it memorably on the occasion of Alan Shepard's splashdown in the Pacific after America's first suborbital space shot (1961). Now largely redundant, it seems never to have been used by astronauts themselves.

President Reagan, emerging from a day of medical tests at a naval hospital in June 1986, pronounced himself 'A-OK'.

Another derivation is that it is a melding of 'A1' and 'OK'.

... SOMETHING IS THE *APPLE OF ONE'S EYE*?

i.e. what one cherishes most. The pupil of the eye has long been known as the 'apple', because of its supposed round, solid shape. Thus to be deprived of the apple is to be blinded and to lose something extremely valuable. Thus: 'He kept him as the apple of his eye' (Deuteronomy 32:10).

... SOMETHING IS IN *APPLE-PIE ORDER*?

There is no certain derivation for this phrase, but it may come from the French *cap-à-pied*, meaning to wear armour 'from head to foot'. This would provide the idea of completeness, with everything in place, though perhaps not the notion of freshness.

Another suggested French origin is the phrase *nappe pliée*, a folded table-cloth or sheet (though this seems a more likely source for the term, 'apple-pie bed'). On the other hand, a folded table-cloth or napkin might convey the idea of crispness and smartness.

... FOR *AULD LANG SYNE*?

It is not just inebriation on New Year's Eve that leads sassenachs into gibbering incomprehensibility when it comes to the singing

of *Auld Lang Syne*. There is genuine confusion as to what the
words mean, how they should be pronounced, and – indeed –
what the correct words are.

The poet Robert Burns adapted *Auld Lang Syne* from an earlier
song which he took down 'from an old man's singing'. He contributed it to the fifth volume of James Johnson's *Scots Musical
Museum* (1787–1803). The refrain, first line and title had all
appeared in print before as the work of other poets. Nevertheless,
what Burns wrote is what people should sing. Here is the first
verse and the chorus:

> Should auld acquaintance be forgot,
> And never brought to min(d)?
> Should auld acquaintance be forgot,
> And days o' lang syne?
>
> (Chorus)
> For auld lang syne, my dear
> For auld lang syne,
> We'll tak a cup o' kindness yet
> For auld lang syne.

In the fourth line of both verse and chorus, 'For the sake of auld
lang syne' should *not* be substituted. 'Auld lang syne' means,
literally, 'old long since' i.e. 'long ago'. Hence, 'syne' should be
pronounced with an 's' sound and not 'zyne'.

. . . MY GIDDY *AUNT*?
See *my*.

. . . *AUNTIE* AS A NICKNAME FOR THE BBC?
– so dubbed mockingly by newspaper columnists, television
critics and the BBC's own employees, becoming familiar from
1955 at the start-up of commercial television, the BBC supposedly
being staid and unambitious by comparison. A BBC spokesman
countered with, 'An auntie is often a much-loved member of the
family.' The corporation assimilated the nickname to such effect
that when arrangements were made to supply wine to BBC clubs
in London direct from vineyards in Burgundy, it was bottled
under the name *Tantine*.

In 1979, the comedian Arthur Askey suggested to me that he
had originated the term during the *Band Waggon* programme in
the late 1930s. While quite probably he did, the widespread use

of the nickname is more likely to have arisen at the time suggested above.

'... A.W.O.L.'?

'Absent Without Leave' (unwarranted absence for a short period, but not desertion). This expression dates from the American Civil War when offenders had to wear a placard with these initials printed on it. During the First World War the initials were still being pronounced individually. Not until just before the Second World War was it pronounced as the acronym 'Awol'.

Burnam explains that the 'o' in the acronym is to make it clear that 'absent *with* leave' is not intended.

The acronym does not mean 'absent without *official* leave'.

... A PERSON HAS AN *AXE TO GRIND*?

i.e. has an ulterior motive, private ends to serve. The expression appears to come from an anecdote related in Benjamin Franklin's essay 'Too Much for Your Whistle'. A man showed interest in young Franklin's grindstone and asked how it worked. In the process of explaining, Franklin – using much energy – sharpened up the visitor's axe for him. This was clearly what the visitor had had in mind all along. Subsequently, Franklin had to ask himself whether people he encountered had 'another axe to grind'.

... *BABY BOOMER*?

i.e. a person born just after the Second World War during the 'baby boom'. This American term was hardly known in Britain until a 'Baby Boomer' edition of the Trivial Pursuit board game arrived in 1986. This was intended to appeal to those who had reached maturity during the 1960s. For a while, British journalists took to using the phrase 'baby boom' and even 'Baby Boomers' in preference to the 'bulge' or 'post-war bulge' which had been used hitherto (and which was a much better way, surely, to describe a pregnancy-related phenomenon?).

In fact, 'baby boom' had also been used to describe the rise in births after the First World War and, specifically, the effect this had when those children became of school age.

In Japan, there is also a phrase for the phenomenon: *dankai no sedai* ('the cluster generation').

... *BABY RUTH* TO DESCRIBE A POPULAR AMERICAN CANDY BAR?

The name does *not* derive from George Herman 'Babe' Ruth (1895–1948), the most popular baseball player in the history of the game, although one story has it that the manufacturers wanted to call the bar a 'Babe Ruth'. They offered him $20,000 but he held out for $50,000. They settled for an approximation and did not have to pay a nickel.

It is also said to take its name from President Grover Cleveland's daughter, who was born in the White House. However, this event took place in 1891 and the bar did not make its first appearance until the 1920s.

More prosaically – and more probably – it was thus dubbed by Mrs George Williamson, whose husband was president of the Williamson Candy Company which originally made the bar. As Burnam 2 suggests, she named it after a granddaughter.

(Babe Ruth had to content himself with giving his name to a home run in baseball.)

... *BACKROOM BOYS* TO REFER TO SCIENTISTS AND BOFFINS?

– and specifically those relied on to produce inventions and new gadgets for weaponry and navigation in the Second World War. In this sense, the term was originated by Lord Beaverbrook (1879–1964) when he was Minister of Aircraft Production. In a broadcast on 19 March 1941, he paid tribute to the Ministry's Research Department: 'Let me say that the credit belongs to the boys in the back-rooms [sic]. It isn't the man who sits in the limelight like me who should have the praise. It is not the men who sit in prominent places. It is the men in the back-rooms.'

In North America, the phrase 'back-room boys' can be traced at least to the 1870s, but Beaverbrook can be credited with the modern application to scientific and technical boffins. His inspiration quite obviously was his favourite film *Destry Rides Again* (1939) in which Marlene Dietrich jumps on the bar of the Last Chance saloon and sings the Frank Loesser song *See What the Boys in the Back Room Will Have*. Beaverbrook once said that, 'Marlene Dietrich singing *The Boys in the Back Room* is a greater work of art than the Mona Lisa' (*SOTC*).

... *BACK TO SQUARE ONE*?

i.e. back to the beginning. This gained currency from the 1930s onwards through its use by radio football commentators in the UK. *Radio Times* used to print a map of the football field divided into numbered squares, to which commentators would refer: 'Cresswell's going to make it – FIVE – There it goes, slap into the middle of the goal – SEVEN – Cann's header there – EIGHT – The ball comes out to Britton. Britton manoeuvres. The centre goes right in – BACK TO EIGHT – Comes on to Marshall – SIX ...' – an extract from the BBC commentary on the 1933 Cup Final between

Everton and Manchester City. The idea had largely been abandoned by 1940, but the phrase lives on.

Partridge, however, prefers an origin in the children's game of hopscotch or the board-game snakes and ladders. The commentators may have done no more than build on this use.

... BRING HOME THE *BACON*?
See *bring*.

... *BAKER'S DOZEN*?
i.e. thirteen. But why? The most likely answer is that it had to do with bakers in fifteenth-century England who gave away an extra loaf with every twelve to avoid being fined heavily for providing underweight produce. The surplus was known as 'inbread' and the thirteenth loaf the 'vantage loaf'.

(A 'Devil's dozen' is also thirteen – the number of witches who would gather when summoned by the Devil.)

... *BALD AS A BADGER*?
Unlike the expression 'bald as a coot' – whose inspiration is obvious as coots look bald – this (more obscure) one takes a little more explanation. Badgers' heads do not look noticeably balder than other animals'. But that is not the part of anatomy in question. The longer expression from which this is extracted is: 'Bald as a badger's bum'. There was once a widely held belief that bristles for shaving brushes were plucked from this area.

... GOES AT SOMETHING *BALDHEADED*?
See *goes at*.

... KEEP THE *BALL ROLLING*?
See *keep*.

... THE *BALLOON'S GONE UP*?
This colourful phrase denotes the start of excitement or action, particularly military activities. It derives from the barrage balloons used during the two world wars to protect targets from air-raids. The mere fact that these (or observation) balloons had 'gone up' would signal that some form of action was imminent.

'... BANG TO RIGHTS'?

i.e. 'you've caught me red-handed' (said by a criminal). In the process of arrest, the criminal might also use the phrase to mean 'it's a fair cop!', i.e. 'you are quite right to have caught me, constable!' Partridge dates this from the 1930s, but the *OED Supp.* finds an American example in 1904.

I think it a very peculiar expression and somewhat unnatural. However, one might note the somewhat rare Americanism 'bang' for a criminal charge or arrest, as in 'it's a bum bang'. Does this have some connection with the banging of the cell door?

... BANJAXED?

This is an Irishism introduced into popular British speech by the broadcaster Terry Wogan in the early 1970s. When he wrote a book called *Banjaxed* in 1979 he helpfully supplied a gloss:

Ban'jax vt Middle Irish (cf Dineen). To hornswoggle, corpse, knacker, rasher, caramelize, malfooster, malavogue, powfagg, keelhaul, macerate, decimate, pulverize, make rawmeish of. Hence *Banjaxed*, reduced to the condition of a pig's breakfast, and *Banjaxing*, tearing a plaster from an hairy leg.

In Partridge, Paul Beale derives it from 'banged about' and 'smashed', and dates its Anglo-Irish use from the 1920s.

... TOUCH WITH A BARGE-POLE?

See *touch*.

... BARKING UP THE WRONG TREE?

i.e. following a false scent. The phrase is American in origin (since about 1832) and appears to come from racoon hunting. As this is done at night (racoons being nocturnal animals) and as, if chased, racoons run up trees, it would be quite possible for a dog, by mistake, to bark under the wrong tree in the dark.

I am slightly worried by the unanimity with which other books accept this explanation.

... A POLITICIAN IS BARNSTORMING?

This comes from the US in the early nineteenth century when actors did indeed go bustling around rural areas performing in

barns and similar venues. Their style was perhaps akin to that
found in melodramas and, thus, 'barnstorming' describes a type
of unsubtle performance. On the other hand, perhaps it was more
the makeshift, improvised nature of the touring which has led to
the word being used about politicians who stump about seeking
votes, although now the term has largely been superseded by
'whistlestopping'.

. . . DON'T LET THE *BASTARDS GRIND YOU DOWN*?
See *illegitimi*.

. . . *BATTLE ROYAL*?
See *waging*.

. . . A PERSON IS *BATTY*?
i.e. mentally deficient, insane (but harmlessly so). This is rather
hard on William Battie (1704–76), author of a *Treatise on Madness*.
After all, he was the psychiatrist and not the patient. On the other
hand, there was Fitzherbert Batty, a barrister of Spanish Town,
Jamaica, who made news when he was certified insane in London
in 1839. Then there is the obvious link to the expressions 'bats'
and 'bats in the belfry' (wildly disturbed by the ringing of bells –
and thus like the ravings of a disturbed person).

This last seems the most likely origin. The first two seem rather
too neat for comfort – smelling of imposition rather than derivation. Besides, there do not seem to be any examples of the word
'batty' in use from before 1900.

. . . SPILLING THE *BEANS*?
See *spilling*.

. . . THE *FIFTH BEATLE*?
See *fifth*.

. . . *BEAVER!*?
– to identify a man with a beard. This cry appears to have been
common, among children, at least since the 1910s and 1920s –
though now redundant. My parents remembered playing a game
when driving in open-topped cars on their holidays. The first

person to spot a 'beaver' scored a point. No doubt this was easy in the reigns of Edward VII and George V when many men – from the sovereign down – were adorned with a full beard of facial hair.

But why *beaver*? Flexner notes the use of the animal's name to describe a high, sheared-fur hat in the US. The beaver's thick dark-brown fur, he says, also refers 'to a well-haired pudendum or a picture showing it, which in pornography is called a "beaver shot".'

I wonder, though, whether beaver as beard does not derive rather from the Middle Ages when the 'beaver' was the part of a soldier's helmet which could be drawn up from the chin as a face-guard. (The 'vizor' was the bit brought down from the forehead.) In Shakespeare's *Hamlet*, the Prince asks, 'Then saw you not his face?' (i.e. that of his father's ghost) and Horatio replies, 'O yes, my lord, he wore his beaver up.'

... MAKE A *BEE-LINE* FOR?
See *make*.

... SOMETHING IS THE *BEE'S KNEES*?
There has always been fascination with bees' knees. From the eighteenth century comes the expression, 'as big as a bee's knee' and, from the nineteenth, 'as weak as a bee's knee'. But the bee whose knees became celebrated in American slang from the 1920s was a very different kettle of fish ...

To say that something was the 'bee's knees' was to convey that it was the best around and absolutely top hole.

I am sure that the particular part of the bee's anatomy singled out was chiefly important (as in the earlier expressions) because of the rhyme. One of the most basic aspects of coining popular expressions lies in rhyme, alliteration and assonance.

Hence, at around the same time, we find 'the kipper's knickers'. But we also encounter, 'the cat's whiskers' (perhaps because of the importance of these in tuning wireless crystal sets in the 1920s), 'the cat's pyjamas' (still new enough to be daring), 'the cat's miaow/ eyebrows/ ankles/ tonsils/ adenoids/ galoshes/ cufflinks/ roller skates'.

Not to mention, 'the snake's hips', 'the clam's garter', 'the eel's ankle', 'the elephant's instep', 'the tiger's spots', 'the leopard's stripes', 'the sardine's whiskers', 'the pig's wings' – 'and just about any combination of animal, fish, or fowl with a part of the body or article of clothing that was inappropriate for it' (Flexner).

... KNOCK SEVEN *BELLS OUT OF SOMEONE*?
See *knocks*.

'... *BELT AND BRACES*' FOR A SYSTEM INVOLVING DOUBLE SUPPORT?
– suggesting that if one falls down, the other may stay up. This is a phrase that seems to have escaped most dictionaries so far (but is included in the Beale revision of Partridge, 1984). It is an engineer's expression. I heard it quite recently used by a BBC engineer to describe the use of two microphones when broadcasting the sovereign's Christmas message. In the days when this was done live, it ensured transmission.

... OMELETTE ARNOLD *BENNETT*?
See *omelette*.

... INHABITANTS OF THE FALKLAND ISLANDS ARE *BENNIES*?
So named by British forces stationed there following the 1982 conflict with Argentina. The uncomplimentary reference was to a not-very-bright character called Bennie in the TV soap opera *Crossroads*. When reprimanded, troops resorted instead to calling the islanders 'Stills' (i.e. 'Still Bennies'). An even later variant by sections of the occupying forces, for some of the islanders, was 'Bubs' – for 'Bloody Ungrateful Bastards'.

The islanders responded by calling the soldiers 'Whennies' after their constant references to past exploits: 'When I was in Belize, when I was in Cyprus ...' (*WWNN*).

... A FOOL IS A *BERK*?
The Morrises charmingly cite Dudley Moore saying of Peter Cook (in a magazine interview), 'It is hard to distinguish sometimes whether Peter is being playful or merely a berk.' The Morrises then go on, coyly, to say, '*Berk* is British slang – originally a bit of Cockney rhyming slang – meaning "fool"' – and leave it at that.

Rhyming slang can be a bit puzzling at times – but not here. The 'berk' is short for 'Berkeley/ Berkshire Hunt' which rhymes with 'cunt'. Spelling the word 'birk' or 'burk(e)' helps obscure the origin. The usage probably does not date from before this century.

... ALL MY EYE AND *BETTY MARTIN*?
See *all*.

... SOMEONE/ SOMETHING IS *BEYOND THE PALE*?
The Pale was the area of English settlement around Dublin in Ireland, dating from the fourteenth century, in which English law had to be obeyed. But there have also been areas known as pales around Calais and in Russia.

The derivation is simple: Latin *palus*, meaning a stake. Hence, anyone who lived beyond this fence was thought to be, if not actually a barbarian, then beyond the bounds of civilisation.

Incidentally, having mentioned Peter Cook and Dudley Moore above (see *berk*), a word of explanation might be given as to the title of the celebrated revue in which they appeared with Alan Bennett and Jonathan Miller. *Beyond the Fringe* was presented in the West End of London in 1961 and went on to Broadway. It had first been shown, however, at the 1960 Edinburgh Festival as part of the main programme of events. It was, thus, 'beyond' the unofficial series of theatrical manifestations at Edinburgh, popularly known as the 'Fringe'. It was rather as though a show on Broadway proper had been given the title 'Beyond Off-Broadway'.

... A WOMAN WEARS A *BIKINI*?
Bikini was originally the name of an atoll in the Pacific Marshall Islands. In July 1946, it was chosen as the site for US atomic bomb tests and the following summer, in France, the word 'bikini' was taken to apply to the skimpy two-piece women's bathing costume which had become all the rage. An unlikely pairing then, but it is a word with an interesting sound and, just possibly, Louis Reard, the French motor engineer who designed the garment, was not too worried when what he called *le minimum* was replaced by a name which expressed the explosive effect of the new fashion.

... OLD *BILL* FOR THE POLICE?
See *Old Bill.*

... *BILLIONS?*
There is often confusion as to what amount a billion refers to
because British and American usage have been at variance. So:
   1 billion (US) = a thousand millions
   1 billion (UK) = a million millions
   1 trillion (US) = a million millions
   1 trillion (UK) = a billion millions
   In other words, the British amounts are *bigger* in each case,
though it is possible that the use of the American values will in
time predominate.

'... *BINGO!*' WHEN THERE'S A FULL HOUSE?
Radford states, 'In the 1700s [Bingo] was the name for the King
of Dominoes game, which only the most skilful players ever
attempted, so complicated was the method of play. The modern
game named Bingo was known before 1914 as Keno or Loo. During
the First World War it became a popular pastime with soldiers
under the name Housey-Housey. It requires no skill at all.'
   But how did it become known as 'Bingo' and turn into a craze
which still flourishes?
   In 1919, an American, Edwin Lowe, saw people playing what
they called 'beano' by putting beans on a numbered card at a
carnival near Jacksonville, Florida. He developed the idea and
launched a craze which netted him a fortune worth tens of
millions of dollars. One of his friends stuttered, 'B .. b .. bingo!'
on winning, and that is how the game is said to have got its name.
   Lowe died at the age of 75 in 1986.
   The word 'bingo' had already been applied to brandy in the
nineteenth century, but – as a result of this development from
'bean-o' – it turned not only into an exclamation on winning
Lowe's game but also into a generalized shout on achieving
anything, like 'Eureka!'

... GOT THE *BIRD?*
See *got.*

24

... WE'RE WRITING WITH A *BIRO*?

There was a Mr Biro. Laszlo Biro (1900–85), a Hungarian by birth, settled in Argentina before the Second World War. In 1943 he patented the capillary attraction system – a method of writing with quick-drying ink, using a ball-point rather than a conventional nib – which is the basis of all ball-point pens today. The success of the pen was helped by its being offered to American and British forces in the Second World War. It would not leak at high altitudes and could be used to write under water.

The word 'biro' – which is also a proprietary brand name – is now often applied indiscriminately to all types of ball-point pen and is pronounced to rhyme with 'giro' rather than the original 'hero'.

... *BISTRO*?

See *Bolshoi*.

... WE'LL FIGHT TO THE *BITTER END*?

Meaning the last extremity, the absolute limit, this has nothing to do with bitterness. The nautical 'bitt' is a bollard on the deck of a ship onto which cables and ropes are wound. The end of the cable that is wrapped round or otherwise secured to the bollard is the 'bitter end'.

... A *BLACK BOX* HAS BEEN RECOVERED FROM AIRCRAFT WRECKAGE?

More properly: 'Flight Data Recorder'. After an aircrash there is usually a scramble to retrieve the plane's 'black box'. This contains detailed recordings of the aircraft's performance prior to the crash. It can be of value in determining what went wrong. The name has been used since the Second World War at least – originally it was RAF slang for a box containing intricate navigational equipment.

In fact, these flight recorders are *orange* – so that, like life-rafts, they may be more easily seen. I expect they acquired the popular name because black is a rather more mysterious colour, appropriate for a box containing 'secret' equipment – (Pye produced a record player with the name in the 1950s) – and because of the lure of alliteration.

... LITTLE *BLACK DRESS*?
See *little*.

... *BLACK FRIDAY* TO DESCRIBE A FRIDAY WHEN DIRE EVENTS OCCUR?

Originally this was a description of Good Friday (when clergymen wore dark vestments). However, there have been several specific 'Black Fridays'.

In Britain, on one such day (15 April 1921), certain trade unions withdrew support from the hardpressed miners, the General Strike was cancelled, and this is recalled in the Labour movement as a day of betrayal.

In the United States, the first Black Friday was on 24 September 1869 when panic broke out on the stock market. During the Wall Street crash of 1929, there were similarly Black Wednesday, Black Thursday – the actual day of the crash – and Black Tuesday.

... *BLACK MARIA* FOR POLICE VAN?

There has been much speculation about 'maria'. It may be connected with the notorious murder of a girl called Maria Marten for which a man was hanged in 1828. Maria and the red barn in which her body was found became subjects of plays and stories, and the most notable melodrama, produced in London in 1840, is part of theatrical history.

An American explanation for the name is that a brawny Negress called Maria Lee who kept a lodging house in Boston, helped to bundle arrested people into the van. The term was current in the USA by 1847 and in Britain by 1869 (*WWNN*).

... THAT FLATTERING SPEECH IS *BLARNEY*?

Kissing the Blarney stone at Blarney Castle near Cork in southern Ireland is supposed to bestow the gift of the gab, but the custom is of relatively recent origin, having not been mentioned in print until the late eighteenth century.

The word 'blarney', however, seems to have entered the language a little while before.

The origin traditionally given is that in 1602, during the reign of Queen Elizabeth I, Cormac Macarthy or Dermot McCarthy (take your pick) was required to surrender the castle as a proof of his loyalty. He prevaricated and came up with so many excuses that (it is said) the Queen herself exclaimed, 'Odds bodikins, more Blarney talk'.

Beyond that, we are unlikely to get any further towards the bottom of the matter.

... A REACTIONARY IS A *BLIMP*?

This name for a type of stupid gentleman derives from the cartoon character called Colonel Blimp created between the wars by David Low (1891–1963) of the London *Evening Standard*. The character, in turn, took his name from an experimental airship/balloon developed during the First World War. Without frames, these were described as 'limp'. There was an 'A-limp' and a 'B-limp'. The aviator Horace Short may have been the man who dubbed them 'blimps'.

Another suggestion is that the name is onomatopoeic. In 1915, a Lieutenant Cunningham of the Royal Navy Air Service is said to have flicked his thumb against the surface of one of the airships and imitated the odd noise that this produced. From that, the name spread.

Alternatively, J.R.R. Tolkien, no less, writing in 1926, hazarded a guess that the name derived from a mixture of 'blister' and 'lump' (which the balloons resembled).

... A WOMAN IS A *BLONDE BOMBSHELL*?

Any dynamic personality with blonde hair – usually a film star, model or show business personality whom the writer would like to portray as striking – gets given this label. The original was Jean Harlow who appeared in the 1933 film *Bombshell*. In Britain – presumably so as not to suggest that the picture was a war epic – it was called *Blonde Bombshell*. The phrase is now a journalistic cliché.

... *BLOODY SUNDAY* TO DESCRIBE A SUNDAY WHEN DIRE EVENTS OCCUR?

As with 'Black Friday' (q.v.), there have been a number of these. In 1887, two men died during a baton charge on a prohibited socialist demonstration in Trafalgar Square, London. In 1905, hundreds of unarmed peasants were mown down when they marched to petition the Tsar in St Petersburg.

More recently, the name was applied to Sunday 30 January 1972 when British troops killed thirteen Catholics after a protest rally in Londonderry, Northern Ireland. Perhaps the epithet sprang to mind much more readily on this occasion because of the 1971 film entitled *Sunday Bloody Sunday* (not referring to violence but to the general malaise and difficulties which arise on that day).

... *BLOOMERS* FOR UNDERWEAR?

Originally, bloomers was the name given to a female fashion of a skirt reaching to just below the knees, under which were worn wide trousers, gathered at the ankles. A close-fitting jacket usually completed the ensemble. The fashion was introduced in New York – though not invented – by Mrs Amelia Jenks Bloomer around 1851, and it was soon adopted in England where it had a sensational vogue for a time and delighted cartoonists.

The trousers were especially appropriate for younger ladies taking up bicycling and the word became a nickname for these undergarments. As they then disappeared under longer skirts, it was applied to the underwear which for a long time preceded knickers and panties.

... SOMEONE HAS *BLOWN THE GAFF*?

i.e. let the secret out, given the game away. Partridge has an earlier (eighteenth-century) form, 'Blow the gab' (i.e. to blab about something) and I suppose 'gaff' could just about have developed from that. 'Gaff' here may mean mouth (gab as gob) and, coupled with 'blow', this gives the idea of expelling air through it and letting things out.

One might compare 'to blow one's top' (to let off steam) evoking the image of a volcano. According to *DOAS*, there is some reported use of 'to gaff' in the US Navy with the meaning 'to reprimand, to bawl out', which is getting close.

... SOMEONE *BLOWS HOT AND COLD*?

Meaning to vacillate or waiver between enthusiasm and apathy, this expression comes from one of Aesop's *Fables*. On a cold day, a satyr comes across a man blowing on his fingers to make them warm. He takes the man home and gives him a dish of hot soup. The man blows on the soup, to cool it. At this, the satyr throws him out, exclaiming that he wants nothing to do with a man who can 'blow hot and cold from the same mouth'.

... A PERSON IS *BLUE-BLOODED*?

Human blood is red, but during the fifteenth century many Spanish aristocrats had fair complexions which made their veins appear bluer than those of darker-skinned, Moorish people. Thus they were said to have blue blood, and the phrase came to describe their social superiority.

... A WOMAN IS A *BLUESTOCKING*?

i.e. literary or studious. So called from the gatherings of cultivated females and a few eminent men who met especially at the home of Elizabeth Montagu in Mayfair, London, a leader of society who encouraged discussion of the latest books and poems instead of banter and gossip over games of cards.

These intellectual conversaziones began around 1750 and the playful nicknames of 'bluestocking ladies' and 'bluestocking clubs' are explained by Boswell in his *Life of Johnson*. He says that a certain Benjamin Stillingfleet, an expert on natural history, was a popular guest, soberly dressed but wearing blue stockings. 'Such was the excellence of his conversation, that his absence was felt as so great a loss, that it used to be said, "We can do nothing without the blue stockings", and thus by degrees the title was established.'

It is also said that Mrs Montagu and her coterie took to wearing blue stockings (*WWNN*).

... *BLURB* TO DESCRIBE A PUFF?

The word given to the notes on the cover or fly-leaf of a book, which describe its contents and merits in encouraging tones (often written anonymously by the author), has a precise origin.

In 1907, Gelett Burgess, the American novelist (1866–1951) is said to have produced a comic book-jacket featuring an alluring female called 'Miss B[e]linda Blurb'. Presumably she was intended

29

to attract readers in the way that the publisher's written, descriptive notes were supposed to do.

Seven years later, Burgess defined the word he had invented in several ways – perhaps best as 'to make a sound like a publisher'. A sort of bland blurt, I suppose one might add.

Burgess also invented the word 'bromide' to describe someone addicted to clichés. The word later came to mean a trite remark or platitude.

'... BOB'S YOUR UNCLE!'?

'And there you are!' 'All will be well.' 'It's as simple as that!' – an almost meaningless expression of the type that takes hold from time to time. It was current in the 1880s but is of no hard and fast origin. It is basically a British expression and somewhat baffling to Americans. There is the story of one such who went into a London shop and had it said to him. 'But how did you know – I do have an Uncle Bob!?' he exclaimed.

In 1886, Arthur Balfour was appointed Chief Secretary for Ireland by his uncle, the Prime Minister, Robert Gascoyne-Cecil, third Marquess of Salisbury. Could this nepotism have been the crucial source?

... BOLSHOI?

– referring to Moscow's principal theatre for opera and ballet, especially in connection with the world-famous Bolshoi Ballet. The building was opened in 1856. *Bolshoi* simply means 'big' in Russian.

Another Russian word that has entered the English language even more fully is *bistro* (or *bistrot*) for a small restaurant or bar. It reaches us via French, but the Russian word says it all. It means 'quick'. However, some would doubt this derivation.

... MAKE NO *BONES* ABOUT?
See *make*.

... *BOONDOCKS* TO DESCRIBE THE BACK OF BEYOND?
During the Second World War, American G.I.s stationed in the Philippines were sometimes sent to the mountain regions. *Bundok* means 'mountain' in Tagalog, the official language of the Philip-

pines. Hence the word 'boondocks' (or 'the boonies') arose for
somewhere obscure, out of the way and 'in the sticks'. (The
Australian equivalent, probably from Aboriginal speech, is 'woop
woop').

. . . ILLEGAL GOODS ARE *BOOTLEG*?

Originally applied to the illegal selling of liquor, the word 'boot-
leg' has in more recent times been applied to such things as
counterfeit records and cassettes. The word arose in the American
Far West during the mid-nineteenth century when illegal liquor
sales were made to Indians on reservations. The thin bottles of
alcohol could be concealed in the vendor's long boots. During
Prohibition, the term 'bootlegging' was applied to the whole
business of selling illegal alcohol.

. . . DIED WITH HIS *BOOTS ON*?

See *died*.

. . . *BOOZE* TO DESCRIBE ALCOHOLIC DRINK?

'Booze' has been used as a noun, in the US, to denote hard liquor
and, in the UK, beer or ale. As a verb, it means to drink heavily.
But why booze? One derivation is from the name of E.C. (or E.S.
or E.G.) Booz, a Philadelphia whisky distiller (*c.* 1840). But the
word was current in the fourteenth century. Middle English
'bousen' meant to drink deeply. Mr Booz may merely have helped
popularize the word.

. . . *BOTTLE* TO DENOTE COURAGE OR GUTS?

An example of the word being used with this meaning can be
found in *Private Eye* (17 December 1982): 'Cowed by the thought
of six-figure legal bills and years in the courts, the Dirty Digger
has "bottled out" of a confrontation with Sir Jams.'

   This usage became well known in Britain through the 1982
advertising slogan, 'Milk's gotta lotta bottle'. But why 'bottle'?
The word has been used in this sense since the late 1940s at least.
One suggestion is that it derives from rhyming slang: either,
'bottle and glass' as 'class' (said to date from the 1920s, this one)
or 'bottle and glass' as 'arse'. But the reason for the leap from class
or arse to courage is not terribly clear.

There is an old-established brewers, Courage Ltd, whose products can, of course, be had in bottles. But I am not sure that this is a totally convincing explanation either.

... *BOWDLERIZE* WHEN WE MEAN TO CUT OUT THE DIRTY BITS?

In 1818, Thomas Bowdler published *The Family Shakespeare*, a ten-volume edition of the dramatist's works with all the dirty bits left out (or, as he put it, 'those words are omitted which cannot be read aloud in a family'). 'Out damn'd spot' becomes 'Out crimson spot', and so on. Bowdler (1754–1825), in consequence, has given his name to any form of literary expurgation.

It is said, in fact, that Bowdler's sister Harriet was hotter on the subject than Thomas himself and that it was she who prepared the first *unsigned* edition. As she was a spinster, perhaps she felt it wrong to show that she understood what she was expurgating.

Whatever the case, one cannot help wondering whether the word caught on because of its closeness to 'disembowel'. It was already current by 1836.

... THE *BOX* TO DESCRIBE TELEVISION?

Now chiefly used, if gradually going out of use, to refer to television sets, 'box' was earlier applied to radios and gramophones. As such, it was one of several somewhat derogatory epithets for TV which arose during the medium's rise to mass popularity in the 1940s and 1950s. In the US, Groucho Marx used the expression in a 1950 letter.

According to Malcolm Muggeridge, the writer Maurice Richardson, sometime television critic of the *Observer*, coined the epithet 'idiot's lantern' or 'idiot lantern' prior to 1957. The *OED Supp.* has an example of 'idiot box' in use from 1959.

An interesting example of the earlier application of 'the box' to a gramophone occurs in a 1924 letter by T.E. Lawrence: 'I covet the idea of being sometimes by myself near a fire with a hope of having a warm solitary place to hide on winter evenings ... I don't sleep here, but come out at 4.30 p.m. – 9 p.m. nearly every evening, and dream, or write, or read by the fire, or play Beethoven and Mozart to myself on the box.'

... PEOPLE ARE MAINTAINING A *BOYCOTT*?

Captain Charles Boycott was an ex-British soldier who acted as an agent for absentee landlords in Ireland's County Mayo during the late nineteenth century. He was extremely hard on the poor tenants and dispossessed them if they fell behind with their rents.

By way of retaliation, the tenants isolated him and refused to have any dealings with him or his family. They were encouraged in this by Charles Parnell of the Irish Land League who said that those who grabbed land from the people evicted for non-payment of rent should be treated like 'the leper of old'. Eventually, the tenants brought about Boycott's downfall by leaving his harvest to rot and he fled back to England where he died in 1897.

The interesting thing about the coining of the word 'boycott' (which became current soon after the above incidents took place in 1880) is that it describes what was done *to* him rather than what was done *by* him.

... *BRAINS TRUST* TO DESCRIBE A GROUP OF PEOPLE WHO GIVE ADVICE?

The expression first arose in the 1930s when President Franklin D. Roosevelt set up a circle of advisers which became known as his '*brain* trust'. The coinage is credited to James M. Kieran, a political reporter with the *New York Times*.

In Britain, the term was borrowed – and turned into a '*brains* trust' – by Howard Thomas when he was launching the popular BBC radio programme of that name in 1941. Actually, the American phrase had originally appeared as *brains*, plural. At first, Thomas's programme in which interesting people answered listeners' queries was called *Any Questions* – a programme name later revised for a more topical long-running discussion series.

The later expression 'think-tank' (also originally from the US) describes a comparable attempt to bring expert advice into government.

... A THING IS *BRAND-NEW*?

'Brand', in this sense, comes from the old word meaning 'to burn' (just as a brand is a form of torch). So, in olden times, a metal object that was brand- (or bran-) new had just been taken out of the flames, i.e. had just been forged. Indeed, Shakespeare has the variation 'fire-new' which points more directly towards the phrase's origin.

... *BRASS MONKEY*?
See *cold*.

... *BRASS TACKS*?
See *get down to*.

... MORE HONOURED IN THE *BREACH*?
See *custom*.

'... *BREAK A LEG!*' TO WISH AN ACTOR LUCK?
This is a traditional theatrical greeting before a performance, especially a first night. It is supposed to be bad luck to wish anyone 'good luck' directly.

Partridge has 'break a leg' as 'to give birth to a bastard', dating from the seventeenth century, but this may be unconnected ... as also might be the fact that John Wilkes Booth, an actor, broke his leg after assassinating President Lincoln in a theatre.

The Morrises pass on a suggestion that it is based on a German good luck expression, *Hals-und-Beinbruch* ('May you break your neck and your leg' – literally, 'neck and bone-break'). Perhaps this entered theatrical speech (like several other expressions) via Yiddish.

Theatrical superstition is understandable, I suppose, in a profession so dependent on luck. However, the euphemism 'Scottish play', invariably used for Shakespeare's *Macbeth*, is based on a well-documented history of bad luck associated with productions of the play. Merely to utter the name would thus be to invoke misfortune.

... *BREAKING THE MOULD*?
i.e. starting afresh from fundamentals. When the Social Democratic Party was established with the Limehouse Declaration of 1981, there was much talk of 'breaking the mould' of British politics, i.e. doing away with the basic system of a Government

party and one chief Opposition party by introducing a strong third party.

Various elegant sources were suggested for this phrase. Ariosto in *Orlando Furioso* (1532) wrote 'Nature made him, and then broke the mould', but clearly that is not appropriate. A much-touted source was Andrew Marvell's *Horatian Ode Upon Cromwell's Return From Ireland* (1650):

> Much to the man is due,
> Who from his private gardens, where
> He lived reserved and austere ...
> Could by industrious valour climb
> To ruin the great work of Time,
> And cast the kingdoms old
> Into another mould.

Roy Jenkins, one of the founders of the SDP, had quoted this passage as early as 1972 in his book *What Matters Now*. But the source is only slightly relevant and there is no real need to search in this area. It is a fairly common way of describing political change, of getting rid of the old system for good, in a way that prevents it being reconstituted. A.J.P. Taylor in his *English History 1914–1945* (1965), for example, writes: 'Lloyd George needed a new crisis to break the mould of political and economic habit'. The image evoked, as in the days of the Luddites, was of breaking the mould from which iron machinery was cast, so completely, that the machinery would have to be re-cast from scratch.

... BRING HOME THE BACON?

i.e. to be successful in a venture. This may have something to do with the Dunmow Flitch, a tradition established in 1111, at Dunmow in Essex. Married couples who could prove they had lived for a year and a day without quarrelling or wishing to be unmarried could claim a gammon of bacon. Also, country fairs used to have competitions which involved catching a greased pig. If you brought home the bacon, you won.

An extra fillip to the remark was given by the mother of the American Negro boxer Jack Johnson (1876–1946) who won the world heavyweight championship in 1910. Afterwards, she commented: 'He said he'd bring home the bacon, and the honey boy has gone and done it.'

... *BRISTOLS* TO DESCRIBE A WOMAN'S BREASTS?

When stuck for the origin of a word, always turn to rhyming slang! Quite often it will supply a connection which otherwise is far from obvious. Here the rhyme is 'Bristol cities' with 'titties' – a use more or less restricted to the UK. As Paul Beale suggests in his revision of Partridge, Bristol City (football team) probably gets chosen because of the initial similarity of the words Bristol and breasts.

... *BROMIDE*?

See *blurb*.

... *BRONX CHEER* TO DESCRIBE A DERISIVE NOISE?

DOAS records that it is said to have originated at the National Theater in the Bronx, New York City, rather than at Yankee Stadium in the same area (though baseball fans were noted users of this form of criticism). *DOAS* goes on to suggest that the phrase may have something to do with 'Spanish "brazo" or Spanish slang and dialect "branca", originally an "affectionate hug", but later the "Olé!" shout of approval voiced by bullfight fans, and now any mass audience noise, whether of approval or disapproval.' This seems pretty unlikely.

The more usual UK equivalent is 'to blow a or give someone the raspberry' (rhyming slang, raspberry tart for fart).

... SOMEONE EARNS *BROWNIE POINTS* FOR DOING RIGHT?

Originating in American business, this phrase has nothing to do with Brownies, the junior version of Girl Guides, and the points they may or may not gain for doing good deeds. Oh no! This has a much more scatological origin, not unconnected with brown-nosing, brown-tonguing, arse-licking and other unsavoury ways of sucking up to someone important.

Note also the Americanism 'Brownie' awarded for doing something *wrong*. According to *DOAS*, 'I got a pair of Brownies for that one' (1942) refers to a system of disciplinary demerits on the railroads. The word is here derived from the inventor of the disciplinary system.

... *BRUSH-OFF* TO DENOTE A REBUFF?

Of American origin, this word is said (by Shook) to derive from a habit of Pullman porters. If they thought you were a poor tipper, they gave you a quick brush over the shoulders and passed on to the next customer. However, perhaps the mere action of brushing unwanted dirt off clothing is sufficient reason for the phrase.

... PASS THE *BUCK*?

See *pass*.

... KICK THE *BUCKET*?

See *kick*.

... SOMEONE IS 'IN THE *BUFF*' OR A 'FILM-*BUFF*'?

First meaning: naked. This seems to derive from the buff-coloured, leather shorts down to which people in the services were sometimes stripped. Although technically speaking they were not naked, the term was extended to apply to those who were completely so.

An English regiment has been known as 'The Buffs' for over three hundred years – not because it goes naked but because of the colour of its uniform.

Second meaning (especially in the US): an enthusiast (e.g. 'film-buff'). This name came from people who liked to watch fires being extinguished or who helped extinguish them in an amateur capacity. They were called 'buffs' either because of their buffalo uniforms or because the heavy buffalo robes they wore to keep them warm in winter (before the fires got started, presumably) somewhat hindered their usefulness. In which case, the term was used as mild form of rebuke by the real fire-fighters.

... IT'S *BUGGINS'S TURN*?

Buggins's turn is an appointment made because it is somebody's turn to receive it rather than because he is especially well qualified to. The name Buggins is used because it sounds suitably dull and humdrum. The earliest recorded use of the phrase is by Admiral Fisher, later First Sea Lord, in a 1901 letter. In a 1917 letter (reprinted in his *Memories*, 1919), he said: 'Some day the Empire will go down because it is Buggins's turn.' It is hard to say whether or not Fisher coined the phrase, though he was a colourful speaker and writer.

But what do people with the name Buggins think of it? In February 1986, a Mr Geoffrey Buggins was reported to be threatening legal action over a cartoon which had appeared in the London *Standard*. It showed the husband of Prime Minister Margaret Thatcher looking through the New Year's Honours List and asking, 'What did Buggins do to get an MBE?' She replies: 'He thought up all those excuses for not giving one to Bob Geldof' (the pop-star and fund-raiser).

The real-life Mr Buggins (who had been awarded an MBE for services to export in 1969), said from his home near Lisbon, Portugal: 'I am taking this action because I want to protect the name of Buggins and also on behalf of the Muddles, Winterbottoms and the Sillitoes of this world.'

The editor of the *Standard* said: 'We had no idea that there was a Mr Buggins who had the MBE. I feel sorry for his predicament, but if we are to delete Buggins's turn from the English language perhaps he could suggest an alternative.'

. . . *BULLDOG BREED* TO DESCRIBE THE BRITISH?

At the outbreak of the First World War in 1914, Winston Churchill spoke at a 'Call to Arms' meeting at the London Opera House. 'Mr Churchill has made a speech of tremendous voltage and carrying power,' the *Manchester Guardian* reported. 'His comparison of the British Navy to a bulldog – "the nose of the bulldog has been turned backwards so that he can breathe without letting go" – will live. At the moment of delivery, with extraordinary appositeness, it was particularly vivid, as the speaker was able by some histrionic gift to suggest quite the bulldog as he spoke.'

Indeed, during the Second World War small model bulldogs were manufactured bearing Churchill's facial pout and wearing a tin helmet.

Used to describe the British as a whole, the phrase is of earlier origin, however. In 1857, Charles Kingsley wrote of, 'The original British bull-dog breed, which, once stroked against the hair, shows his teeth at you for ever afterwards.' In 1897, the British had been called 'boys of the bulldog breed' in a late Victorian music-hall song, *Sons of the Sea, All British born*, by Arthur Reece.

'John Bull' as a British symbol (sometimes shown accompanied by a bulldog) dates from *before* John Arbuthnot's *The History of John Bull* (1712).

... *BUM*?

i.e. bottom, buttocks or (as in *SOED*) 'the posteriors'. The simplest origin for this old word would seem to be from 'bottom', but this is clearly ruled out by the *OED* which fancies some 'echoic' source (i.e. one imitating a sound). Hence, bum would seem to come from the 'bump' which a person makes as he sits down.

... SOMETHING NONSENSICAL IS *BUNK*?

In 1820, a congressman from Buncombe County, North Carolina – Felix Walker was his name – made a totally worthless speech to the House of Representatives in Washington during a debate on the Missouri Compromise. He justified himself by saying, 'I was not speaking to the House, but to Buncombe', and the name stuck although the spelling was simplified as 'bunkum', then 'bunk'. Hence also to 'debunk', to draw attention to nonsense, or deflate, the creation of William E. Woodward in a 1920s book called *Bunk* (an exposé of Henry Ford, famous for saying 'History is more or less bunk').

... GONE FOR A *BURTON*?

See *gone for*.

... WE *BUTTONHOLE* ANOTHER PERSON?

i.e. detain a reluctant listener. This does not derive from buttonhole – the hole through which a button passes – or from the flower(s) worn in the slit on a coat-lapel. No, the verb is really 'to buttonhold', i.e. to stop a person going away by holding on to one of his buttons.

... *BY AND LARGE* TO MEAN GENERALLY SPEAKING?

Originally, this was a nautical term. To sail by and large meant to keep a ship on course so that it was sailing at a good speed even though the direction of the wind was changing (Longman). Brewer puts it thus: 'To sail slightly off the wind, making it easier for the helmsman to steer and less likely for the vessel to be taken aback.'

... PLOTTERS HAVE FORMED A *CABAL*?

The word is from the Hebrew *qabbalah* meaning 'accepted by tradition' and used in connection with a Jewish mystical system of theology and metaphysics. It is *not* true to say that it gained its modern meaning of a council of intriguers from the initial letters of Clifford, Ashley, Buckingham, Arlington and Lauderdale, ministers in the reign of Charles II who signed the Treaty of Alliance with France in 1672. Their initials merely conformed to a word already in existence and did not create it through an acrostic or acronym.

... *CADDY* IN GOLF?

Caddy is no more or less than a shortened form of the word 'cadet' (from the French for the younger of two brothers). Such people were often used for running errands or providing ancillary services.

... *CAESAR SALAD*?

Julius Caesar has given his name to less things than you might expect. In recent times a 'Caesar haircut' was one like those seen on busts of Caesar (and popularized by Marlon Brando in the 1953 film of *Julius Caesar* – although, in fact, he was playing Mark Antony).

The 'Caesarian section' method of childbirth is *not* so named because Julius Caesar was born that way. It was illegal under Roman law, except where the mother was dead. The part of the Caesarian Laws dealing with this aspect was called the Caesarian

Section. An even simpler derivation is from the Latin word *caesus*, past participle of *caedere*, to cut.

Which brings us to Caesar salad, beloved of Hollywood diners-out. It took its name from its creator, Caesar Gardini who ran Caesar's Place restaurant in Tijuana, Mexico. In the great tradition of kitchen creativity, he had to improvise a salad when more people turned up to eat than he had prepared food for. The ingredients included lettuce, garlic, olive oil, croutons, cheese, and eggs, all lightly tossed.

... *CALAMITY JANE* FOR A FEMALE PROPHET OF DOOM?
Martha Jane Canary (1852–1903) of Deadwood, South Dakota, behaved like a cowboy but was generally unlucky in nefarious activities and brought catastrophe on her associates. Eleven of her twelve husbands died untimely deaths. She claimed to have been an Indian scout and pony-express rider. She dressed, swore and shot like a man, and eventually went into show business.

Doris Day portrayed her in a 1953 film biography. 'Calamity Jane' became a common nickname for female prophets of doom, but this does not reflect the nature of Mary Jane Canary. What she did was to threaten 'calamity' to any man who offended her (*WWNN*).

... *CAMELOT* FOR PRESIDENT KENNEDY'S COURT?
In January 1961, the inauguration of a stylish young US President, with a glamorous wife at his side, aroused hopes of better things to come, following the sober Eisenhower years. But this in itself was not enough for people to apply the epithet to members (and hangers-on) of John F. Kennedy's administration.

What triggered it was the fact that the Lerner-Loewe musical *Camelot* (about King Arthur and Queen Guinevere's court) had opened on Broadway in December 1960. Following the President's assassination, Jackie Kennedy gave an interview to Theodore H. White in *Life* magazine and said: 'At night, before we'd go to sleep, Jack liked to play some records; and the song he loved most came at the very end of this record [*Camelot*]. The lines he loved to hear were: "Don't let it be forgot, that once there was a spot, for one brief shining moment that was known as Camelot ..."

'There'll be great Presidents again – and the Johnsons are wonderful, they've been wonderful to me – but there'll never be another Camelot again.'

One observes how the President's widow had a hand in creating the legend.

... SOMEONE IS *CAMP*?

I can quite clearly remember when I first encountered this word. Although I have since discovered it has been used since at least the beginning of the century, it was explained to me in 1963 by a man who displayed certain traits described by the word. He said it derived from prostitutes (male or female) who used to trail along behind the military and were thus 'camp followers'.

This has always struck me as being a perfectly good enough origin for a word meaning 'outrageously effeminate' and signifying one who flaunts his homosexuality. The word has since been extended in its use to refer to anyone, male or female, who ostentatiously, exaggeratedly, self-consciously, somewhat vulgarly and theatrically flaunts himself or herself, without necessarily being homosexual.

Susan Sontag, the American critic, bestowed a certain respectability on the word in a 1964 article 'Notes on Camp' in the *Partisan Review*. It was about this time that the word entered general speech.

As to what it means, I once interviewed Kenneth Williams, in Britain, most people's ideal of a camp actor, on the set of the film *Carry on Camping* (1968). I asked him for his definition of the word and he referred me to the *Oxford Dictionary's* 'that which is fundamentally frivolous', which is an interesting though not exactly precise gloss. (Actually, the *OED* contains no such definition.)

As to sources other than the one suggested above, there are plenty to choose from. How about the Italian word *campeggiare*, 'to stand out'?

Or the acronym said to have been found in the New York police files: 'KAMP' – 'known as male prostitute'?

Or, in English, the sort of 'camping' that was used to describe the sixteenth-century theatrical convention of boys dressing up to play women's roles.

Or, in French, the seventeenth-century *se camper* – camping it up – derived from the big silk billowing tents in which Louis XIV's army travelled? In Moliere's *Les Fourberies de Scapin*, written at the French court, Scapin instructs, 'Camp about on one leg ['*Campe-toi sur un pied*']. Put your hand on your hip. Strut like a comedy king.' A contemporary French dictionary (the Oxford, 1968) gives *se camper*, 'to posture boldly'. The French *campagne*, 'countryside' has also been suggested, as the place where strolling players performed. Surely, somewhere here – and most likely in the French – we have the origin?

... HOLD A *CANDLE* TO?
See *hold*.

... SET ONE'S *CAP* AT?
See *set*.

... SOMEONE MUST *CARRY THE CAN*?
i.e. bear responsibility, take the blame, become a scapegoat. Longman suggests that this was originally a military phrase referring to the duties of a man chosen to get beer for a group. He would have to carry a container of beer to the group and carry it back when it was empty. Thus, he (usually a rookie) had to perform a menial task and take responsibility for it, though he may not have benefited from it.

... SOMEONE IS IN THE *CART*?
i.e. in trouble (compare 'on the carpet'). Perhaps this comes from the fact that prisoners used to be taken in a cart to punishment or execution? Or, if a horse was in the cart (because it was ill or dead) the owner would be in a spot.

... LET THE *CAT OUT OF THE BAG*?
See *let*.

... NO ROOM TO SWING A *CAT*?
See *swing*.

... *CATGUT*?
i.e. sheep, horse or ass intestines used in the making of strings for musical instruments. Shakespeare got it right in *Much Ado About*

43

Nothing: 'Is it not strange, that sheeps' guts should hale souls out of men's bodies?' Cats' intestines do not come into it and it is not known how this mistaken expression arose, unless the word was intended originally as a pejorative way of describing the *sound* made by badly played violin strings, whatever their actual source.

... *CATHOUSE* FOR A BROTHEL?

Morris traces this term (more American than a British usage) from the fact that prostitutes have been called 'cats' since the fifteenth century, 'for the simple reason that the urban female cat attracts many toms when it is on heat and mates with them one after the other.' As early as 1401, men were warned, he says of the risk of chasing 'cat's tail', i.e. women, hence the slang word 'tail' to denote the female genitals (compare 'pussy').

... SOMETHING DOESN'T HAVE A *CAT-IN-HELL'S CHANCE*?

i.e. none whatsoever. Morris, who is rather good on 'cat' phrases provides the original saying which makes the meaning much clearer. It is, 'No more chance than a cat in hell *without claws*'. A cat is hopeless without weapons.

... IT'S RAINING *CATS AND DOGS*?

See *raining*.

... *CATS HAVE NINE LIVES*?

This comes from a proverbial saying dating at least from the sixteenth century. But why are cats supposed to have so *many*? Well, they have an obvious capacity for getting out of scrapes, literally landing on their feet in almost all cases. In ancient Egypt, cats were believed to have rid the country of a plague of rats and were thus venerated. The sacred number three when itself multiplied by three may have led to the nine figure.

... *CAVIARE TO THE GENERAL*?

i.e. of no interest to the public. A famously misunderstood phrase, having nothing to do with giving expensive presents to military gentlemen. In Shakespeare's *Hamlet*, the Prince refers to a play which, he remembers, 'pleased not the million, 'twas caviare to the general' (i.e. the general public).

The Arden edition of Shakespeare notes that in 1599–1601, when the play was written, caviare was a novel delicacy. *OED* adds, it was 'generally unpalatable to those who have not acquired a taste for it'.

... BY A LONG *CHALK*?
See *long*.

... *CHARLIE FARNSBARNS* TO DENOTE A TWIT WHOSE NAME YOU CAN'T REMEMBER?
Noting that this moderately well-known expression (in the UK at least) had passed by Partridge and his reviser, Paul Beale, I mentioned it to Beale in November 1985, suggesting that it sounded military to me, even pre-Second World War, though I had heard the comedian, Ronnie Barker, use it in a monologue quite recently.

He came back with this:

'Charlie Farnsbarns was a very popular equivalent of, e.g. "Mrs Thing" or "Old Ooja", i.e. "Old whatsisname". Much play was made with the name in *Much Binding in the Marsh* [late 1940s BBC radio series], but whether [Richard] Murdoch and [Kenneth] Horne actually invented it, or whether they borrowed it "out of the air", I'm afraid I don't know. They would mention especially, I remember, a magnificent motorcar called a "Farnsbarns Special" or something like, say, a "Farnsbarns Straight Eight". This was in the period, roughly, 1945–50, while I was at school – I recall a very jolly aunt of mine who was vastly amused by the name and used it a lot.'

I suspect it came out of the services (probably the RAF) in the Second World War. 'Charlie' (as in 'Proper Charlie', 'Right Charlie') was a slightly derogative name to apply to anyone. 'Farnsbarns' has the numbing assonance needed to describe a bit of a nonentity.

... A PAID DRIVER IS A *CHAUFFEUR*?
The first motor cars ran on a steam-operated principle. So the drivers had to heat up (Fr. *chauffer*) the vehicles before they would start. The name for these 'warmer-uppers' (also used in French to describe the fireman on a steam engine) has since been applied in English to the person paid to drive and look after the vehicle.

... MALE *CHAUVINIST PIG*?

See *male*.

... WE'RE *CHEESED OFF*?

i.e. fed up. I suppose 'cheese' and 'off-ness' rather go together so one might think of cheese as having an undesirable quality. Hence, also, when you subject cheese to a bit of stress in the form of heat it goes brown. It gets 'browned off', if you like. (It has also been suggested that the 'brown' link to cheese has rather more to do with the colour of its rind than with toasting.)

An origin seems to be trying to break out here. However, it may not be anything specifically to do with cheese that gives us the expression. It could derive from 'cheese off', an expression like 'fuck off', designed to make you go away. 'Cheesed off' may just be the state of rejection (Partridge). It also resembles 'pissed off'.

... *CHE SERA SERA* FOR 'WHATEVER WILL BE, WILL BE'?

In 1956 Doris Day had a hit record with the song *Whatever Will Be Will Be* which made use of this foreign phrase. She had sung it, somewhat painfully, but importantly for the plot, in the re-make of Alfred Hitchcock's *The Man Who Knew Too Much* in that year. Ten years later, Geno Washington and the Ram Jam Band had a hit with a song entitled *Que Sera Sera*. So where does the phrase come from? Is it 'che' or 'que'? What language is it?

There is no such phrase as *'Che sera sera'* in modern Spanish or Italian, though 'che' is an Italian word and 'sera' is Spanish.

If you were to say *'Que sera? sera?'* in Spanish that would translate as 'What will be? will be?', which is not quite right, or *'Lo que sera, sera'* (which makes sense but is not the wording of the song).

However, in Christopher Marlowe's *Dr Faustus* you will find in Faustus's first soliloquy:

> What doctrine call you this? Che sera, sera,
> What will be, shall be.

This is an old spelling of what would be put, in modern Italian, as *'Che sara, sara.'* In *Faustus*, it is probably Old French. Are you following this?

The idea behind the proverbial saying is simpler to trace. 'What must be, must be' can be found as far back as Chaucer's 'Knight's Tale' (*c.* 1390): 'Whan a thyng is shapen, it shal be.'

However, *'che sera sera'* is the form in which the Duke of Bedford's motto has always been written and so presumably that, too, is Old French or Italian.

... CHEVY CHASE?

A young American comedy actor arose bearing this name in the 1970s. He appeared notably on NBC's *Saturday Night Live* and in films like *Foul Play*. In fact, he was born Cornelius Crane Chase in 1943. So why did he adopt the name 'Chevy' except to get away from Cornelius or why was he given this nickname?

Could it be that he wanted to allude to Chevy as in the abbreviated form of Chevrolet, the American motor car which derives its name from Louis Chevrolet, a Swiss engineer?

Or could he have wanted to allude to the fifteenth-century ballad *Chevy Chase* which describes an old dispute between the Percy and Douglas families on the Scottish border, arising from a hunting accident? ('Chevy' or 'chivvy' is a huntsman's call meaning 'chase or harass the fox'.)

No, nearer home is the suburb of Washington D.C. known as Chevy Chase which, nevertheless, was most probably named after the fifteenth-century ballad by colonists who settled there. As such, in the US, 'Chevy' is set to become the inevitable nickname for someone with the surname Chase.

... PEOPLE *CHEW THE RAG*?

As in the expression 'to chew something over', the word 'chew' here means simply to say, i.e. something that is carried on in the mouth like eating. The 'rag' part relates to an old meaning of the word, in the sense 'to scold' or 'reprove severely'. 'Rag' was also once a slang word to describe the tongue (from 'red rag', probably).

So, to chew the rag means to grouse or grumble over something at length. Or it can mean simply to discuss matters with a degree of thoroughness (as in 'to chew the fat').

... CHICKEN À LA KING?

Cooked chicken breast served in a cream sauce with mushrooms and peppers does not have a royal origin. Rather, it is said to have been named after E. Clark King, a hotel proprietor in New York, when the dish was introduced in the 1880s (*OED Supp*).

Another story is that it was dreamed up at Delmonico's restaurant by Foxhall Keene, son of the Wall Street operator and sportsman J.R. Keene, and served as *chicken à la Keene* (Flexner). Yet another version is that the dish was created at Claridge's in London for J.R. Keene himself after his horse won the Grand Prix (Shook).

... A PERSON HAS A *CHIP ON HIS SHOULDER*?

i.e. bears a grudge in a defensive manner. Indeed, I once heard someone who was peculiarly prone to this posture described as 'having a bag of chips on his shoulder'.

The image has more to do with chips of wood than chipped potatoes and seems to have originated in the US where it was known by the early nineteenth century. A boy or man would, or would seem, to carry a chip on his shoulder daring others to dislodge it, looking for a fight. For once, there is general agreement about the source of this expression.

'... THE *CHIPS ARE DOWN*'?

i.e. a situation is at a crucial stage. This expression comes from chips used in some betting games. When they are down is the moment when the bets are placed but the outcome still is not known.

... *CHOP-SUEY*?

Shook says, 'In New York, on August 29 1896, the Chinese statesman Li Hung-Chang had his chef create *chop suey* which was unknown in China. It was an attempt to create a dish that would appeal to both American and Oriental tastes.'

But *OED Supp*. turns up a reference from 1888 (from an American source): 'A staple dish for the Chinese gourmet is now chow chop svey [*sic*], a mixture of chickens' livers and gizzards, fungi, bamboo buds, pigs' tripe, and bean sprouts stewed with spices.'

Whatever the case, the dish seems probably to owe more to origins in America than China, though the meaning of the words *shap sui* in Cantonese is clear enough: 'mixed bits'.

... *CHOW* FOR A BREED OF DOG?

... and 'chow mein' for a Chinese dish'? Could a diner's worst fears be justified?

Well, 'chow' in Mandarin means to cook or fry (and so 'chow mein', from *chao mian*, means 'fried flour').

In Cantonese, 'chow' means food and Chow dogs were, it is true, originally bred to be eaten and were clearly labelled as such (*chow-chow*, in full).

... WE'RE *CHUFFED* WHEN WE'RE PLEASED *AND* DISAPPOINTED?

Correspondence in *The Times* in 1980 pointed up how this word has managed to maintain two completely opposed meanings. As a boy in Liverpool in the 1950s, I was aware (like the Beatles-to-be) that 'I'm dead chuffed' meant 'I'm dead pleased'.

However, equally, 'I'm chuffed' can mean 'I'm fed up.' This is what is known as a Janus word because it faces in two different directions and has two opposed meanings.

I would like to think that the 'pleased' meaning predominates. When Paul McCartney of the Beatles returned to Liverpool to receive the Freedom of the City in November 1984 he declared that he was 'well chuffed'. A reader of *The Times* suggested that, in any case, 'dis-chuffed' would make a much better opposite.

Paul Beale in Partridge suggests a development (in military circles) from the word 'chow' (meaning food in general). This might account for the pleased or well-sated meaning. *SOED* mentions an 1832 dialect use of 'chuff' meaning 'churlish, gruff, morose' which may account for the opposite.

... *CHUNDER* FOR 'BE SICK'?

For reasons one can only guess at, there are numerous colourful Australianisms for 'sick' and this is one of them. Like many a pom I was introduced to this one by Barry Humphries via the 'Barry Mackenzie' column in *Private Eye* in the late 1960s. It has always been rather difficult to work out quite what Humphries himself invented and what was taken from general Australian 'slanguage'.

According to *The Dictionary of Australian Quotations* (1984), 'Barry Humphries states that, to the best of his knowledge, he

introduced the words "chunder" and "chundrous" to the Australian language. Previously "chunder" was known to him only
as a piece of Geelong Grammar School slang.'

The dictionary quotes one of his songs (from 1964):

> Oh, I was down by Manly Pier
> Drinking tubes of ice-cold beer
> With a bucket full of prawns upon me knee.
> But when I'd swallowed the last prawn
> I had a Technicolor yawn
> And I chundered in the old Pacific sea.

It is probably the case that 'chunder' was merely re-popularized
by Barry Humphries. Macquarrie (the Australian dictionary)
gives 'orig. uncert.', though the usual derivation concerns people
about to be sick on board ship. They shout to those on lower
decks: 'Watch under'. I am not sure whether this is entirely
convincing.

Partridge passes on another explanation: that it is rhyming
slang for Chunder Loo, i.e. spew, from Chunder Loo of Akin Foo,
'a cartoon figure in a long-running series of advertisements for
Cobra bootpolish in the *Bulletin* (Australian newspaper) from 8
Apr. 1909.'

Among equally delightful Australianisms for 'to be sick', I
might mention:

'to do a Technicolor yawn' (as above);
'to cry ruth' ('ruth' has to be said in a loud, rasping manner,
     and you'll get the picture);
'to talk on the big white telephone';
'to enjoy yourself in reverse';
'to pebbledash a bungalow';
'to park a tiger';
'to yodel on the lawn';
'to do a liquid laugh'.

These may never have been exclusively Australian. Partridge has
the variant 'to park a custard' as a piece of (British) naval slang
dating from the 1930s. By 1982 it was in the *Official Sloane Ranger
Handbook* as being spoken by Sloanes.

... THE MAN ON THE *CLAPHAM OMNIBUS*?
See *man*.

... MR *CLEAN*?
See *Mr*.

... A PERSON IS ON *CLOUD NINE*?
– or is it 'cloud seven'? – meaning 'in a euphoric state.' *DOAS* just gives 'cloud seven' but it is obvious from the examples in the *OED Supp.* that both forms have coexisted from the 1950s. I myself have only been acquainted with 'cloud nine' or 'upon cloud nine'.

The derivation appears to be American, in particular from terminology used by the US Weather Bureau. Cloud nine is the cumulonimbus cloud which may reach 30–40 thousand feet. As the Morrises note, 'If one is upon cloud nine, one is high indeed.'

The Morrises neatly record the reason for cloud nine being more memorable than cloud seven: 'The popularity ... may be credited to the *Johnny Dollar* radio show of the 1950s. There was one recurring episode... Every time the hero was knocked unconscious – which was often – he was transported to cloud nine. There Johnny could start talking again.'

... WE *COCK A SNOOK* AT SOMETHING?
The snook (like 'snoot' or 'snout') is another word for one's nose. So, to cock a snook is to thumb one's nose. Indeed, the gesture of pressing one's thumb against the nose and spreading the fingers is sometimes called a 'snooks'. There is probably a connection with the word 'sneak', for one who tells tales.

A 'snooker' was at one time a similarly derisive term for a raw army cadet. In 1875, when the game of snooker was devised by Colonel Sir Neville Chamberlain (1856–1944) while serving in India, the name was applied to the raw technique of a player who, not having ever played it before, was a 'snooker'.

... *COCKROACH*?
i.e. a voracious beetle infesting kitchens. The name has nothing to do with cocks or roaches (fish) but derives from the Spanish *cucaracha*.

The tarantula spider, meanwhile, derives its name from Taranto in southern Italy. Those bitten by the spider were said to suffer from tarantism (dancing mania), the effect being that they danced a tarantella.

... I SHOULD *COCOA*?
See *I should*.

... IT'S *COLD ENOUGH TO FREEZE THE BALLS OFF A BRASS MONKEY*?
The monkey in this colourful saying may not be an animal. A brass monkey was the name given to the plate on a warship's deck on which cannon balls or other ammunition were stacked. In cold weather, the brass would contract, tending to cause the stack of balls to fall down.

'Monkey' appears to have been a common slang word in olden gunnery days – there was a type of gun or cannon known as a monkey and a 'powder monkey' was the name for a boy who carried powder to the guns.

One has to say, though, that this derivation rather spoils the descriptiveness of the phrase.

... FINE-TOOTH *COMB*?
See *fine-tooth*.

'... *COME HELL AND/OR HIGH WATER*'?
i.e. 'come what may'. This cliché (as Partridge describes it) seems curiously lacking in pedigree. The *OED Supp*. finds no examples earlier than this century. And I have to admit defeat, too.

... NO *COMMENT*?
See *no*.

... *CONDOM*?
i.e. prophylactic sheath. Nobody knows why it is called this. It is not after the town of Condom in south-western France. Indeed, early eighteenth-century use of the term tended to be 'cundum' or 'condon' suggesting a different source. No 'Dr Condom' who prescribed this method of contraception has been discovered either.

Perhaps it will remain a mystery. Nor is there much logic to slang words for sheaths. The British call them a 'French letter', the French, *une capote anglaise* ('English great-coat').

McConville and Shearlaw in *The Slanguage of Sex* (1984) wonder whether the 'French' appellation (as in 'French safe' or 'Frenchie' or 'French tickler') derives from an old term for condom, 'frog skin'. On the other hand, the French obsession with *l'amour* has probably more to do with it. The Germans call condoms *parisiennes*.

But why do the French themselves see fit to think of England in this context. . . ?

... BEHAVIOUR IS *CONDUCT UNBECOMING*?

In this precise form and as part of the longer phrase 'conduct unbecoming the character of an officer and a gentleman' this seems to have appeared first in the (British) Naval Discipline Act (10 August 1860), Article 24, but the notion has also been included in disciplinary regulations of the other services, and in other countries, if not in quite these words.

This is merely an excuse to quote from a delightful letter I once received on the subject from Malcolm Macdonald, the novelist:

The only lecture I remember from a chilly few weeks at Mons officer Cadet School, Aldershot, (1955) was on The Manual of Military Law, especially on Section 40: Scandalous Conduct Unbecoming the Character of an Officer and a Gentleman. (It contrasted neatly with Section 41, for Other Ranks, which ran: Conduct Prejudicial to Good Order and Military Discipline.) Each section the lecturer dealt with was covered by an example taken from the Manual itself. The one for Section 40 ran: 'Captain R.M. Smythe of the 40th Punjabi Horse, charged under Section 40 of the Army Act (Scandalous Conduct Unbecoming ... etc) in that he, at a Government Ball at Mysore on the 14th of December 1892, did grasp Mrs Ponsonby, wife of Major C.F. Ponsonby of Tucker's Irregulars, by the breasts and did prance around the ballroom with her, neighing the while like a horse.'

An example used for Section 41: 'Trooper Scrope, C Company, 4th Battalion, 15th/41st Lancers, is charged under Section 41 of the Army Act (Conduct Prejudicial to Good Order and Military Discipline) in that he on foot parade in Buller Square, Thursday 14th August 1908, did throw down his rifle and, divesting himself of his tunic and accoutrements, did cry out: "I'll soldier no more. You may do as you please!" *or words to that effect.*'

Another section (I've forgotten the number) dealt with rape and was at pains to point out to the licentious soldiery that 'consent' obtained by deception was no defence to the charge. The example here concerned a bandmaster who persuaded a drum-major's daughter who dreamed of an operatic career that what he did to her behind the cricket pavilion was actually a novel form of breathing exercises straight from La Scala.

Thank you, Malcolm.

... THE OLD CONTEMPTIBLES?
See *old*.

... WE TAKE A COOK'S TOUR?
... when we are merely taking a tour, though possibly of rather greater extent than we meant to? Thomas Cook (1809–92) was the founder of the world's original and most famous travel agency. His first tour was in 1841 when he took a party of fellow tee-totallers on a railway trip in the British Midlands.

... COOL MILLION?
In Henry Fielding's novel *Tom Jones* (1749) we can read: 'Mr Watson rose from the table in some heat and declared he had lost a cool hundred...'. In Charles Dickens's *Great Expectations* (1861): 'She had wrote a little [codicil] ... leaving a cool four thousand to Mr Mathew Pocket'. In Anthony Powell's *Hearing Secret Harmonies* (1975), Lord Widmerpool comments on a smoke-bomb let off at a literary prize-giving: 'I wouldn't have missed that for a cool million.'

But why 'cool'? *SOED* says drily that it 'gives emphasis to the (large) amount'. Is it because a large amount of money is rather chilling, lacking in warmth? This is not very satisfactory. Perhaps the word 'cool' in this context anticipates its more modern connection with jazz, as something thrilling, to be approved of.

... AN ACTOR HAS CORPSED?
When an actor corpses, it means that he has been overtaken by such involuntary laughter that he is unable to go on speaking his lines. This is quite a common occurrence and is hard to explain. On the whole, the nightly repetition of familiar lines is such a dull procedure that it is commonly held that actors are quite capable of thinking of other matters while they speak them. Nevertheless, when some (perhaps spontaneous) joke or action occurs it can trigger off such a reaction.

Presumably, the term 'corpsing' is used because the actor is rendered as incapable as a dead body. When another actor 'confuses or puts (him) out, or spoils his acting by some blunder' (*SOED*), or makes him forget his lines, it is the equivalent of killing him by stopping his performance.

Diana Rigg (*No Turn Unstoned*, 1982) recalls what happened to John Philip Kemble when he was playing Mark Antony in *All For Love*. 'He happened to look up, and, perceiving a pedantic old figure, who was leaning over the upper box, with a listening trumpet to his ear, he began to smother a laugh, but no longer able to contain himself, to the great astonishment of the audience, his laugh became loud and immoderate, and it was some time before he was able to finish the character.'

More recently, the actor Anthony Sher in his book *Year of the King* (1985) described what happened to him during a performance of *Tartuffe*: 'During the rape-on-the-dining-table scene ... everything just stops for about thirty seconds while [Alison Steadman] and I join the audience screaming with laughter. A most peculiar event, breaking all the rules... Why is an actor's unintentional giggling called a "corpse"? It seems to me quite the opposite. It proves that he's very much alive, and can still tell how silly this all is: him dressed up as someone else speaking words written by a third party.'

... SOMEONE *COULDN'T RUN A WHELK-STALL*?

This pleasantly obscure way of describing incompetence appears – until an earlier instance turns up – to have originated with John Burns, the Labour MP. In the *South-Western Star* for 13 January 1894 he is quoted as saying: 'From whom am I to take my marching orders? From men who fancy they are Admirable Crichtons ... but who have not got sufficient brains and ability to run a whelk-stall?'

Partridge has 'that's no way to run a whelk-stall' as the British equivalent of the US '[that's] a hell of a way to run a railroad'.

... SENT TO *COVENTRY*?

See *sent*.

... *CRAP*?

i.e. faeces, rubbish, utter nonsense. In 1979, the Greater London Council, after earnest consideration, declined to erect a blue plaque to commemorate the former home of the Victorian sanitary engineer, Thomas Crapper. The council's historic buildings committee decided that 'memorable though Crapper's name might be in popular terms', evidence from the Patent Office showed that he was not a notable inventor or pioneer in his field.

It has to be said, though, that there was indeed a 'Thomas Crapper Ltd, sanitary engineers by appointment to King George V' and the company's shop in Chelsea (featured in the opening moments of the 1963 film *The Servant*) did at one time exist.

But did Thomas Crapper give part of his name to excretion? Or did his surname become another word for 'privy'? Well, he invented a refinement of the lavatory – a valve-and-syphon system which automatically shut off the water after its job had been done. His story is told in *Flushed with Pride: The Story of Thomas Crapper* (1969) by Wallace Reyburn, a book which I am sure is invaluable.

Mr Crapper was born in 1837 and died in 1910. And yet the *OED Supp.* finds this use of the word in 1846: '"Fenced, in a dunniken" ... "What? Fenced in a crapping ken?"' which proves that the word 'crap' was being used in this situation when Mr Crapper was a mere thirteen years old and presumably had not as yet made his mark in the lavatory.

Partridge gives the verb 'to crap' as coming from the mid-eighteenth century. This proves little as Partridge was notoriously unreliable about dating. But it is clear that the connection between Mr Crapper and the word 'crap' is no more than an amazing coincidence.

'Crapper' = privy derives from 'crap' and that word comes from Middle English *crappe* (residue, rubbish) and was well established in the US by the 1860s (Flexner). It may, however, be that the use of the words 'crap-house' and 'crapper' were reinforced because of the existence of the British sanitary engineer.

... A PERSON IS *CRAZY LIKE A FOX*?
i.e. 'apparently crazy but with far more method than madness' (Partridge). This hardly seems to be true of foxes, so the expression was perhaps formed in parallel with the older 'as cunning as a fox'.

But foxes always get into expressions like these. Interviewing the actress Judy Carne in 1980, I asked about Goldie Hawn, her one-time co-star on the US TV series *Rowan and Martin's Laugh-In*. She said: 'She's not a dizzy blonde. She's about as *dumb* as a fox. She's incredibly bright.'

... THERE EXISTS A *CREDIBILITY GAP*?

'The difference between what is claimed as fact, especially in matters of official government policy, and actuality...' says Radford. 'The phrase was first used in 1966 by Gerald Ford, then an American Republican Congressman, in connection with the discrepancy between the actual escalation of American participation in the Vietnam War, and the claim by the Johnson Administration that no change had taken place in policy.'

Well, maybe. But Safire digs further back: 'Coinage of the phrase in print probably belongs to an anonymous *New York Herald Tribune* headline writer. On May 13 1965, reporter David Wise wrote a piece that had the word "credibility" in the same lead with the word "gap" though not tied together. The headline read "Dilemma in 'Credibility Gap'". The phrase was given currency by *Washington Post* reporter Murray Marder on December 5, 1965, in a story about "growing doubt and cynicism concerning Administration pronouncements ... The problem could be called a credibility gap."'

However, according to Safire, in *early* 1965, 'G.I.s in South Vietnam began sporting buttons reading "Ambushed at credibility gap".'

... EATING *CROW*?

See *eating*.

... CHEWING THE *CUD*?

i.e. thinking deeply about something, especially the *past*. This refers to the ruminative look cows have when they chew the 'cud' – that is, bring back food from their first stomach and chew it in their mouths again. 'Cud' comes from Old English *cwidu*, meaning what is chewed.

... A WIFE GIVES A *CURTAIN LECTURE*?

– a somewhat dated term for the private reproof given by a wife to her husband. This refers to the scolding that took place in bed, after the curtains around the bed (as on a four-poster) had been closed (Longman).

Sometimes, the variation 'Caudle lecture' is used. This derives from Douglas Jerrold's *Mrs Caudle's Curtain Lectures*, a series published by *Punch* in 1846 in which Mr Caudle suffered the naggings of his wife after they had gone to bed.

... A *CUSTOM IS 'MORE HONOUR'D IN THE BREACH THAN THE OBSERVANCE'*?

As Burnam 2 says, 'Few remarks are more universally misapprehended' than Hamlet's reply to Horatio.

So what does it mean? It is usually taken to mean that whatever custom is under consideration has fallen into sad neglect. But, says Burnam, 'Hamlet's meaning, clearly, is that celebrating the King's drunken revelries ... is a custom that would be better "honour'd" if it were not followed at all ... Change Shakespeare's "more" to "better" and you have his meaning.'

... A PERSON HAS *CUT AND RUN*?

i.e. escaped or run away. This is one of many phrases of nautical origin and describes what happened when, in order to make a quick getaway, instead of the lengthy process of hauling up a ship's anchor, the anchor cable was cut. This was easier to do, of course, when the anchor was attached to a hemp rope.

... WE DON'T LIKE THE *CUT OF SOMEONE'S JIB*?

i.e. don't like the look of them. Nautical origin. The cut (or condition) of the jib or foresail signified the quality of the vessel as a whole.

... *DAGMARS* TO DENOTE MOTOR-CAR BUMPERS?

For a while, in the 1950s, this was what Americans called the sticking-out bits. I wondered why until I learned that in a TV show called *Broadway Open House* there was an actress called Dagmar (Virginia Ruth Egnor) who was well endowed in the bumper area. She took the role assumed in Britain in the 1950s by Sabrina and in the 1980s by Samantha Fox.

... *DALEK?*

The most famous characters in the BBC's long-running science-fiction TV series *Dr Who* are undoubtedly the Daleks – armed pepper-pot creatures who go around screeching, 'Exterminate! Exterminate!' The Daleks made their first appearance in the first year of the programme's existence, 1963, and have come back from time to time since. It is possible that the word 'dalek' has been used to describe anyone who behaves like an unpleasant automation.

The *OED Supp.* cites an explanation for the name given by Terry Nation, the begetter of *Dr Who* and the Daleks: 'Who are the Daleks? Dr Who's most dangerous enemies, written into his second adventure in 1963 by Terry Nation, who named them after an encyclopedia volume covering DAL-LEK' (quoting *Radio Times*, 30 December 1971).

But Nation admitted in an interview published in 1973 (for *The Doctor Who Tenth Anniversary Special*) that this story had been invented merely to satisfy journalists. In fact, in his own words, the name 'simply rolled off the typewriter'.

... *DANDELION* FOR A PLANT?

Unlike some supposed French derivations (cf. 'marmalade'), the name of this flower really does come from *dent de lion* – lion's tooth – i.e. from the supposed resemblance of the outline of the widely toothed leaves. The Italians call it, similarly, *dente di leone* and the Spanish, *diente de leon*.

It should be noted, however, that the French themselves will have none of this. They call it *pissenlit*, which sounds most unsavoury and is (a little bit). Drinks made from the dandelion are a powerful diuretic and could make you wet the bed.

According to *Harrap's (French) Slang Dictionary* (1984), *manger les pissenlits* or *bouffer du pissenlit par la racine* means 'to be dead and buried, to be pushing up the daisies'. It is all very complicated...

... *DANDER UP*?

See *gets one's*.

... AN IMPORTANT DAY IS A *D-DAY*?

Although D-Day has come to mean the day, 6 June 1944, on which the Allies began their landings in northern France in order to push back German forces, it has a more general use. Like H-Hour, D-Day is a military way of detailing elements in an operation. The 'D' just reinforces the 'Day' on which the plan is to be put into effect and enables successive days to be labelled 'D-Day plus one' etc. As it happens, the Normandy landings were due to begin on 5 June but were delayed by bad weather. But whatever day they had started on would still have been D-Day. And H-Hour, the moment of action on that day, would also still have been what it actually was.

The form was used in the First World War and can also be used in non-military situations to denote an important day when something is due to begin.

... SOMEONE IS A *DEAD RINGER* FOR SOMEONE ELSE?

i.e. very closely resembles him. The origin here is very definitely in horse racing and comes from the US. There, the word 'ringer' has been used since the last century to describe a horse fraudulently substituted for another in a race. Although perhaps this could take place if the horse due to run had died, the 'dead' element in this expression is probably no more than a way of saying 'exact' (as in 'dead heat').

... DEATH SENTENCE?
See *pronounced.*

... SOMETHING HAS BEEN DEEP-SIXED?
During the Watergate affair of 1973–4 (that rich source of colloquialisms), former presidential aide John Dean told of a conversation he had had with another Nixon henchman, John Ehrlichman: 'He told me to shred the documents and "deep-six" the briefcase. I asked him what he meant by "deep-six". He leaned back in his chair and said, "You drive across the river on your way home at night, don't you? Well, when you cross over the bridge on your way home, just toss the briefcase into the river".' (Ehrlichman, before going to prison, denied this conversation ever took place.)

As such, the word clearly means, 'to dispose of, with emphasis; to destroy or deliberately lose' (Safire). It comes from an American nautical saying used by the men who took soundings. When they said 'by the deep six' they meant six fathoms which is thirty-six feet. In naval circles, 'to deep six' equally means 'to jettison overboard'.

DOAS notes an extension of this meaning in jive and jazz use since the 1940s: the deep six means the grave.

... DEEP THROAT?
– to denote an anonymous source. Because that was the name given to the source within the Nixon White House who fed *Washington Post* journalists Carl Bernstein and Bob Woodward with information which helped in their Watergate investigations (1972–4). It has been suggested that 'Deep Throat' never existed but was a cover for unjustified suppositions. However, the reporters explained:

Woodward had promised he would never identify him or his position to anyone... In newspaper terminology, this meant the discussions were on 'deep background' ... Woodward explained the arrangement to managing editor Howard Simons one day. He had taken to calling the source 'my friend', but Simons dubbed him Deep Throat, the title of a celebrated pornographic movie. The name stuck.

All The Presidents' Men (1974)

61

Indeed, *Deep Throat* was the most fashionable American porno movie of the late 1960s. The censor would not allow it to be shown in Britain but everyone knew that it concerned a woman, played by Linda Lovelace, whose clitoris was placed in the back of her throat enabling her to engage in a very special form of sex. It is said that the film grossed in excess of $600 million (*SOTC*).

... A RACE IS A *DERBY*?
(Pronounced 'darby' in the UK, 'durby' in the US.) *The* Derby is the most famous horse race over the flat in the world. It is run every June at Epsom race course in Surrey. Every other Derby in the world derives its name from this one. It was started in 1780 by the twelfth Earl of Derby who is said to have discussed the idea of a race for three-year-old fillies, over dinner with his friend, Sir Charles Bunbury. Tradition has it that they tossed a coin over which of them the race should be named after and Derby won. (Somehow the idea of a race called the Kentucky Bunbury would have been hard to take seriously.)

Another race, The Oaks, run two days after the Derby, takes its name from an estate of the Earl of Derby near Epsom. It was first run in 1779.

... BETWIXT THE *DEVIL AND THE DEEP BLUE SEA*?
i.e. having two courses of action open, both of them dangerous. Burnam suggests it is wrong to interpret this as meaning 'between Satan and the bottom of the ocean'. He says that 'devil' here is the seam of a wooden ship's hull. It is very difficult to obtain access to and thus described as 'the devil to get at' when caulking.

The Morrises say that this was a plank fastened to the side of a ship as a support for guns. 'It was difficult of access and, once you were there, a perilous place to be, but better than the deep blue sea.'

Either way, it is a similar expression to 'between Scylla and Charybdis'.

... THE *DIE IS CAST*?
This has nothing to do with dying or 'dye'. The 'die' here is the singular of 'dice', so when the die is cast, the player must accept whatever fate has in store for him.

When Caesar crossed the Rubicon he is supposed to have said, *iacta alea est* ('the die is cast').

... A MAN *DIED WITH HIS BOOTS ON*?
i.e. died violently, or was hanged summarily (sometimes 'died in his boots or shoes'). Naturally, this comes from the American West in the nineteenth century. It was firmly ensconced in the language by the time of the 1941 Errol Flynn film *They Died With Their Boots On*, about General Custer and his death at Little Big Horn.

In one sense it can suggest an ignominious death (say, by hanging) but in a general way it can refer to someone who dies 'in harness', going about his work, like a soldier in the course of duty.

'To die with one's boots *off*' suggests, of course, that one dies in bed.

... PEOPLE DANCE IN A *DISCO*?
Now almost universally known, 'disco' is a contraction of the French word *discothèque*. This word was devised for a place where people danced to records and first began to be used in the early 1950s. It is an adaptation of the French word *bibliothèque*, 'a library' (from the Greek meaning a 'book repository'), and seems to have been invented, initially at least, with a view to conveying the idea of a 'record library' rather than a dancing place.

... *DISCUSSING UGANDAN AFFAIRS*?
See *Ugandan*.

... GIVE A *DOG A BAD NAME*?
See *give*.

... HAIR OF THE *DOG*?
See *hair*.

... LOVE ME, LOVE MY *DOG*?
See *love*.

... PUTTING ON THE *DOG*?
See *putting*.

... *DOG-DAYS* IN MID-SUMMER?

Nothing to do with dogs getting hot under the collar, contracting rabies or anything like that.

The ancients applied this label to the period between 3 July and 11 August when the Dog-star, Sirius, rises at the same time as the sun. At one time this seemed to coincide with the overwhelmingly hot days of high summer.

... LOOKING LIKE A *DOG'S BREAKFAST*? AND
... DRESSED UP LIKE A *DOG'S DINNER*?

When the first saying suggests something scrappy and the second something showy, what are we led to conclude about the differing nature of a dog's breakfast and dinner?

A dog's breakfast might well (before the invention of tinned dog food) have consisted of the left-over scraps of the household from the night before. So that takes care of that, except that there is also the phrase 'cat's breakfast', meaning a mess. Could both these derive from a belief that dogs and cats might on occasions appear to eat their own sick?

A dog's dinner might well not have differed very much ... except in the case described in II Kings 9. Of Jezebel, it says that, after many years of leading Ahab astray, she 'painted her face, and tired her head', but failed to impress Jehu, whose messy disposal of her fulfilled Elijah's prophecy that the 'dogs shall eat Jezebel by the wall of Jezreel'.

So, if this is the origin, a specific dog's dinner is being evoked by the phrase.

... *LA DOLCE VITA*?

Put into the English language as a result of Federico Fellini's film *La Dolce Vita* (1960), this phrase suggests a high society life of luxury, pleasure and self-indulgence. It is an Italian phrase simply meaning 'sweet life'. I'm not sure how much of a set phrase it was in Italian before it was adopted by everybody else.

... WE HAVEN'T SEEN SOMEONE FOR *DONKEY'S YEARS*?

i.e. for a very long time. It is not very hard to believe that what we have here is a contortion of the phrase 'donkey's ears' (which are, indeed, long.) As such, what we have is a form of rhyming slang: donkeys = donkey's ears = years.

This also helps to explain the alternative expression, 'I haven't seen him for *yonks*', where 'yonks' may well be a distortion of year and donk(ey)s.

Brewer, however, gives the less fun derivation that 'donkey's years' is an allusion to the 'old tradition' that one never sees a dead donkey.

'... DON'T EAT OYSTERS UNLESS THERE'S AN R IN THE MONTH'?

'The oyster is unseasonable and unwholesome in all months that have not the letter R in their name,' wrote Richard Buttes in *Diet's Dry Dinner* (1599).

This is an old belief, hard to dispose of, but no longer tenable. Before modern refrigeration came along, oysters did 'go off' in the warmer months from May to August which, as it happens, do not have an R in them. Now oysters may be eaten at any time.

... A THING IS A *DOOBRY*?

Well, we say it because we cannot think what else to call it. It's a 'thing', a 'thingy', a 'thingamy', a 'thingumajig', a 'thingumabob', or a 'whatsit'. But really I am including this word (a) because I do not know how to spell it, and (b) because I have yet to find it given much prominence in a dictionary, although it is undoubtedly on people's lips.

Paul Beale in Partridge has it as 'doobri', 'an elaboration of *doofah*, a gadget' or, applied to a person, as the short form of 'doobri-firkin'.

I am pretty sure people were saying 'doobry' at Oxford in the mid-1960s. Kenny Everett, the disc jockey, used it in the 1970s.

Talking of whom, I might also mention a 'thingerooni', which is just the sort of thingerooni he would say. Adding the suffix '-eroo' to words is a recognised linguistic practice (e.g. 'flopperoo') and is not frantically modern. The *OED Supp.* cites American discussions of the phenomenon in the 1940s and 1950s.

I have yet to find any recognition of the longer '-erooni' suffix, though that is hardly of recent origin either. In Alfred Hitchcock's film *Pyscho* a character, in need of a drink, says 'I'm dying of thirsterooni'. That was filmed in 1960. More recently a 'smack-eroonie' has meant a kiss.

... HAWKS AND *DOVES*?
See *hawks*.

... BAKER'S *DOZEN*?
See *baker's*.

... *DRESSED UP TO THE NINES*?
i.e. very smartly dressed. As with 'donkey's years', this phrase may have come to us by a pronunciation shift. If you were to say dressed up 'to then eyne', that would mean in Old English 'dressed up to the eyes' (*eyne* being the old plural of eye). The snag with this is that no examples of the phrase being used occur before the eighteenth century.

I do not accept the definition which suggests that it refers to the setting of a standard with ten as the highest point one could reach. If you were up to the nines you were very nearly the best. (Longman). (Compare the catchphrase, 'How would you rate her on a scale of one to ten?' which was all the rage after the film *10* in 1979.)

Nor do I agree with Ewart that it has anything to do with setting oneself up to match the Nine Muses of Greek and Roman mythology.

Nor with the mystic number nine (Partridge).

Nor am I swayed by the suggestion that the 99th Regiment of Foot was renowned for smartness of dress. Hence anyone well turned out was 'dressed up to the nines'.

It all remains a bit of a mystery.

... *LAME DUCK*?
See *lame*.

... COMBATANTS ENTER WITH THEIR *DUKES UP*?
Describing a summit between Soviet and American leaders, *Time* (20 October 1986) stated 'Reagan and Gorbachev both came to office not with their hands outstretched but with their dukes up.' If dukes means fists, why so?

Shook explains: 'The Duke of Wellington had such a large nose that "duke" became a synonym for "nose". Then, so the theory goes, a man's fist became a "duke buster". In time this was shortened, and fists were simply called "dukes".

The Morrises prefer another theory: that it is to do with Cockney rhyming slang, viz. Duke of Yorks = forks = fingers (used to express the whole hand or fist). Though it is an involved explanation, I agree with it.

E

...SOMEONE IS *EATING CROW*?

i.e. having to do something distasteful. This expression, mostly confined to the US, stems, so it is said, from an incident in the British-American war of 1812–14.

During a ceasefire, a New England soldier went hunting and crossed over into the British lines where, finding no better game, he shot a crow. An unarmed British officer encountered the American and, by way of admiring his gun, took hold of it. He then turned it on the other and forced him to eat part of the crow.

Warning him to keep away, the British officer handed back the gun, only to have it turned on him. He was also forced at gunpoint to eat some of the crow.

Later, when the British officer complained of this violation of the ceasefire to his American counterpart, the soldier was brought in and, when asked if he recognised the British officer, replied: 'Yes, I dined with him yesterday.'

That is the story, and a very neat source for the phrase it is too and, for once, no one seems to dispute that this is indeed the origin of the phrase.

...*EATING HUMBLE PIE*?

i.e. submitting to humiliation. The 'humbles' or 'umbles' were those less appealing parts of a deer (or other animal) which had been killed in a hunt. They would be given to those of lower rank and perhaps served as 'humble pie' or 'umble pie'.

So, although this kind of 'humble' had nothing to do with humility, it was natural that the meanings should get blended.

Although this food sense of the word '(h)umble' has been

current since the fifteenth century, the expression incorporating it seems to come from no earlier than the nineteenth.

'... *EAT YOUR HEART OUT!*'?

As a swanking exultation, a minor singer having just finished a powerful ballad might exclaim, 'Eat your heart out, Frank Sinatra!' Although current at the end of the last century, this expression acquired popularity in the mid-twentieth century, largely (I would say) through its use in show business circles.

As such, it is another of those Jewish expressions so popularized. Originally, 'to eat one's heart out' meant simply 'to pine' and Leo Rosten in *Hooray For Yiddish!* (1983) suggests convincingly that it is a translation of the Yiddish, *Es dir oys s'harts.*

... *ECONOMICAL WITH THE TRUTH?*

On 18 November 1986, the British Cabinet Secretary, Sir Robert Armstrong, was being cross-examined in the Supreme Court of New South Wales. The British Government was attempting to prevent publication in Australia of a book about M15, the British secret service. Defence counsel Malcolm Turnbull asked Sir Robert about the contents of a letter he had written which had been intended to convey a misleading impression. 'What's a "misleading impression"?' inquired Turnbull. 'A sort of bent untruth?'

Sir Robert replied: 'It is perhaps being economical with the truth.' This explanation was greeted with derision not only in the court but in the world beyond and it looked as though a new euphemism for lying had been invented.

In fact, Sir Robert had prefaced his remark with, 'As one person said ... ' and, when the court apparently found cause for laughter in what he said, added: 'It is not very original, I'm afraid.'

Indeed not. Dr E.H.H. Green, writing to the *Guardian* on 4 February 1987, said he had found a note penned by Sir William Strang, later to become head of the Foreign Office, in February 1942. Describing the character of the exiled Czech president Benes, Strang had written: 'Dr Benes's methods are exasperating; he is a master of misrepresentation and ... he is apt to be economical with the truth.'

The notion thus appears to have been a familiar one in the Civil Service for a very long time – and not only there. Mark Twain is

reported to have said, 'Truth is a mighty valuable commodity, we
need to be economical with it.' And, before him, Edmund Burke
remarked, 'We practise an economy of truth, that we may live to
tell it the longer.'

... LAID AN *EGG*?
See *laid*.

... *EGG ON*?
i.e. encourage, incite. Nothing to do with eggs. The meaning is
really 'to edge on'.

... SURE AS *EGGS IS EGGS*?
See *sure*.

... ONE OVER THE *EIGHT*?
See *one*.

... SOMETHING IS BEING DONE AT THE *ELEVENTH
HOUR*?
i.e. at the last moment. This expression alludes to the parable of
the labourers, of whom the last 'were hired at the eleventh hour'
(St Matthew 20:9).

On the other hand, the phrase was used with different re-
sonance at the end of the First World War. The Armistice was
signed at 5 a.m. on 11 November 1918 and came into force at 11
a.m. – 'at the eleventh hour on the eleventh day of the eleventh
month'.

... *EMMY* FOR A SHOW BUSINESS AWARD?
American TV's equivalent of the Oscar has a most obscure origin.
The image orthicon tube is an important part of the television
camera and, if you can believe it, image became immy became
emmy. The statuettes so called were first awarded by the American Academy of Television Arts and Sciences in the 1940s.

The film Oscar is traditionally said to take its name from a
comment made by Margaret Herrick, a secretary at the American
Academy of Motion Picture Arts and Sciences in about 1931. On
seeing the statuette (awarded since 1928), she declared: 'Why, it

looks just like my Uncle Oscar,' – i.e. one Oscar Pierce, a wheat and fruit grower.

... *EQUERRY*?

i.e. an officer in charge of the horses of a king or similar exalted person (now an officer of the British Royal household who attends a member of the Royal family). Oddly, this name has nothing to do with Latin *equus*, meaning horse, but is derived from French *écurie*, meaning stable which (although having to do with horses) leads to a meaning more akin to the title 'esquire' (which is derived from the Latin *scutarius*, meaning shield-bearer).

... TAKEN DOWN AND USED IN *EVIDENCE*?

See *anything you say*.

... ALL MY *EYE*?

See *all*.

... APPLE OF ONE'S *EYE*?

See *apple*.

... *EYEBALL TO EYEBALL*?

(meaning in close confrontation). Use of this expression is of comparatively recent origin. In the missile crisis of October 1962, the US took a tough line when the Soviet Union placed missiles on Cuban soil. After a tense few days, the Soviets withdrew. Secretary of State Dean Rusk (*b*. 1909) was speaking to an ABC news correspondent, John Scali, on 24 October and said; 'Remember, when you report this, that, eyeball to eyeball, they blinked first.' Columnists Charles Bartlett and Stewart Alsop then helped to popularize this as 'We're eyeball to eyeball and the other fellow just blinked.'

Before this, 'eyeball to eyeball' was a Black American serviceman's idiom. Safire quotes a reply given by the all-Black 24th Infantry Regiment to an inquiry from General MacArthur's HQ in Korea (November 1950), 'Do you have contact with the enemy?'

'We is eyeball to eyeball.'

... A PERSON MUST *FACE THE MUSIC*?

i.e. accept whatever punishment is coming. Two theories: one is
that an actor or entertainer must not only accept the judgement of
the audience but also of the (often hard to impress) musicians in
the orchestra pit before him. He literally 'faces' the music.

But that seems a bit feeble. More likely is the second, akin to the
expression 'to be drummed out' of something. At one time, if a
soldier was dismissed from the army for dishonourable conduct,
he would literally be drummed out in a ceremony which included
having a description of his crime read out and his insignia
stripped from his uniform.

... SWEET *FANNY ADAMS*?

See *sweet*.

... AN ACHIEVEMENT IS A *FEATHER IN ONE'S CAP*?

The giving of feathers is associated with bravery – and with its
complete opposite.

American Indians are perhaps the most notable wearers of
feathered costume to signify their bravery in battle. However, in
1346, the English Black Prince was awarded the crest of John,
King of Bohemia, which showed three ostrich feathers, after he
had distinguished himself at the Battle of Crécy. This symbol has
since been carried by every Prince of Wales.

Later, any knight who had fought well might wear a feather in
his helmet. Hence, the phrase means an honour or achievement of
which one can be proud.

In the First World War, being awarded a white feather took on the opposite meaning. Women would hand them to men who had not enlisted, as a pointed encouragement to do so.

... FIT AS A *FIDDLE*?
See *fit*.

... *FIFTH BEATLE*?
i.e. someone who has missed out on success. The original 'Fifth Beatle' was Brian Epstein (1934–67), the group's manager, so dubbed, much to his annoyance, by Murray the K, an American disc jockey, in 1964. Others could more fittingly have merited the title – Stu Sutcliffe, an early member of the group who was eased out and died before fame struck, Pete Best, who was replaced as the drummer by Ringo Starr, and Neil Aspinall, road manager, aide and friend.

... *A FIFTH COLUMN* IS AT WORK?
– meaning traitors, infiltrators. During the Spanish Civil War, the Nationalist General, Emilio Mola, was besieging the Republican-held city of Madrid with four columns. He was asked in a broadcast whether this was sufficient to capture the city and he replied he was relying on the support of the *quinta columna*, the fifth column, which was already hiding inside the city and which sympathized with his side. This remark, made in October 1936, rapidly became known and was helped on its way when Ernest Hemingway used the phrase as the title of a play in 1938.

... WE'LL GO THROUGH SOMETHING WITH A *FINE-TOOTH COMB*?
i.e. examine it very closely. It is a small point to make but people often speak this phrase as though it were a fine *tooth-comb* rather than a *fine-tooth* comb. What they should be saying is that the comb has fine-teeth (enabling the smallest pieces of dirt to be removed) rather than praising the excellence of the tooth-comb they are using.

... HANGS *FIRE*?
See *hangs*.

... NEITHER FISH, FLESH etc?
See *neither*.

... HAND OVER FIST?
See *hand*.

... FIT AS A FIDDLE?
i.e. extremely healthy. It is odd how this name for the violin has produced so many idioms – 'to play second fiddle', 'to have a face as long as a fiddle', 'fiddle about', 'fiddle-faddle', 'on the fiddle', and so on, most of them self-explanatory.

But why 'fit as a fiddle'? It is hard to say. First, there is the alliteration – as ever an important factor in these matters – and the *OED Supp.*'s first citation (1603) – 'as fine as a farthing fiddle' would seem to support this.

More likely perhaps, a fiddler, when playing quickly, has to be so dextrous with his fingers and bow that he is assumed to be especially lively and awake, and thus could the phrase as we have it now be a contraction of 'as fit as a fiddler'?

According to Charles Earle Funk (quoted by the Morrises) there was an expression 'to have one's face made of a fiddle', meaning to be exceptionally good-looking. Repeatedly one comes back to the idea of a fiddle being something admirable (cf. 'play first fiddle'), and perhaps there is no more to it than that.

... SOMETHING FIT ONE TO A T?
i.e. perfectly. Simple, you might think: a T-square is used by draughtsmen to draw parallel lines and angles. But Shook complains that 'to a T' was in use in the seventeenth century before the T-square got its name. 'A more likely explanation is that the expression was originally "to a tittle". A tittle was the dot over the *i*, so the phrase meant "to a dot" or fine point.'
(See also *jot and tittle*.)

... IN LIKE FLYNN?
See *in*.

... YOUNG FOGEY?
See *young*.

... *FOURTH ESTATE* TO DESCRIBE THE PRESS?

Thomas Macaulay wrote (1828) concerning the House of Commons: 'the gallery in which the reporters sit has become the fourth estate of the realm' – the other three being the Lords Spiritual, the Lords Temporal and the Commons – and Macaulay has often been credited with coining this phrase. But so have Thomas Carlyle, William Hazlitt, Lord Brougham and Edmund Burke. Burke, for example, is said to have pointed to the press gallery, remarking: 'And yonder sits the Fourth Estate, more important than them all.'

The phrase was originally used to describe various forces outside Parliament – such as the army (as by Falkland in 1638) or the mob (as by Fielding in 1752). When Hazlitt used it in 'Table Talk' in 1821, he meant not the Press in general but just William Cobbett. A couple of years later, Brougham is reported to have used the phrase in the House of Commons referring to the Press in general. So when Macaulay used it in the *Edinburgh Review* in 1828, it was apparently already an established usage.

Then Carlyle used it several times – in his article on Boswell's *Life of Johnson* in 1832, in his history of *The French Revolution* in 1837, and in his lectures 'On Heroes, Hero-Worship, & the Heroic in History' in 1841. But, just to keep the confusion alive, on the last occasion Carlyle attributed the phrase to Burke, who had died in 1797.

(I am indebted to Nicolas Walter's letter to the *Observer* of 29 December 1985 for the above summary.)

It has been suggested that the BBC (or broadcasting in general) has become the *Fifth* Estate.

... CRAZY LIKE A *FOX*?

See *crazy*.

... A PERSON IS DANCING THE *FOX-TROT*?

Allegedly named after the US comedian Harry Fox whose 1913 *Ziegfeld Follies* contained the steps for it, the word first appears (according to Flexner) in the 1915 Victor Record catalogue.

The dance nevertheless uses a name that existed before to describe an aspect of horsemanship. *SOED* has 'a pace with short steps, in changing from trotting to walking' (presumably because a fox does something similar) and the *OED Supp.*'s earliest citation is from 1872.

... A SELF-EMPLOYED PERSON IS A *FREELANCE*?
The word, redolent of the Middle Ages, when an unattached
soldier for hire – a mercenary – would have been appropriately
called a 'free lance', is in fact a nineteenth-century coinage. The
coiner was Sir Walter Scott in *Ivanhoe* (1820): 'I offered Richard
the services of my Free Lances.' He was writing *about* the Middle
Ages but not using a word *of* the Middle Ages. By the end of the
century, shortened to 'freelance' the word was being used in its
modern sense of 'a self-employed person', particularly with reference to writers and journalists.

... *FRENCH LETTERS*?
See *condom*.

... BEYOND THE *FRINGE*?
See *beyond the pale*.

... A PERSON HAS BANGED HIS *FUNNY BONE*?
SOED has 'that part of the elbow over which the ulnar nerve
passes, so called from the peculiar sensation experienced when it
is struck.' Shook (and everybody else) goes further and suggests
that it is a pun on the Latin *humerus*, the medical name of the long
bone in the upper arm. I do not think so, though. How would this
medical joke have gained common currency?

... BLOWN THE *GAFF*?
See *blown the gaff*.

... A SENILE PERSON IS *GAGA*?
This is a straightforward copying of the French word *gaga* which means either 'senile' or a 'senile person'. It is also possible to say in French that an old man is completely gaga, thus: *C'est un vieux gâteux*.

'Gaga' may have developed from *gâteux* in some way. Or it may just be imitative of the way such a person would sound if he tried to speak.

Rosie Boycott's suggestion, in *Batty, Bloomers and Boycott* (1982), that it has anything to do with the Impressionist painter Paul Gauguin (1848–1903) seems unlikely. He may have been mentally disturbed in old age but the word was known in French by 1875, when he was not.

... A LEG IS *GAMMY*?
From 'Focus on Fact' in *Private Eye* (1981): 'The Llewellyns are descended from medieval knight, Sir Dafydd Gam, who got an arrow in his eye at Agincourt ... hence the expression "gammy" eye, leg etc.'

Indeed, 'Davy Gam, Esquire' is mentioned in Shakespeare's *King Henry V* (IV.viii.106) as having fallen at Agincourt. It appears that David ap Llewellyn of Brecon was called Gam because of a squint.

'Gammy' is a dialect form of 'game' (lame, crippled) which is '18th century dialect of unknown origin' (*COED*). Brewer gives it

77

as 'a dialect form of the Celtic *cam* meaning crooked. It is of comparatively modern usage.'

So, although the origin of 'gammy' may be from the Celtic fringe, it was not derived from Dafydd Gam, merely applied to him.

... RUN THE *GAMUT/GAUNTLET*?
See *run*.

... CONSPIRATORS ARE LIKE A *GANG OF FOUR*?
The original 'Gang of Four' was led by Jiang Qing, unscrupulous widow of Chairman Mao Tse-tung – so labelled in the mid-1970s, when the four were tried and given the death sentence for treason and other crimes (later commuted to life imprisonment). The other three members were Zhang Chunqiao, a political organizer in the Cultural Revolution, Wang Hogwen, a youthful activist, and Yao Wenyuan, a journalist. Chairman Hua Kuo-feng attributed the phrase to his predecessor. Apparently, on one occasion Mao had warned his wife and her colleagues: 'Don't be a gang of four.'

The nickname was applied also to the founders of the British Social Democratic Party in 1981 – Roy Jenkins, David Owen, William Rodgers and Shirley Williams.

... A HOMOSEXUAL IS *GAY*?
It was at the end of the 1960s that homosexuals most noticeably hi-jacked the word 'gay' when the Gay Liberation Front (in the US) came out of the closet and used such slogans as 'Say it loud, we're gay and we're proud' and '2-4-6-8, gay is just as good as straight.'

However, within such circles the word 'gay' had been used in the homosexual sense since at least the 1930s and on both sides of the Atlantic. In the last century 'gay' was used to describe female harlots and there is an earlier history of the word being applied to female licentiousness. It may have gravitated towards its homosexual use from there (like camp, q.v.).

The French still manage to distinguish between the old and new meanings of the word (at least when writing): 'gay or joyful' is still *gai*; 'gay as homosexual' is *gay*.

Although one regrets the loss of the word to mean 'joyful, light-hearted', perhaps this usage goes some way towards making up for the pejorative use of 'bent', 'queer' and 'poof' for homosexuals.

'Poof' (also 'pouf', 'poove', 'poofdah', the Australian 'poofter') dates back at least to the 1930s, although 'puff' was apparently tramps' slang for a homosexual by 1870. *Private Eye* certainly popularized 'poof' in the 1960s but clearly did not invent it, as has been claimed.

... GAZUMPED?

– when a higher bid is accepted during a house purchase. This specific meaning became noticeably popular in England and Wales from the early 1970s onwards. The process described can only occur in those countries where a vendor is allowed to break a verbal agreement to sell if he or she receives a later, better offer. In Scotland, where the 'sealed bid' system operates, such gazumping is not possible.

But why the word 'gazump' (alternatively spelt 'gazoomph', 'gasumph', 'gazumph', 'gezumph')? The *OED Supp.* has citations from 1928 onwards (from English sources) suggesting that the word had always had something to do with swindling. One suggested origin was in the motor trade, though the *OED Supp.* labels the word, 'origin uncertain'.

It occurs to me that it might come from 'goes up!' (meaning the price) – rather along the lines of the term 'gazunder', meaning chamber pot. But that may be a bit far-fetched.

The other suggestion is that it is a Yiddish word (*gezumph*) – it certainly looks like one – but it does not appear in the Yiddish dictionaries I have consulted.

... CAVIARE TO THE *GENERAL*?
See *caviare*.

... A TALL PERSON IS A *GENTLE GIANT*?
The alliteration is important and the application to any tall, strong person has become a journalist's cliché. A policeman killed by an IRA bomb outside Harrods store in London (December 1983) was immediately dubbed 'the gentle giant'. Terry Wogan, the disc jockey, had used the expression allusively to describe the BBC's Radio 2 network (cf. 'the big one', beloved of advertising folk).

Larry Holmes (*b.* 1950), the world champion boxer, is another to whom the label has been attached, like James Randel Matson (*b.* 1945), the US track and field champion.

In 1967, there was an American film entitled *The Gentle Giant*. This was about a small boy in Florida who befriends a bear which later saves his disapproving father's life.

Going back even further, the journalist William Howard Russell wrote of Dr Thomas Alexander who served in the Crimean War as a surgeon, as a 'gentle giant of a Scotchman'. There really is no new thing under the sun.

... A *GENTLEMAN AND A SCHOLAR*?
See *scholar*.

... *GENTLEMAN'S AGREEMENT* HAS BEEN REACHED?
SOED says that this is of US origin and gives no citations before 1929. It means an agreement which is not enforceable at law and only binding as a matter of honour.

A.J.P. Taylor in his *English History 1914–1945* (1965) has a footnote: 'This absurd phrase was taken by [von] Papen from business usage to describe the agreement between Austria and Germany in July 1936. It was much used hereafter for an agreement with anyone who was obviously not a gentleman and who would obviously not keep his agreement.'

... *GERTCHA!*?
This word had a burst of popularity in about 1980 when it was used in TV advertisements for Courage Best Bitter in the UK. Various grim-faced drinkers sat around in an East End pub and shouted it out during breaks in the music. But what was it supposed to mean?

Dave Trott, the copywriter responsible for using the word, suggested it derived from the expression, 'Get out of it you.' This is supported by Partridge who was on to it, as 'gercher' in 1937. The *OED Supp.* has 'Get away/ along with you.'

The line got into the commercial from a song composed by the Cockney singers Chas and Dave who originally pronounced it 'Wooertcha'.

... *GESUNDHEIT!* WHEN WE SNEEZE?

It is the German for 'health' but it also has the rhythm of 'God bless you' and of a musical finish (as to a music-hall joke).

Sneezing was believed to be the expulsion of an evil spirit, hence the need for such exclamations. The Romans cried *absit omen!* ('flee, omen!')

... WE OUGHT TO *GET DOWN TO BRASS TACKS*?

i.e. get down to essentials, fundamentals. Various theories have been advanced for this phrase, seemingly of American origin.

In old stores, brass tacks were positioned a yard apart for measuring. When a customer 'got down to brass tacks' it meant he or she was serious about measuring the fabric rather than just guessing.

Then there is a suggestion that brass tacks were the fundamental element in nineteenth-century upholstery. 'To get down to brass tacks' was to deal with a fault in the furniture by getting down to basics.

Another suggestion is that 'brass tacks' is rhyming slang for 'facts', but I doubt this.

... A PERSON *GETS GIVEN THE SACK*?

The suggestion is that this dates from the days when a worker would carry the tools of his trade around with him, from job to job, in a bag which he would leave with his employer. When his services were no longer required, he would be given the bag back.

There is a similar seventeenth-century French expression: *on lui a donné son sac*. Brewer unfortunately declines to make any connection with the habit of Turkish sultans who, when wishing to get rid of members of their harems, would put them in a sack and drop them in the Bosporus.

Would that there was a more convincing explanation.

... SOMETHING *GETS ONE'S DANDER UP*?

i.e. gets one ruffled or angry. Originally from the US in the nineteenth century, this has a much older flavour to it. A 'dander' (according to the *SOED*) has two meanings: it is a 'calcined cinder' and is a form of 'dandruff'. But it is hard to see quite how these could lead to the expression.

Donder is Dutch for thunder, 'dander' has also been dialect for a fit of shivering and 'dunder' for the 'lees or dregs of cane-juice, used in the West Indies in the fermentation of rum (corrupted from the Spanish *redundar*, to overflow).' I expect the notion of 'ferment' must have led in one way or another to 'dander' being used in the idiomatic phrase.

Flexner 2 has *dunder* as a Scottish word for 'ferment'. That is as near as we are likely to get, I expect.

... AN ANNOYING THING *GETS ONE'S GOAT*?

Apparently another Americanism that has passed into general use, this expression can also be found in French as *prendre la chèvre*, 'to take the milch-goat'. One is always suspicious of explanations which go on to explain that, of course, goats were very important to poor people and if anyone were to get a man's goat ... etc. One is even more unimpressed by the Morrises' explanation: 'It used to be a fairly common practice to stable a goat with a thoroughbred [horse], the theory being that the goat's presence would help the high-strung nag to keep its composure. If the goat were stolen the night before a big race, the horse might be expected to lose its poise and blow the race.'

Shook, interestingly, wonders whether it has anything to do with a 'goatee' (a beard like a goat's). If you got someone by the goat, it would certainly annoy them.

All one can do is to point to the number of idioms that do refer to goats – 'act the goat', 'giddy goat', 'scapegoat' and, once more, point to the alliteration.

... GENTLE *GIANT*?
See *gentle*.

... THAT SOMEONE IS TALKING *GIBBERISH*?
Dr Johnson thought this word derived from an Arabian alchemist called Geber in the eleventh century who had, in turn, translated into Latin the writings of an eighth-century alchemist called Jabir ibn Hayyan. He wrote in a mystical jargon because, if his writings had been discovered, he might have been put to death.

The most obvious derivation is from 'gibber' which, like 'jabber', means to speak fast and inarticulately (compare 'gabber' and 'gab'.) But it appears to have an earlier source than this. Which might just confirm Dr Johnson's theory. Partridge meanwhile thinks it may have developed from 'Egyptian', like 'gypsy'.

... LOOK A *GIFT-HORSE IN THE MOUTH*?
See *look*.

... *GIN AND IT*?
See *martini*.

'... *GIVE A DOG A BAD NAME*'?
– meaning, if we say bad things about a person, they will stick. Longman thinks this is a shortened form of the saying to 'give a dog a bad name and hang him', which means that 'if a dog is said to bite or be bad-tempered, it might as well be killed because no one will trust it any more.'

... *GNOMES OF ZURICH* FOR SWISS BANKERS AND FINANCIERS?
This term was used to disparage the tight-fisted methods of speculators in the Swiss financial capital who questioned Britain's creditworthiness and who forced austerity measures on the Labour government of Prime Minister Harold Wilson when it came to power in 1964. George Brown, the Secretary of State for Economic Affairs, popularized the term.

Harold Wilson had, however, himself used it long before in a speech to the House of Commons on 12 November 1956, referring to 'all the little gnomes in Zurich and other financial centres.'

... GET ONE'S *GOAT*?
See *get one's*.

... A MAN *GOES AT/ FOR SOMETHING BALDHEADED*?
i.e. without regard for the consequences. An American expression from the nineteenth century, this suggests that a man would tackle a problem as though he had just rushed out of his house without wearing a hat.

However, earlier sources for it have been suggested – notably that the Marquis of Granby, a colonel of the Blues, led a cavalry charge at the Battle of Warburg (1760) despite his hat and wig falling off. Quite how this could have led to the American origination, I'm not sure.

The Dutch for 'audacious' is *bald dadig*. Indeed, one way and another, I am suspicious about the Granby explanation, colourful though it is.

. . . GO FOR IT?

This was a popular exhortation of the mid-1980s, mostly in America. For example, in June 1985, President Reagan's call on tax reform was, 'America, go for it!' Victor Kiam, an American razor entrepreneur entitled his memoirs *Going For It!* (1986), and 'Go for it, America' was the slogan used by British Airways in the same year to get more US tourists to ignore the terrorist threat and travel to Europe.

Originally, the phrase came from aerobics. Jane Fonda, for example, on her work-out tape cried, 'Go for it, go for the burn!' (where 'the burn' is a sensation felt during exercise).

At about the same time and probably pre-dating it, another popular expression was 'Go for gold!' (i.e. a gold medal). As far as I can tell, this slogan was first used by the US Olympic team at the Lake Placid Winter Olympics in 1980. Other teams, including the British, had taken it up by the time of the 1984 Olympics.

Just to show, as always, that there is nothing new under the sun: in 1832, there was a political slogan 'To stop the Duke, go for gold' – which was somehow intended, through its alliterative force, to prevent the Duke of Wellington from forming a government.

. . . GO, MAN, GO?

This was a term of encouragement originally shouted at jazz musicians in the 1940s. Then it took on wider use. At the beginning of the number *It's Too Darn Hot* in Cole Porter's *Kiss Me Kate* (film version, 1953) a dancer cries: 'Go, girl, go.'

TV newscaster Walter Cronkite reverted famously to 'Go, baby, go!' while describing the launch of Apollo XI in 1969 and this form became a fairly standard cry at rocket and missile departures thereafter. *Time* magazine reported it being shouted at a test firing of a Pershing II missile (29 November 1982).

'Crazy, man, crazy' originated at about the same time as 'Go, man, go', but was perhaps better suited to rock'n'roll usage than the earlier bop.

One wonders whether T.S. Eliot's 'Go go go said the bird' ('Burnt Norton', *Four Quartets*, 1935) or Hamlet's 'Come, bird, come' (the cry of a falconer recalling his hawk) relate to these cries in any way?

... GONE FOR A BURTON?

Early in the Second World War, an RAF expression arose to describe what had happened to a missing person, presumed dead. He had gone for a Burton, meaning that he had gone for a drink or, as another phrase had it, 'he'd bought it.'

Folk memory has it that 'Gone for a Burton' had been used in advertisements to promote a Bass beer known in the trade as 'a Burton' (though, in fact, several ales are brewed at Burton-on-Trent). More positive proof is lacking.

Another fanciful theory is that RAF casualty records were kept in an office above or near a branch of Burton Menswear in Blackpool. I think we may discount his theory.

... GONE TO POT?

i.e. gone to ruin. This could refer to the custom of putting a dead person's ashes into an urn or pot. After that happens, there is no more to be done.

Ewart, on the other hand, prefers to think 'the phrase comes from the melting-pots into which broken items of metal, gold and silver, were thrown when they could no longer be used in their original form as they were either damaged, or stolen.'

The Morrises think it means left-over meat and vegetables all chopped up and ready for their last appearance as stew or hash in the pot. This is supported by *SOED* which sees the phrase as shortened from 'go to the pot' (lit. 'to be cut in pieces like meat for the pot').

Whatever the case, the phrase has nothing whatsoever to do with the other type of 'pot', namely marijuana. This word is said to come from the Mexican Spanish word *potiguaya*, meaning marijuana leaves.

. . . PEOPLE BELONG TO THE LIST OF THE *GOOD AND THE GREAT*?

This is the list to which British governments resort when they need people to serve on Royal Commissions and committees of inquiry. In 1983, according to a leading article in *The Times*, the list then stood at some 4,500 names. For the previous eight years custodians of the list had 'pertinaceously sought more women, more people under 40 and more from outside the golden triangle of London and the South-East' in an attempt to 'break the stereotype enshrined in Lord Rothschild's parody of it as containing only 53-year-old men who "live in the South-East, have the right accent and belong to the Reform Club".'

In the 1950s, apparently, the Treasury division which kept the list was actually known as the 'G and G'. On one occasion it really did nominate two dead people for service on a public body.

. . . *GONE WEST*?

i.e. died. Popularized during the First World War (according to Partridge) but of much earlier origin, the simple idea here is to liken a death to the setting of the sun.

I cannot get too excited about an alternative suggestion that the phrase arose because Tyburn, where hangings were carried out for several centuries, was situated near what is now Marble Arch on the main route *westwards* out of London.

'. . . ALL *GOOD THINGS MUST COME TO AN END* . . . '?

See *all*.

. . . A MAN HAS BEEN KICKED IN THE *GOOLIES*?

i.e. testicles. Simple, really. *Goli* is Hindustani for a bullet, ball or pill.

. . . *'GORDON BENNETT!'*?

Of the dictionaries I have before me at the moment, only Partridge mentions this expression at all and, even so, does not try to explain why we use it in the United Kingdom (to where its use is entirely restricted, as far as I am aware).

My inquiries into this odd expletive began in about 1982. The first person I consulted – a cheery Londoner with the absolute confidence of the amateur etymologist – assured me that it was short for 'Gawd and St Benet!' Quite who St Benet was and why people invoke his name, I never found out.

But, shortly afterwards, on a visit to Paris, I found myself staring up in amazement at a street sign which bore the legend 'Avenue Gordon-Bennett'. I felt like exclaiming: *'Mon dieu et St Benet!'*

Reading Churchill's *History of the Second World War*, I came across one Lieut.-Gen. Gordon Bennett. Knowing how many slang expressions have come out of the services, I wondered whether he had done something to impress himself upon the language.

Next I talked to a man I met at the annual convention of the Institute of Concrete Technology. (It falls beyond the scope of this book, I am afraid, for me to reveal what I was doing there.) He told me he thought the expression was current in the 1930s. Had not Gordon Bennett been a comedian?

Indeed, there were comedians called Billy Bennett, Wheeler and Bennett, Bennett and Moreny, though why any of *them* should have been commemorated by having a street named after them in Paris (even had their first names been Gordon) is anybody's guess.

'Ah,' said the concrete man, 'the *French* Gordon Bennett was probably the man who gave his name to a motor race in the early 1900s.'

In fact, he was not French at all, but American, and there were two of him. James Gordon Bennett I (1795–1872) was a Scot who went to the United States and became a megalomaniac newspaper proprietor. James Gordon Bennett II (1841–1918) was the even more noted editor-in-chief of the *New York Herald* and the man who sent Henry Morton Stanley to find Dr Livingstone in Africa.

But why should either of these gentlemen have a street named after him in Paris, not to mention a motor race, as well as giving his moniker for a British expletive?

James Gordon Bennett II (for we must concentrate upon him) was quite a character. He was exiled to Paris after a scandal but somehow managed to run his New York newspaper from there (the cable bills ran up and up, so he bought the cable company). He disposed of some $40 million in his lifetime. He offered numerous trophies to stimulate French sport and, when the motor car was in its infancy, presented the Gordon Bennett cup to be competed for.

On one occasion he tipped a train guard $14,000 and, on another, drew a wad of 1,000 franc notes from his back pocket (where they had been causing him discomfort) and threw them on the fire. He became, as the *Dictionary of American Biography* has it, 'one of the most picturesque figures of two continents.'

This, if anything does, probably explains why it was *his* name that ended up on people's lips and why they did not go around exclaiming, 'Gordon of Khartoum!' or 'Gordon Selfridge!' or anything else. Gordon Bennett was a man with an amazing reputation.

I do not take very seriously suggestions that a stunned public shouted 'Gordon Bennett!' when Stanley found Livingstone. Nor that there were cartoons of Stanley 'phoning his editor (from the jungle?) and saying, 'Gordon Bennett, I've found him!' The truth of the matter seems to be that people found some peculiar appeal in the name 'Gordon Bennett' – but the important thing is that the first name was 'Gordon'.

People, understandably, shrink from blaspheming. 'Oh gawd!' is felt to be less offensive than 'Oh God!'. At the turn of the century, it was natural for people to water down the exclamation 'God!' by saying 'Gordon!' The name Gordon Bennett was to hand.

A decade or two later, in similar fashion – and with a view to circumventing the strict Hollywood Hay's Code – W.C. Fields would exclaim 'Godfrey Daniel!' in place of 'God damn you!'

Now who was Godfrey Daniel . . . ?

. . . A PERFORMER HAS *GOT THE BIRD*?
i.e. he is rejected by the audience. What do audiences do when they do not like something? They boo or they hiss. What would an audience of hissers sound like? A flock of geese, perhaps. And that is the bird in question (originally the expression was 'to get the big bird').

. . . BRIDES *GO UP THE AISLE*?
Sir Thomas Bazley fired off a letter to *The Times* in July 1986:

Sir, You report that Miss Sarah Ferguson will go up the aisle to the strains of
Elgar's 'Imperial March'. Hitherto, brides have always gone up the nave.
        Yours faithfully...

Quite right, of course. The nave is the main route from the
west door of a church to the chancel and altar; the aisles are the
parallel routes, at the side of a church, separated from the nave by
pillars.

Nevertheless, the phrase 'up the aisle' in connection with
weddings holds strong. Could it be that the assonance of the 'i'
sound in 'bride' and 'aisle' has something to do with people
preferring the inaccurate to the accurate?

...WE'LL TAKE IT WITH A *GRAIN OF SALT*?
This comes from the Latin *cum grano selis* and simply means that
something would be better treated sceptically just as food is
sometimes made more palatable if it is accompanied by a pinch of
salt.

... DON'T TEACH YOUR *GRANDMOTHER TO SUCK EGGS*?
i.e. try to tell her things which, from her age and experience, she
might be expected to know anyway. According to Partridge,
variations of this very old expression include advice against
instructing grandmothers to 'grope ducks', 'grope a goose', 'sup
sour milk', 'spin', and 'roast eggs'.

I have heard it suggested that, in olden times, sucking eggs
would be a particularly important thing for a grandmother to be
able to do because, having lost her teeth, it would be about all she
was capable of eating.

... A WOMAN IS A *GRASS WIDOW*?
– meaning that she is temporarily apart from her husband
(because his job or some preoccupation has taken him elsewhere)
or is divorced.

According to Longman, the phrase originally referred to an
*un*married woman who had sexual relations with one or more men
- suggesting perhaps that she had these relations secretly on a bed
of grass or straw rather than lawfully in the marriage bed. Chiefly,
though, it meant that she had had a child out of wedlock.

Radford comes up with something a little different, saying that the expression is from British India where women and children were sent up to the cool hill country (where grass grows) during the hottest season of the year. Separated from their husbands they were thus 'grass widows'. I rather incline to this version, though the expression seems to have been in existence before the British went to India.

... PEOPLE CLIMB ABOARD THE *GRAVY TRAIN*?
i.e. obtain access to a money-spinning scheme. This was an American expression originally – *DOAS* says it started in sporting circles. The alternative expression is 'to climb aboard the gravy boat'. This is a bit easier to understand. Gravy boats exist for holding gravy in, and take their name from their shape. So, if money means gravy, it is not too hard to see how the expression arose.

According to *Webster's Dictionary*, 'train' and 'boat' are equal American terms. 'Train' less so in the UK, I feel, in the figurative and literal sense.

... THE GOOD AND THE *GREAT*?
See *good*.

...'*GREAT SCOTT!*'?
As with 'Gordon Bennett!' (q.v.) one is dealing here with a watered-down exclamation. 'Great Scott!' is not a million miles from sounding like 'Great God!' and yet is not blasphemous. Can one be precise about which particular Scott is being invoked?

The Morrises say the expression became popular in the mid-nineteenth century when US General Winfield Scott (1786–1866) was the hero of the Mexican War (1847) and 'probably our most admired general between Washington and Lee.'

No rival candidate seems to have been proposed and the origination is certainly American.

... BEWARE *GREEKS BEARING GIFTS*?
The allusion here is to the most famous Greek gift of all – the large wooden horse which was (according to Virgil) built by the Greeks as an offering to the gods before they returned home after besieging Troy unsuccessfully for ten years. It was taken within the

gates of Troy by the Trojans, but it contained men who leapt out, opened the city gates and helped destroy the city. The Greeks were able to broach the enemy lines in this way.

Virgil in his *Aeneid* (II, 49) has Laocoon warn the Trojans not to admit the horse by saying *timeo Danaos et dona ferentes* ('I still fear the Greeks, even when they offer gifts').

... SOMETHING/SOMEBODY IS A *GREEN GODDESS*?
Diana Moran was a keep-fit demonstrator on BBC breakfast television at its inception in 1983. A well-preserved lady in her forties, with blonde hair, she wore distinctive green exercise clothing and was promoted as the 'Green Goddess'.

Previously the name had been applied to Second World War fire engines, Liverpool trams, to a crème de menthe cocktail, a lettuce salad, and to a lily.

Clearly, the alliteration contributed to the popularity of the phrase. Did it all start with William Archer's play entitled *The Green Goddess* in 1923 (filmed 1930)?

... *GREEN ROOM*?
See *see you on the green.*

... A SAILOR DRINKS *GROG*?
Grog is rum diluted with water. It was introduced by the British Admiral Edward Vernon (1684–1757) in an attempt to prevent scurvy among his crewmen in 1740. It did not work. Vernon's nickname was 'Old Grog' because of his addiction to a cloak made of grogram, a coarse material of silk and wool.

The nickname was then given by sailors to public houses ashore – 'grog shops', places where spirits were sold.

... *GROOVY*?
i.e. very good (especially of music). Although this word was very popular in the pop world of the 1960s, *DOAS* takes it back to the mid-1930s and use among 'swing' musicians and devotees. It comes from 'in the groove', referring to the way a gramophone or phonograph stylus or needle fits neatly into the groove on a record.

. . . *GROTTY*?
– a very 1960s word and now rather quaint, meaning 'seedy, down-at-heel, crummy, unpleasant, nasty, unattractive, less than good'. It is fairly obviously a form of the word 'grotesque' and is very much associated with the Mersey culture that accompanied the Beatles out of Liverpool in 1962–3. Indeed, George Melly in his book *Revolt Into Style* (1970) credits the Liverpudlian play-wright Alun Owen with the coinage. Owen put it in his script for the first Beatles film, *A Hard Day's Night* (1964). It may have been in general Scouse (Liverpudlian) usage before this but the Beatles' use of the word undoubtedly popularized it.

As for 'grotesque' itself, I have heard it derived from the name of Mrs Grote, the wife of a nineteenth-century Greek historian. She was peculiar in one or two ways: she 'dressed in discordant colours, with her petticoats arranged to show her ankles and feet'; she wore a man's hat and a coachman's cloak when driving her dogcart; and, she had 'unwholesome attachments to other women' (Ronald Pearsall, *Collapse of Stout Party*, 1975). This, alas, is more a case of life imitating the dictionary than the other way round. 'Grotesque' is of Italian and Greek origin and derived from the 'grotto' style of ornamentation.

. . . A MORAL GUARDIAN IS A MRS *GRUNDY*?
The name has a 'grudging' air to it and comes from a comedy, *Speed the Plough* (1798), by Thomas Morton, in which one of the characters frequently asks, 'What will Mrs Grundy say?'

Compare this name for a censorious person, upholder of con-ventional morals, with that of 'Mrs Whitehouse', an actual person who campaigned on a similar basis in Britain from the 1960s to the 1980s. Mary Whitehouse (*b*. 1910) established the National Viewers' and Listeners' Association in 1965 with the avowed intention of 'cleaning up TV'. Her name was often invoked like Mrs Grundy's.

. . . *GUILLOTINE* FOR EXECUTION EQUIPMENT?
the French physician, Dr Joseph-Ignace Guillotin (1738–1814) did not invent the guillotine. The idea of severing a man's head with a contraption incorporating a vertically descending blade was based on a device already used in Italy and elsewhere. It

was at first called a *louison* or *louisette* after Dr Antoine Louis (1723–92) who adapted this 'painless' and 'humane' method of execution.

What Dr Guillotine did was to push a resolution through the French Constituent Assembly adopting the device as the official means of executing criminals, in 1792. It was thus in position ready for the thousands of executions resulting from the French Revolution in 1789.

Dr Guillotin's family did not take kindly to having their name attached to such a device and, after his death, changed their name rather than put up with it. He had narrowly escaped being guillotined himself.

La Veuve ('The Widow'), as the guillotine was nicknamed, was pensioned off at last in 1981 when the French National Assembly abolished the death penalty.

... *GULAG ARCHIPELAGO* TO DENOTE THE SOVIET SLAVE LABOUR CAMP SYSTEM?

Alexander Solzhenitsyn's book *The Gulag Archipelago 1918–1956* introduced the Gulag concept to Western readers. It is not an actual archipelago. As Safire observes, 'the metaphor Solzhenitsyn had in mind was a series of islands – or camps – in the sea of the USSR.'

GULAG is an acronym made up from the Russian words for the main administration of correctional labour camps – *Glavnoye Upravleniye Ispravitelno-trudovykh Lagerei.*

... *SON OF A GUN*?
See *son.*

... A PERSON HAS A *GUNG-HO* ATTITUDE?

In Chinese, *kung* plus *ho* mean 'work together'. Lieut.-Colonel (later General) Evans F. Carlson of the US Marines borrowed these words to make a slogan during the Second World War. In 1943, a film about the Marines had the title *Gung Ho!* From there, the expression came to have adjectival use denoting an attitude that is enthusiastic, if a little wildly so.

Carlson had served as an observer with the Chinese Eighth Route Army during 1937–9 (Morris).

... THE *HAIR OF THE DOG* (THAT BIT US)?
i.e. we'll take another drink to help cure a hangover the morning after.

It used to be believed that a bite from a mad dog could be cured if you put hair from the same dog's tail on the wound.

... HOW THE OTHER *HALF LIVES*?
See *how*.

... A BAD ACTOR IS A *HAM*?
Well, it could be short for 'hamateur'. Or it could have something to do with Hamlet (who makes a very good speech on how not to be a ham). Or maybe it has something to do with hamfistedness. Or with Hamish McCullough (1835–85) who was known as 'Ham' and toured Illinois with his troupe, known as 'Ham's actors'. Or with a song *The Hamfat Man*, about a bad actor.

Whatever the case, the word seems to come to us, like so many, from nineteenth-century America. The *OED Supp.* says that apparently it is short for 'hamfatter' – in other words, an actor who used fat from ham chops to take off his makeup.

As applied to an amateur radio operator the term (coined in the 1920s) is more likely to refer to the amateur status.

... A PERSON IS MAKING MONEY *HAND OVER FIST*?
A similar expression 'pulling it in' provides the explanation here. If you are pulling in a rope on board ship or hoisting a sail, you pass it between your two hands and, in so doing, unavoidably put one hand over the fist of the other hand.

... HANGED, DRAWN AND QUARTERED?

The last time anyone one was hanged, drawn and quartered was in 1867 when three Fenians received this penalty. As the gentlemen in question may or may not have been in a position to observe, it did not quite happen in the order as stipulated in the phrase.

It should really be 'drawn, hanged and quartered' as is made clear by the words of a British judge sentencing Irish rebels in 1775: 'You are to be *drawn* on hurdles to the place of execution, where you are to be *hanged* by the neck but not until you are dead; for, while you are still living, your bodies are to be taken down, your bowels torn out and burned before your faces; your heads then cut off, and your bodies *divided each into four quarters*, and your heads and quarters to be then at the King's disposal; and may the Almighty God have mercy on your souls.'

... SOMETHING *HANGS FIRE*?

i.e. is hesitant, holds back. This expression comes from gunnery when the gun is slow to fire.

... 'HAPPINESS IS ... '?

Samuel Johnson declared in 1766: 'Happiness consists in the multiplicity of agreeable consciousness.'

Then, along came E.Y. Harburg with the lyrics to his song *Happiness is a Thing Called Joe* (1942). However, it was Charles M. Schultz (*b.* 1922), creator of the *Peanuts* comic strip, who really launched the 'Happiness is ... ' format. In *c.* 1957 he had drawn a strip 'centring around some kid hugging Snoopy and saying in the fourth panel that "Happiness is a warm puppy."' This became the title of a best-selling book in 1962 and let loose a stream of promotional phrases using the format, including: 'Happiness is egg-shaped', 'Happiness is a cigar called Hamlet' (UK advertising slogans), 'Happiness is being elected team captain – and getting a Bulova watch', 'Happiness is a $49 table' (US advertising slogans), 'Happiness is seeing Lubbock, Texas, in the rear view mirror' (song title), and many, many more.

No wonder Lennon and McCartney wrote a song called *Happiness is a Warm Gun* (1968) (*SOTC*).

... HAPPY AS A SANDBOY?
People suggest that the similar expression 'happy as Larry' comes
from the name of the boxer, Larry Foley (1847–1917), but no one
seems sure why a sandboy should be singled out for his good
humour.

The *SOED* has 'jolly as a sandboy' and suggests that he was
a boy who hawked sand. The *OED Supp.* finds a quotation
from Pierce Egan (1821): 'As happy as a sandboy who had un-
expectedly met with good luck in disposing of his hampers full of
the above-household commodity.'

I wonder, rather, whether it had something to do with birds –
sandpipers and sand martins? Or, perhaps, the gist is simply that
sandboys were like urchins – boyish, charming, happy.

... HARVEST MOON?
See *shine on*.

... MAD AS A HATTER?
See *mad*.

... HAWKS AND DOVES TO DENOTE THOSE FOR AND
AGAINST TOUGH MILITARY ACTION?
The term 'war hawk' was coined by Thomas Jefferson in 1798.
The choice of bird is as appropriate for a tenacious, lethal,
attacking attitude as is the traditional use of the dove to represent
peace.

The modern division into hawks and doves, much used during
the Vietnam war of the 1960s, dates from the Cuban missile crisis
of 1962.

... A PERSON HAS GONE HAYWIRE?
i.e. is behaving in an uncontrolled and crazy manner. This phrase
is of fairly recent American origin – turn of the century, perhaps
– and derives from the wire used to hold bales of hay together. If
cut, the wire can whip around in a fearsome way.

According to *DOAS*, there is another use of the word 'haywire'
in American slang. Something is described as 'haywire' if it is
dilapidated and might be held together with such, just as in
English usage we might say something is 'held together with bits
of string'.

... EAT YOUR *HEART OUT*?
See *eat*.

... 'COME *HELL AND/OR HIGH WATER*...'?
See *come*.

... '*HI-DE-HI*'?
The spirit of the traditional British holiday camp was recreated in a popular BBC TV series with this title, starting in 1980. The title comes from a song written before but taken up during the Second World War, particularly by army instructors greeting their troops. Hence the exchange, 'Hi-de-hi!'/'Ho-de-ho!'

There was, in fact, one real army colonel who was court-martialled for making his troops shout 'Ho-de-ho' when he yelled 'Hi-de-hi!'

The original song may have derived from 'hi-de-ho', a shout used by 1930s jazz and dance bands in the US.

A campers' song, peculiar to Butlin's, went:

> Tramp, tramp, tramp, tramp.
> Here we come, to jolly old Butlin's every year.
> All come down to Butlin's, all by the sea.
> Never mind the weather, we're as happy as can be.
> Hi-de-hi! Ho-de-ho!

... WE'RE FACED WITH *HOBSON'S CHOICE*?
i.e. no choice at all. It seems generally agreed that there was an actual Mr Hobson. Thomas Hobson (1544–1631) hired horses from a livery stable in Cambridge. 'When a man came for a horse,' recorded Sir Richard Steele in the *Spectator*, No. 509 (1712), 'he was led into the stable, where there was great choice, but he obliged him to take the horse which stood next to the stable door; so that every customer was alike well served according to his chance, and every horse ridden with the same justice. From whence it became a proverb, when what ought to be your election was forced upon you, to say Hobson's choice.'

Hobson had earlier been celebrated in Fuller's *Worthies* and in two epitaphs by Milton. The poet Thomas Ward wrote in 1630:

> Where to elect there is but one
> 'Tis Hobson's choice, – take that or none.

The tendency to use the expression to indicate a choice between two equally unpalatable alternatives should be resisted.

A pleasing modern version of Hobson's choice is Henry Ford's offer regarding the Model T Ford motor: 'People can have it any colour – so long as it's black.'

. . . NOT FIT TO *HOLD A CANDLE TO ANOTHER*?

In the pre-electric light era, an apprentice might have found himself holding a candle so that a more experienced workman could do his job. Or, in the days before street lighting, a linkboy would carry a torch for another person. Holding a candle, in either of these ways, was a necessary but menial task. If a person was so incompetent that he could not even do that properly, then he really was not fit for anything.

There seems to have been no suggestion of anything to do with examining eggs by holding them up to the light (as has been suggested) or even of one person being *compared* with another. The meaning of the phrase is better expressed as 'not fit to a hold a candle *for* another'.

. . . WE NEED SOMETHING LIKE A *HOLE IN THE HEAD*?

A colourful expression, hardly needing explanation. Leo Rosten in *Hooray for Yiddish!* (1982) describes it as 'accepted from Alaska to the Hebrides' and 'directly from the Yiddish: *loch in kop* . . . it was propelled into our vernacular by the play *A Hole in the Head* by Arnold Schulman, and more forcibly impressed upon mass consciousness by the Frank Sinatra movie (1959) . . . "Hole in the head" was used with vigor, in Yiddish/English/Yinglish, for a century B.S. (Before Sinatra).'

. . . THE *HOLOCAUST*?

i.e. the mass murder of Jews by the German Nazis during the 1939–45 war. A holocaust is an all-consuming conflagration and is not perhaps the most obvious description of what happened to the Jews under the Nazis, though many were burned as well as being gassed or killed in some other way.

The term seems to have arisen because 'genocide' hardly sounded emotive enough. The use of 'the Holocaust' for this purpose dates only from 1965 when A. Donat published a book about it entitled *The Holocaust Kingdom*. The use was finally settled when an American TV mini-series called *Holocaust* (1978) was shown and caused controversy in many countries.

... NEWLY-WEDS GO ON *HONEYMOON*?

Shook: 'Among the Germans, a newly-married couple drank mead (wine made with honey) for a period of about one month after the ceremony. That period of a month – or moon – put the *moon* in "honeymoon".' Now, more usually, the word is used to describe the holiday a bride and groom traditionally take after the wedding.

Other languages follow the same pattern, e.g. French *lune de miel*; Italian *luna di miele*.

Any suggestion that 'moon' comes into it because love wanes after the honeymoon, should be rejected...

... *HOOK, LINE AND SINKER*?

See *lock, stock and barrel*.

... TO SLING ONE'S *HOOK*?

See *slung*.

... A PROSTITUTE IS A *HOOKER*?

The Hooker family of Conklin, New York State, had a tussle with authority in the early 1980s. There were official objections to them putting on their car licence plates '1-Hooker', '2-Hooker', and so on. 'Our ancestor was repeatedly decorated by the President, so how can our name be offensive?' they argued. And they won their case.

It would indeed have been a hard thing if they had been prevented from using the plates on the grounds that 'working girls' derive their title from an American Civil War general of that name. Alas, however much we might want to believe that derivation, it is not true.

The word 'hooker' has nothing to do either with any notion of prostitutes 'hooking' their clients or with ladies of the night on the Hook of Holland. It appears to have come from Corlear's Hook, or 'the Hook', a part of Manhattan where tarts used to ply their trade in the early nineteenth century.

However, although this may let the Hooker family of Conklin, New York State off the hook, it is equally true that General Joseph Hooker (1814–79) did have something to do with prostitutes. He may not have given his name to them originally but he may have helped *popularize* the use during the Civil War when he had a famous set of camp-followers. Charles Francis Adams, son of the sixth US president, called Hooker a 'man of blemished character whose headquarters was a place that no self-respecting man liked to go and no decent woman could go, for it can only be described as a combination of bar-room and brothel.' An area of Washington D.C. became known as Hooker's Division on account of the General's proclivities.

The *OED Supp*. has a citation from the US in 1845, showing obviously that 'hooker' was well established in this sense before the General and the Civil War came along.

... A PERSON IS A *HOOLIGAN*?
i.e. a destructive young ruffian, a vandal. This derives from the English form of the common Irish name 'Houlihan' or, maybe, from 'Hooley's gang' (of which there was said to be one in North London in the late nineteenth century).

A farce shown in London in 1824 had a tipsy, unreliable valet called 'Hoolagan', but that may not be significant. There is also said to have been a music-hall song towards the end of the nineteenth century about a quarrelsome Irish family with the name Hooligan. Newspaper police-court reports from 1898 talk of 'Hooligan gangs' and may derive from an actual case, trace of which has been lost.

But there was an actual Patrick Hooligan who seems to have operated as something of a Fagin in London and was imitated by other such operators. He is described in a book called *The Hooligan Nights* (1899).

Which of the Hooligans came first and started it all off is impossible to say with certainty.

... A MAN IS A *HOORAY HENRY*?
i.e. a loud-mouthed upper-class twit (in Britain). The archetypal Sloane Ranger husband is also called Henry though he may not be quite as bad as a 'Hooray'. *The Official Sloane Ranger Handbook*

(1982) says Hoorays 'are aged between 18 and 30; main interest, getting drunk together.' They are thought to make a meaningless braying noise to show enjoyment. This is best rendered in print by putting 'hooray'.

According to Jim Godbolt (in an article for *Harpers and Queen*, October 1984), the term was coined by him in the basement of 100, Oxford Street, in January 1951. For ten years that basement had been used as a jazz club but, following the emergence of Humphrey Lyttelton, an old Etonian and ex-Guardsman, as trumpeter and bandleader, an upper class contingent began to be drawn there to listen to the newly respectable music.

Godbolt recalls how he had just finished reading a collection of short stories by Damon Runyon: 'In one of these, "Tight Shoes", he introduces a character called Calvin Colby, Runyon describing him as "Strictly a Hurrah Henry". The appellation hadn't properly registered with me and I remarked to (a friend): "The Hooray Henrys are at it again." I got an amused reaction and Hooray Henry went into jazz lingo and then into common usage.'

Anyone claiming to have coined anything has to be treated with caution but jazz historian Godbolt's claim sounds pretty convincing to me.

. . . WE *HOOVER* THE CARPET?

The manufacturers of Hoover vacuum cleaners would, of course, like to protect the proprietary name but the fact is that people use the word as noun or verb whether or not they are actually talking about a specifically Hoover model.

The original Hoover was started as an invention by James Murray Spangler in 1908. It was taken up by William H. Hoover whose company, until that time, manufactured high-grade leather goods, harnesses and horse collars. Spangler's idea was developed to include the principle of carpet vibration to remove dust. This gave Hoovers their exclusive feature – the gentle beating or tapping of the carpet to loosen dirt and grit embedded in it. An agitator bar performed this function, together with strong suction and revolving brushes – giving the Hoover the 'triple action' enshrined in the slogan 'It beats as it sweeps as it cleans.'

It remains ironic that the name honoured by the machine is that of the merchandiser and not the inventor.

... 'ABANDON *HOPE* ... '?
See *'abandon ...'*

... SOMETHING IS A *HORSE OF A DIFFERENT COLOUR*?
i.e. another matter altogether. Shook demonstrates the bizarre
lengths to which some etymologists will go to find an origin for a
perfectly simple phrase. According to him, it 'may have grown
out of an English archaeological phenomenon, the White Horse of
Berkshire, which is an outline of a horse 374 feet long, formed by
trenches in a chalk hillside. It is customary for neighbourhood
citizens to clean the weeds from the trenches every so often, thus
making it "a horse of a different color".'

... STRAIGHT FROM THE *HORSE'S MOUTH*?
See *straight*.

'... *HOW THE OTHER HALF LIVES*'?
i.e. how people live who belong to a different social group (e.g.,
and especially, the rich). Longman suggests that this phrase may
have been launched through the title of a book (1890) by Jacob
Riis (1849–1914), a US newspaper reporter, describing the
conditions in which poor people lived in New York City. Indeed,
the expression seems basically to have referred to the poor but has
since become used about any 'other half'.

Maybe, but even Riis alludes to the core-saying in these words:
'Long ago it was said that "one half of the world does not know
how the other half lives".' The *OED Supp.* finds this proverb in
1607, in English, and, in French, in *Pantagruel* by Rabelais (1532).

... ACCORDING TO *HOYLE*?
See *according*.

... EATING *HUMBLE PIE*?
See *eating*.

... A *HUNDRED DAYS* TO DENOTE A TRIAL PERIOD?
During the 1964 British general election campaign, the Labour
leader, Harold Wilson declared: 'What we are going to need
is something like what President Kennedy had after years of
stagnation – a programme of a hundred days of dynamic action.'

102

In fact, Kennedy had specifically ruled out a 'hundred days' saying that his programmes could not be carried out even in a thousand days – hence the passage to that effect in his inaugural address. According to Ted Sorensen in his book *Kennedy* (1965), the President-elect had said: 'I'm sick of reading how we're planning another "hundred days" of miracles and I'd like to know who on the staff is talking that up. Let's put in [the speech] that this won't all be finished in a hundred days or a thousand.'

Whoever had been 'talking up' was evoking a phrase used to describe the period of dynamic action in the special session of the US Congress summoned by President Franklin D. Roosevelt to deal with the Depression in 1933.

This use in turn stemmed from the original 'hundred days' during which Napoleon Buonaparte ruled between his escape from Elba and his defeat at the Battle of Waterloo in 1815 (although this was actually 116 days). The hundred days originally referred to by Louis de Chabrol, prefect of Paris, was the period between Louis XVIII's absence from Paris and his return. Chabrol said to the King: *Cent jours se sont écoulés depuis le moment fatal où votre majesté quitta sa capitale.* ('A hundred days, sire, have elapsed since the fatal moment when your majesty was forced to quit your capital in the midst of tears.')

... A TYPE OF SHOE IS A *HUSH PUPPY*?

These light, soft shoes were popular in the 1960s, in Britain and America. But in the US, you *eat* hush puppies. Either way, has cruelty been committed against these obviously once-noisy puppies?

In the southern US, hush puppies are 'tasty bits of deep-fried corn meal batter often served as accompaniment to fried fish', say the Morrises. In the period of reconstruction after the Civil War, when food was scarce, 'many a mother fried up bits of corn batter to quiet the plaintive cries of hungry children – and dogs – with the words "Hush, child. Hush, puppy!"'

That takes a bit of swallowing. Flexner has it that it is 'so named because hunters tossed pieces of it to their hounds to quiet them with the admonition "hush puppy".' Which is marginally more believable.

A better explanation (from the Morrises), also from the South, is that a hush puppy was a salamander, also known as a 'water dog' or 'water puppy'. People reduced to eating these may have said, 'Hush, don't say anything about it.'

In 1961, the Wolverine Shoe and Tanning Corporation, an American company, registered 'Hush Puppies' as a trade name. Room suggests that the name was adopted because it conjures up softness 'hush' and suppleness 'puppies'. Pictures of beagle-like dogs, not salamanders, were shown on the display material.

The only connection between the food and the shoe seems to have been a would-be homeliness.

... PUBLICITY IS *HYPE*?

In the publishing world particularly, 'hype' is applied to publicity stunts in which, it may be felt, the book is rather less important or substantial than its promotion. As such, the word would seem to come from US slang expressions referring to deception, short-changing and confidence tricks, and dating from about the 1920s. Some give the origin of the word as a short form of 'hyperbole', which is quite complimentary; others say it is a short form of 'hypodermic' (i.e. something used to give someone or something an unnatural boost).

I

... *I DO* OR *I WILL* WHEN TAKING MARRIAGE VOWS?
'Wilt thou have this Woman to thy wedded wife .. ?'
'Wilt thou have this Man to thy wedded husband .. ?'

The response in each case, according to the 1649 Anglican *Book of Common Prayer* is 'I will'. So where does 'I do' come in?

The simple answer is that it occurs in the Order of Confirmation in the same prayer book. 'Do ye renew the solemn promise and vow that was made ... at your baptism?' Response: 'I do'.

But in some US marriage services, the question is posed, 'Do you take so-and-so .. ?' to which the response has to be 'I do'. Having heard this so often in Hollywood films, it is not surprising that British people are a little confused. Jan de Hartog's play *The Four Poster* was turned into a musical with the title *I Do! I Do!* (c. 1966).

'*Will* you' is said to be more popular among the American clergy, '*Do* you' among those who conduct civil ceremonies.

... *ILLEGITIMI NON CARBORUNDUM*?

This cod-Latin phrase – supposed to mean 'Don't let the bastards grind you down' – was used by US General 'Vinegar Joe' Stilwell as his motto during the Second World War, though it is not suggested he devised it. Partridge gives it as 'illegitimis' and gives its origin in British army intelligence very early on in the war.

'Carborundum' was the trade name of a very hard substance called silicon carbide, used in grinding.

The same meaning is also conveyed by the phrase, 'Nil carborundum ...' (as in the title of a play by Henry Livings, 1962) –

a play upon *nil desperandum* ('never say die,' lit.: 'there is nought to be despaired of').

Perhaps because it is made up, the phrase takes all sorts of forms, e.g. 'Nil illegitimis . . . ', 'Nil bastardo illegitimi . . . ', 'Nil bastardo carborundum . . . ' etc. When the Rt. Rev. David Jenkins, the Bishop of Durham, was unwise enough to make use of the phrase at a private meeting in March 1985, he was reported by a cloth-eared journalist as having said, 'Nil desperandum illegitimi . . . '

. . . A QUICK SEDUCER IS *IN LIKE FLYNN*?

This is the Australian use of the phrase – appropriately so because Errol Flynn (1909–59), the film actor, was Australian-born. It pays tribute to his legendary bedroom prowess and the phrase means the person is 'seizing an opportunity offered, especially a sexual one'.

According to *The Intimate Sex Lives of Famous People* (by Irving Wallace *et al*, 1981), Flynn took to despising the expression when it became popular, particularly among servicemen, during the Second World War. It 'implied he was a fun-loving rapist', though 'in fact, Flynn's reputation stemmed partly from his having being charged with statutory rape'. After a celebrated trial, he was acquitted. Nevertheless, he 'boasted that he had spent between 12,000 and 14,000 nights making love'.

Partridge turned up an American version which refers to Ed Flynn, a Democratic machine politician in the Bronx, New York City, in the 1940s. Here the meaning is 'to be in automatically', as his candidates would have been.

. . . *'I SHOULD COCOA!'*?

This is a slightly dated British English exclamation meaning 'certainly not!' Longman adds a word of caution: 'This phrase is not recommended for use by the foreign student.'

But why 'cocoa'? As always, when in difficulty with a phrase origin, turn to rhyming slang. 'Cocoa' is from 'coffee and co-coa', rhyming slang for '(I should) say/ think so!' – often used ironically.

. . . THE SEVEN YEAR *ITCH*?

See *seven*.

... A TYPE OF INTELLECTUAL LIVES IN AN
IVORY TOWER?

i.e. secluded and protected from the harsh realities of life. There is a very precise origin here: Sainte-Beuve, the French literary critic, was writing in 1837 about the seclusion of the Comte de Vigny (the French poet, dramatist, and novelist) in a turret-room. He described it as his *tour d'ivoire*.

... *JACUZZI* FOR A SWIRLING BATH?

For some reason it is often a surprise to find that the word for a familiar object comes from the name of the man who invented it. Such is the case with 'the jacuzzi', the hot tubs used especially in California and other sybaritic places for relaxation and leisure, from the late 1960s onwards.

Candido Jacuzzi (who died aged 83 in 1986) was not that inventor, however. What he – an engineer and inventor mainly in the aviation world – did do was to make a portable pump so that his baby son Kenneth could be treated in the bath at home for his rheumatoid arthritis instead of having to go to a public pool.

In 1968, a third-generation member of the family, Roy Jacuzzi, saw the commercial possibilities of using the pump to make a whirlpool bath. Roy, who became president and managing director of the Jacuzzi Whirlpool Bath Company, has said that Candido thought the idea of a swirling bath for leisure was a little crazy.

... AN OLD LAVATORY IS A *JAKES*?

This is an archaism but an interesting one. Just as there is a current (mostly American) use of the name 'john' for a lavatory, so, in Elizabethan times (and later) there was a use of 'jakes' (a form of John/ Jack) for the same thing.

It is said that this derives from the name of Sir John Harrington (1561–1612) who invented a flush lavatory, hence 'Jake's place', once a respectable euphemism (according to Vernon Noble, *Speak Softly – Euphemisms and Such*, 1982). Sir John, Queen Elizabeth's 'saucy godson', installed a WC at Hampton Court and even

published instructions as to how such devices could be manufactured, but either because of the difficulty of installation or
frequent breakdowns – or perhaps because people simply could
not be bothered – more than a century and a half elapsed before
the household version was generally adopted.

It would be nice to believe all this, but one cannot be sure.
SOED has 'c. 1530' for the use of 'jakes' to mean a privy, which
would effectively eliminate Sir John.

And, as for the American use of 'john', the Morrises record the
first appearance of the word in print in this sense. It is contained
in an official regulation of Harvard College published in 1735.
'The expression in full was "Cousin John" ... the regulation read:
"No Freshman shall go into the Fellows' Cousin John".'

... A PERSON IS *JAYWALKING*?
i.e. being a pedestrian who ignores the rules in a motorized zone.
This word is an American coinage from the turn of the century.
'Jay' was a slang term for a rustic or countrified person. So
jaywalking was inappropriate in a city where newfangled auto-
mobiles were likely to interrupt the reveries of visitors from
quieter parts.

... A HOUSE IS *JERRY-BUILT*?
i.e. in other words: built unsubstantially of bad materials, the
shoddy result of bad workmanship. There are various contenders
here.

SOED suggests no origin but dates it 1881, which rules out any
connection with the German type of 'jerry' or with buildings
erected by German prisoners-of-war.

A strongly advanced contender is that there were two brothers
called Jerry who were notoriously bad builders in Liverpool. But
there is no supporting evidence for this theory except that there
is said to have been a use of the word 'jerry-building' in a
Liverpool paper of 1861 (Partridge).

More ingenious is the theory that it must have something to do
with the French word *jour*, meaning day, and that workers paid
on a daily basis were unlikely to make a good job of things. Or
that, as with the nautical term 'jury' ('jury-rigging', 'jury mast')
the word suggests something temporary.

As for the link with Jericho, of which the walls came tumbling down, well, this is quite the most intriguing and likely explanation, in my view.

... *JERUSALEM ARTICHOKE*?
... when it has nothing to do with Jerusalem? The name derives from a corruption or mishearing of the Italian *girasole articiocco*, meaning sunflower artichoke.

... THE CUT OF SOMEONE'S *JIB*?
See *cut*.

... *JOEY* FOR A HANDICAPPED PERSON?
– or someone behaving like one. An unfortunate coinage. The children's TV programme *Blue Peter* featured a quadraplegic spastic called Joey Deacon who was unable to communicate in normal language. His 'autobiography' had earlier been dramatized for adult TV viewers in 1974. The idea was to promote a caring attitude in young viewers. Alas, cruelly, the word 'Joey' came to be used by children in quite the wrong way, as in 'You are a joey', or 'That was a real joey thing to do'.

... *JOHN BULL*?
See *Bulldog Breed*.

... THAT A SIGNATURE IS A *JOHN HANCOCK*?
(American use only.) John Hancock (1737–93), a Boston merchant, was one (if not the first) of the signatories of the American Declaration of Independence in 1776. His signature is quite the largest on the document and he is variously reported to have done it 'so the King of England could read it without spectacles' and said, 'There! I guess King George [or John Bull] will be able to read that!'

Hence if you ask someone to give their 'John Hancock', or to 'put your John Hancock on the dotted line', it is their signature or autograph you are after.

The Morrises add that in the western US, in the early nineteenth century, the expression changed to 'John Henry', though it is not clear which John Henry was being referred to.

'...JOLLY D!'?
A slightly dated English exclamation of delighted agreement,
short for 'jolly decent!' Probably from the Second World War,
perhaps public school or RAF usage. Certainly it was in use by the
1940s and, as 'Oh, jolly d!', became a catchphrase of 'Dudley
Davenport' (Maurice Denham) in the BBC radio series *Much
Binding in the Marsh* (c. 1944–5).

... KEEPING UP WITH THE *JONESES*?
See *keeping*.

... EVERY *JOT AND TITTLE*?
i.e. the least item or detail – as one might say 'no jot or tittle was
missing'. The expression is included in the Authorized Version of
the Bible (1611): 'Till heaven and earth pass, one jot or one tittle
shall in no wise pass from the law, till all be fulfilled' (St Matthew
5:18).
   'Jot' means *iota*, the smallest Greek letter; 'tittle' (from Latin
titulus) means the dot over the letter *i*.
   ('Not one iota' comes from the same source.)
   Not a lot of people know this. Hence, presumably, the rather
unfortunate mangling of the phrase by Jack Valenti in a BBC
Radio interview. He referred to 'every tit and jottle' of something
or other. (See also *fits one to a T*.)

... *JUMBO* FOR 'ELEPHANTINE'?
'Jumbo' was the name of a famous African elephant, a notably
large one and the first to be seen in England. It was exhibited at
the London Zoo from 1865 to 1882. The beast was then sold
to Barnum and Bailey's circus in the United States where it
unfortunately died when a railway engine ran into it in 1885. Its
stuffed remains are preserved in New York City's Museum of
Natural History.
   Every other jumbo since – on the ground and in the air – takes
its name from this 'all-famous and gigantic' original. *SOED*
suggests the name may have been derived from *mumbo-jumbo*, the
West African name for a divinity or bogey. It might equally well
come from the Swahili word *jumbe*, meaning chief.

... A MAN HAS BEEN TRIED BEFORE A *KANGAROO COURT*?
i.e. by a self-appointed court which has no proper legal authority.
Macquarie, the Australian dictionary, ironically calls this chiefly
an American and British colloquialism. The term was already
being used in Texas by 1853. But surely there must be some link
to the land of the kangaroo?

'Kangaroo court' is a term used to describe the disciplinary
proceedings sometimes to be found among prisoners in gaol. As
Australia was the great nineteenth-century British penal colony,
perhaps if one wanted to refer to such a set-up, to call it a
'kangaroo' court was no more than to say 'of the type you would
find in Australia'.

Australian usage has 'kangaroo' as rhyming slang for a screw,
meaning a warder in a prison. Perhaps that, too, has something to
do with it? The Australian verb 'to kangaroo' means to release the
clutch of a motor car unevenly so that it moves forward in a jerky
manner, like the hops of a kangaroo. This might be a way of
conveying the irregular operations of a kangaroo court though the
term clearly pre-dates the motor car?

... A LAVATORY IS A *KARZY*?
This word has limited British use and I had always assumed that
it was spelt *khazi* and had some connection with India. However,
Partridge – while drawing attention to other spellings viz. *kharsie*
and *carzey* – derives it from the more English *carsey*, a low
Cockney word for a privy and dating from the late nineteenth
century. A carsey was also a den or brothel and presumably
derives from the Italian *casa*, meaning house.

. . . WE MUST *KEEP THE BALL ROLLING*?

i.e. keep the conversation going, maintain the flow of events. The American Shook has it that this image is taken from 'the British game of bandy, which we call hockey'. Partridge says it comes from association football. Brewer wisely just says it derives from 'ball games'. An alternative (according to *SOED*) is 'to keep the ball *up*', i.e. in the air, as in tennis.

The meaning is surely clear without specifying a game.

. . . PEOPLE ARE TRYING TO *KEEP UP WITH THE JONESES*?

i.e. striving not to be outdone by their neighbours. Yes, but why the Joneses in particular? A straightforward answer. *Keeping up with the Joneses* was the title of a comic strip by Arthur R. 'Pop' Momand which appeared in the New York *Globe* from 1913 to 1931.

It is said that Momand had at first intended to call his strip 'Keeping up with the Smiths' but refrained because his own neighbours were actually of that name and some of the exploits he wished to report had been acted out by them in real life.

. . . WE PUT THE *KIBOSH* ON SOMETHING?

i.e. put an end to, squelch, spoil, veto it (as in the First World War song: *When Belgium Put the Kibosh on the Kaiser*). One explanation is that it comes from the Irish *cie bais* (which is pronounced 'kibosh') meaning a cap of death. Certainly some of the earlier recorded uses of the expression are Irish. *OED Supp.* has this from *Lays and Legends of Northern Ireland* (1884): 'The Rector pull'd out an' oul' fourpinny-bit . . An' handed the pill that wid kibosh the fun.'

SOED wonders whether it is Yiddish. Rosten, who should know, says that the word and its meaning are known in Yiddish but cannot decide whether it is Yiddish in origin. In *The Joys of Yiddish*, he reviews all the options, Yiddish, Irish and heraldic, at great length and concludes: 'Why do I bother you with this *megillah*, for a word that may not come from Yiddish at all? . . . I want to give you one little example of the prolonged, irksome, frustrating and unbelievable *tsuris* to which a writer subjects himself when he rashly undertakes to write a book such as this.'

113

... A DEAD MAN HAS *KICKED THE BUCKET*?

Ewart confidently asserts that it is not the kind of bucket used for carrying water with which we are dealing here. A 'bucket beam' was a wooden frame on which pigs were hung after being slaughtered. Hence the odd *post mortem* spasm would involve kicking the bucket. Brewer adds that this is an East Anglian usage and derives from the Old French word *buquet*, meaning a balance. From this we also get the idea that a bucket is a yoke. So when one kicks (off) the bucket one gets rid of the yoke or burden of life.

A more basic origin is that of a suicide who stands on a bucket and kicks it away in order to hang himself.

... CHICKEN À LA *KING*?
See *chicken*.

... A TYPE OF DRINK IS A *KIR*?

Chilled, dry white wine mixed with a drop of *crème de cassis* (an alcoholic blackcurrant syrup) takes its name not from the man who invented it but from a notable imbiber: Canon Felix Kir, a French Resistance hero and Mayor of Dijon who died in 1968 aged 92. His favourite tipple was white Aligoté burgundy with *cassis*. The drink, known as *blanc cassis* had been popular long before he gave his name to it. However, in a letter to *The Times* (12 November 1983), Sir Patrick Reilly insisted that the Canon always drank *red* wine with his *cassis*. So I do not really know where that leaves us. But it is a delicious drink.

... SOMEONE IS HAVING *KITTENS*?

i.e. behaving in a hysterical manner. Morris explains that, in medieval times, if a pregnant woman was having pains, it was 'believed she was bewitched and had kittens clawing at her inside her womb'. Witches could provide potions to destroy the imagined 'litter'. As late as the seventeenth century an 'excuse for obtaining an abortion was given in court as "removing cats in the belly"'.

... WE PUT MONEY IN A *KITTY*?

i.e. the pool in card games. Shook says it comes from 'kit', short for 'kitbag', which was used among soldiers as a receptacle to pool their money. I can find no support for this theory, but no one seems to have a better idea.

... WOMEN WEAR *KNICKERS*?

– short, of course, for knickerbockers. Many of the original Dutch settlers in New York (originally New Amsterdam) were called Knickerbocker. Dutchmen wore loose knee-pants or breeches and they, via a common process, came to be called 'knickerbockers' especially after the garments had been shown in the illustrations for Washington Irving's book *Knickerbocker's History of New York* (1809). The term has also been applied to the wide trousers, gathered just below the knee, favoured by golfers.

In Britain, shortened to 'knickers', the word has been more usually applied to female underwear formerly called 'drawers' and which, initally at least, looked like the old Dutch breeches.

The excellent expression 'Don't get your knickers in a twist' (meaning 'don't get worked up or confused about something') is, for this reason, probably denied to the Americans.

... SOMETHING COMES WITH *KNOBS ON*?

As in the similar phrases, 'with bells on' or 'with brass knobs on', this is a way of saying (somewhat ironically) that something comes with embellishments. It has proved hard to find an example of its use before the 1930s. The *OED Supp.* has a 1931 citation from J.J. Farjeon. I have found a 1932 one from a theatre review by Herbert Farjeon. (Perhaps, if they were related, it was a family expression?) It goes: 'A massive company has been assembled at His Majesty's theatre to restore what is called "the Tree tradition" with an overwhelming production of *Julius Caesar*, which I need hardly tell anyone who knows anything about the Tree tradition means plenty of lictors and vestal virgins or, to sum the matter up in the base vernacular, *Julius Caesar* with knobs on.'

... ONE *KNOCKS SEVEN BELLS* OUT OF SOMEONE?

i.e. beats him severely, if not knocks him out. It's nautical, but why seven out of the eight bells available aboard ship?

... SOMEONE WHO FAILS HAS *LAID AN EGG*?
The origin of this lies in the game of cricket where a zero score
was called a 'duck's egg' because of the obvious resemblance
between the number and object. In the US, in baseball, there
developed a similar expression, 'goose egg'. The more general
use came from sporting metaphors, e.g. *Variety*'s famous headline at the time of the 1929 crash: 'WALL STREET LAYS AN
EGG'.

(Although the Morrises and Shook and other American sources
give cricket as the source of the expression, the *OED Supp.* says
the origin is American.)

... SOMETHING OR SOMEONE IS A *LAME DUCK*?
i.e. handicapped by misfortune or by incapacity. On the London
Stock Exchange, this was the name given to a defaulter. In the
nineteenth century, it was a stigma to be shunned. The money-
conscious Mr Osborne in William Thackeray's *Vanity Fair* was
suspicious of the financial position of Amelia's father: 'I'll have no
lame duck's daughter in my family' (ch. xiii).

In the US, the term has come to be applied to a President or
other office-holder whose power is diminished because he is
about to leave office. In *c*.1970, it was also applied to British
industries unable to survive without government financial
support.

The image evoked by the phrase is obvious enough, but why
'duck'? Shook suggests it had to do with Exchange Alley in the
City of London. People who could not pay their debts were said to
'waddle out of the alley'.

116

... A PERSON IS A *LANDLUBBER*?

– if he is at sea and might prefer to be on land. It is not that he is a 'land-lover' (thought he might be) but that he is a 'lubber' – a big, clumsy, stupid fellow. By 1579, 'lubber' was a seaman's name for a clumsy novice. The addition of 'land-' only served to emphasize the insult. Presumably such a person would be equally clumsy on land as on sea.

'... *LANG MAY YER LUM REEK*'?

Well, perhaps not many of us say this, but it is a Scotticism which has passed into wider use, if not quite as much as 'auld lang syne'.

It means, 'May you have long life', when you are wishing someone health and prosperity. But how? Think of a nickname for Edinburgh – 'auld reekie' (which means 'old smokey') – and you more or less have it.

A 'lum' is a chimney, so the phrase literally means, 'long may your chimney smoke'. Rather charming.

... THE *LATE UNPLEASANTNESS* TO REFER TO THE LAST WAR?

I suppose, if we say it at all, we do so because it is a euphemistic way of dealing with something horrid. It is a slightly facetious euphemism.

The earliest use of the phrase I have come across is the (pseudonymous?) American writer, 'Petroleum V. Nasby' who referred thus to the American Civil War. The *OED Supp*. has another American source dating from 1868 and from its various citations gives the impression that it was quite a common expression.

... BREAK A *LEG*?

See *break*.

... A PERSON IS WEARING A *LEOTARD*?

It was with something approaching glee that I learned in April 1986 of the appointment of a Monsieur François Leotard as France's Minister of Culture.

Leotard? Could he possibly be descended from Jules Leotard (c.1830/42–70), the French acrobat, who gave his name to the body-coverings beloved of ballet dancers and other performing artists?

It was rather as though Britain's Minister for the Arts had been called Frank Tights.

The original Leotard is also said to have invented the 'flying trapeze' and thus may have been the original *Daring Young Man on the Flying Trapeze* – at least, Colin MacInnes says he was in his book *Sweet Saturday Night*. George Leybourne's lines 'He flies through the air with the greatest of ease' and 'His figure is handsome, all girls he can please' were included in the song *The Man on the Flying Trapeze*, published in 1860, so it is possible they referred to Leotard. The man himself was paid £180 a week to perform without a net between himself and the diners at the Alhambra, Leicester Square, in London.

Leotard wrote: 'Do you want to be adored by the ladies? A trapeze is not required, but instead of draping yourself in unflattering clothes, invented by ladies, and which give us the air of ridiculous mannikins, put on more natural garb, which does not hide your best features.'

... WE *LET THE CAT OUT OF THE BAG*?

A trick played upon unsuspecting purchasers at old English country fairs was when a sucking-pig was advertised for sale. The pig would be shown to the buyer, then put in a sack while the deal was finalized. A quick substitution would then be effected, and the buyer would take away a sack with a less valuable *cat* in it. If he opened the sack and discovered the fraud, he would 'let the cat out of the bag' – and that is one fairly reasonable suggestion as to why this image is evoked. The same idea lies behind the expressions 'to buy a pig in a poke' (where poke means bag) and 'to be sold a pup'.

... A PERSON IS WEARING *LEVIS*?

meaning jeans, denims. Each of these words has an interesting origin. Let's take them in reverse order. 'Denim' (*de Nimes*) is derived from the town of Nimes, in southern France, the source of the material *serge de Nim* or *Nimes*. 'Jeans' come from the French for Genoa (*Genes*), in Italy, where a similar cloth, *jene fustian*, was once made.

Trousers were made out of these materials before they became famously American. 'Levis' or 'levis' (meaning Levi's) are the specific type of blue denim jeans originated by Levi Strauss of San Francisco. He pioneered the industry which makes this especially American garment and his company is still a world leader in it. Apparently, he turned up in the California Gold Rush in 1850 with a roll of tent canvas under his arm. He got a tailor to run up out of it the tough trousers needed in those parts. When he ran out of canvas, his brothers in New York imported the material from its original French source.

... A PERSON IS A *LIMEY*?

An old American (and then Australian) name for a British person, this term derives from the free issue of lime-juice made to British sailors to protect them from scurvy, especially in the eighteenth century. It is short for 'lime-juicer'.

... PEOPLE DANCED THE *LINDY HOP*?

This was a vigorous dance popular in the 1930s which evolved into the jitterbug of the 1940s and perhaps even led on to the jive and rock'n'roll of the 1950s.

Its name comes from an age perhaps more inclined to celebrate progress than our own. In 1927, Colonel Charles Lindberg, the American pilot, flew the Atlantic – the first non-stop solo crossing – and set off a tremendous, euphoric response. Most reference books connect the dance which began to flourish shortly after the flight with Lindberg's nickname, 'Lindy'.

... A WOMAN WEARS A *LITTLE BLACK DRESS*?

i.e. a simple dress suitable for most social occasions and sometimes abbreviated to 'l.b.d.'. In December 1978, Baroness David de Rothschild paid £1,500 at Christie's in London for the original legendary dress, the creation of Coco Chanel (at a sale of the late designer's clothes and jewellery). Chanel had died at 87 in 1971.

However, it appears Chanel was not the sole creator of the l.b.d. J. Ironside in *Fashion Alphabet* (1968) states: 'This highly useful garment was at first almost the trademark of the British designer, Molyneux, who perfected it as an "after six" look in the cocktail party era between 1920 and 1939. The ultimate in sophistication then, it is still very much in demand.'

Georgina O'Hara in *The Encyclopedia of Fashion* (1986) puts it this way: 'Heavily promoted by Chanel and Molyneux in the 1920s and 30s, the little black dress has been popular at some point in almost every decade.'

... *LOBSTER NEWBURG*?
i.e. lobster cooked in a rich, thick, creamy sauce flavoured with brandy, sherry or wine, with paprika or cayenne pepper and egg yolks. This was a speciality of Delmonico's, the fashionable New York restaurant of the late nineteenth century. (In 1895 it was being called 'Lobster à la Newburg'.)

Originally, so the story has it, it was named 'Lobster Wenberg', after a particular customer, Ben Wenberg, a sea-captain who supplied the cayenne pepper and also related how a similar South American dish had been prepared. When he fell out of favour with the management – for fighting in the restaurant – his name was anagrammatised, more or less, into 'Newburg'.

... *LOCK, STOCK AND BARREL*?
– meaning the whole lot. This term comes to us from the armoury where the lock (or firing mechanism), stock and barrel are the principal parts which go to make up a gun.

Compare the expression 'hook, line and sinker' (for the depths to which a person swallows a story), which comes from the component 'catching' parts of fishing tackle.

'... NOT BY A *LONG CHALK*'?
i.e. not by any means. This seems to refer the method of making chalk marks on the floor to show the score of a player or team. A 'long chalk' would mean a lot of points, a great deal.

... AN OLD PERSON IS *LONG IN THE TOOTH*?
Before regular teeth-cleaning was actively encouraged, many people had to have their teeth out or see them reduced by decay. This was most obvious in old people who suffered from receding of the gums and bone in the jaw. When the mouth is not effectively cleaned, the gums gradually recede and the teeth appear tc be longer – hence the expression, long in the tooth.

... WE GO TO THE *LOO*?

i.e. to the lavatory. Let us take a deep breath before tackling this one, as everybody has a favourite theory:

The present Earl of Lichfield was told by the historian Sir Steven Runciman that 'loo' derived from the name of Lichfield's great-great-aunt, Lady Louisa Anson, about a hundred years ago. During a houseparty in Ireland, the host's two youngest sons took her name-card from her bedroom door and put it on the guest lavatory. Henceforward, aristocrats talked of 'going to Lady Lou'.

It comes from the French word *lieu*, meaning place. Old Parisian hotel lavatories had a notice to the effect, '*On est prié de laisser ce* lieu *aussi propre qu'on le trouve*' ('Please leave this place as you would wish to find it').

When chamber-pots were emptied out of windows into the street, the emptier would cry, 'Guardy-loo' from the French *gardez l'eau*' ('mind the water').

At the time of the French Revolution, lavatories were sometimes known as *lieux d'aisances* ('places of easement').

It is an anglicized form of *lieu*, as in the expression 'time off in *lieu* (pronounced 'loo')' – in place of work done.

It is a pun on Water-loo.

It is nautical in origin, from 'looward' or 'leeward' (the sheltered side of a boat).

Shepherds would relieve themselves in a 'lee' (pronounced 'lew'), a shelter made of hurdles.

Macquarie calls it a 'mincing' form of 'lavatory', whatever that may mean.

A bordalou was a portable piss-pot carried by ladies in the eighteenth century (it could be hidden in a muff.)

Professor A.S.C. Ross who examined the various options in a 1974 edition of *Blackwood's Magazine* favoured a derivation, 'in some way which could not be determined', from Waterloo. However, I should not have thought it took a great deal of effort to see how that word could give rise to the short form. People have always sought euphemistic ways of referring to the lavatory, so at one time they probably said 'I must go to the water-closet' and, wishing not to be explicit, substituted 'Water-loo' as a weak little joke.

I still have a lingering affection, though, for a simple derivation which involves the French *l'eau*, meaning water.

Whatever the case, the word was established in well-to-do English society by the early part of the twentieth century and was swept into general middle-class use, as a respectable euphemism, after the Second World War.

... ' DON'T *LOOK A GIFT-HORSE IN THE MOUTH*'?

As with 'long in the tooth,' we are dealing here with age as shown by tooth-length, but in this case the association with horses is quite clear. If you are offered a gift of a horse (such is the suggestion) you would be ill-advised to look in its mouth. You might discover information not to your advantage.

The first known use of the saying is by St Jerome in AD 420. In the Preface to his commentary on the Epistle to the Ephesians, he wrote: *Noli ... ut vulgere proverbium est, equi dentes inspicere donati* ('Do not, as the common proverb says, look at the teeth of a gift horse').

' ... *LOVE ME, LOVE MY DOG*'?

– meaning, 'If you are inclined to take my side in matters generally, you must put up with one or two things you don't like at the same time.'

This is an old proverbial saying. Of all people, St Bernard wrote in a sermon, *Qui me amat, amat et canem meum* ('Who loves me, also loves my dog'). Alas, to spoil a good story, this was a different St Bernard to the one after whom the breed of dogs is named (the former was St Bernard of Clairvaux; the latter was St Bernard of Menthon.)

... WE'VE BEEN *LUMBERED*?

i.e. put in an impossible position (sometimes 'dead lumbered').

Not too clear, this one. In one sense, of course, lumber is simply timber, wood. The verb 'to lumber' used to mean 'to arrest, put in prison' and the phrase 'in lumber' can mean 'in prison', so I suppose these might have contributed to the present meaning.

Ewart, however, prefers a derivation from 'lumber-room', i.e. the room in a house in which disused or useless articles of furniture are dumped. People who cannot bear to part with objects like this often prefer to give them to other people rather than throw them away. Recipients of such questionable gifts from the lumber-room might be said to have been lumbered with them. Maybe.

Brewer notes that lumber (from Lombard) was also the name given to a pawnbroker's shop. Perhaps the owners of these shops, if they were not careful, sometimes lent money in return for items they would never be able to get rid of if they were not re-claimed – and were thus 'lumbered'?

... LANG MAY YER *LUM REEK*?
See *lang*.

... A DRUNK IS A *LUSH*?
SOED wonders whether the word merely develops from the other meaning of lush – lax, flaccid, soft, tender (of vegetation, for example). I suppose a drunk, by being wobbly and weak at the knees, might just about merit these adjectives.

The fact is, though, that 'lush' is slang for beer. Quite how this occurred is a bit of a mystery. There was a London actors' drinking club called 'The City of Lushington' which was founded in the eighteenth century. There may have been a London brewer called Lushington. And Dr Thomas Lushington (1590–1661), chaplain to Bishop Corbet, was a noted tippler.

The use of 'lush' for an alcoholic seems to have originated in the US by the beginning of the nineteenth century, building on the English origins of the slang name for beer.

Brewer adds that it may also come from Old French *vin lousche* (thick or unsettled wine).

... A POSSE MIGHT *LYNCH* A MAN?
i.e. administer its own justice by summarily executing him. It seems to have an eponymous origin, but which Mr Lynch was responsible? Was it:

James Lynch FitzStephens, a Mayor of Galway in Ireland who, in 1493, had to hang his own son on a murder charge because no one else would do it? (But this hardly denotes lynch law.)

Colonel William Lynch (1742–1820) of Pittsylvania County, Virginia, who took the law into his own hands and formed a vigilante band (c.1780) and devised what became known as the Lynch Laws (though he was not famous for hanging people)?

Charles Lynch (1736–96), a justice of the peace in Virginia? He was said to have had a notorious record for condemning malefactors to be hanged. The evidence against him seems suspect, however. Although he tended to throw people into jail illegally, he did not hang them.

I would settle for either of the Americans – and probably William Lynch. This view is supported by the *OED Supp.* However, as Burnam 2 points out, even he did not really behave in the way that 'to lynch' came to mean.

There is another possible origin, not eponymous. An old English word *linch* meant punishment by whipping or flogging, and this was sometimes imposed by the 'Lynch courts' of Virginia. So, who can say?

Oh yes, and why 'posse'? The word comes from the medieval Latin phrase *posse comitatus* ('power of the county') which was later used in the US to describe a body of men summoned by the sheriff to put down a riot.

... THE REAL MCCOY?
See *real*.

... A HITCHCOCK FILM HAS A MACGUFFIN?
This was the name given by Alfred Hitchcock (1899–1981) to something which had existed long before he thought of it. By MacGuffin he meant a device in a thriller writer's plot, the hinge upon which the whole story revolves.

Talking to François Truffaut about the film *Notorious*, Hitchcock said:

'After talking it over with Ben Hecht [the scriptwriter], we decide that the girl is to sleep with the spy in order to get some secret information. Gradually we develop a story and now I introduce the MacGuffin: four or five samples of uranium. The producer said, "What in the name of goodness is that?" I said, "This is uranium; it's the thing they're going to make the atom bomb with." And he asked, "What atom bomb?" This, you must remember was in 1944, a year before Hiroshima ...'

Jonathon Green adds a further gloss to this definition in his book *Newspeak* (1984) when he quotes Hitchcock as calling the device a 'demented red herring' – after which the characters in his films chase but which in the end has absolutely no relevance to the plot or its solution.

But why did Hitchcock choose the name MacGuffin?

... WE WEAR A MACINTOSH?
The first raincoat made of macintosh cloth appeared in 1830. It took its name from Charles Macintosh (1766–1843). He developed a method, devised by James Symes (1799–1870), for binding

125

together two layers of fabric with india rubber dissolved in naphtha to produce a waterproof. But it was Macintosh who patented the method (in 1823) and took the glory. Nowadays, waterproof garments tend to be treated with silicone which allows air to permeate the fabric, making it more comfortable to wear.

As will be apparent, the garment should be spelt without a 'k', although perhaps in the majority of cases it is spelt with one – when it is not abbreviated to 'mac'.

... MAD AS A HATTER?

The Mad Hatter in Lewis Carroll's *Alice's Adventures in Wonderland* was not the original of this phrase, merely the encapsulation of a popular belief. Dr Alice Hamilton of the Howard Medical School in the US is credited with discovering that people working as hat-makers could be affected by the nitrate of mercury used to treat felt. Inhaling the vapour could affect the brain.

Needless to say, there is also a specific 'mad' hatter who is said to have given rise to the craze. He was Robert Crab, a seventeenth-century eccentric who lived at Chesham, gave all his goods to the poor, and lived on leaves and grass.

The Morrises favour a derivation from the Anglo-Saxon word *atter*, meaning poison (closely related to adder, the British snake whose bite can cause fever). This is preferred because the phrase was current long before hat-making was a recognized trade.

Lewis Carroll may not have been thinking of a hatter at all, in using the expression, but referring to a man notable for the top hat he wore. It is said that Carroll suggested to Sir John Tenniel, who drew the book's original illustrations, that he make the character resemble Theophilus Carter, a furniture dealer from near Oxford. He was a bit potty, too – one of his inventions was an alarm-clock bed which tipped its occupant out onto the floor. It was shown at the Great Exhibition in London in 1851.

... WE MAKE A BEE-LINE?

i.e. go directly. From the belief that bees fly in a straight line back to the hive. But do they?

... *MAKE DO AND MEND*?
Popularized in Britain during the Second World War (when there were Make-Do-And-Mend departments in some stores), this phrase was designed to encourage thrift and the repairing of old garments, furniture, etc., rather than expenditure of scarce resources on making new.

It achieved near-slogan status and was probably derived from 'make and mend' which was a Royal Navy term for an afternoon free from work which could be devoted to mending clothes.

... WE *MAKE NO BONES ABOUT* MATTERS?
– meaning, go straight to the point, not conceal anything. Longman suggests that the phrase originally referred to finding no bones in a bowl of soup – the soup was therefore easy to swallow quickly, and there was nothing to complain about.

Brewer takes a different view and derives it from bone, meaning dice. This way, to 'make no bones' is not to make much of or not to coax the dice in order to show favour.

... A MAN IS A *MALE CHAUVINIST PIG*?
This phrase (sometimes abbreviated to M.C.P.) erupted in 1970 at the time of the launch of the Women's Movement in the US and elsewhere. It denotes a man who is sunk in masculine preoccupations and attitudes. The use of 'pig' was a reversion to the traditional fat, porky use of the word after a recent slang borrowing to describe the police (mostly in the US).

'Chauvinism' itself is a venerable eponymous word and originally referred to excessive patriotism. Nicolas Chauvin was a French general during Napoleon's campaigns who became famous for his excessive devotion to his leader.

I wonder who first coined the phrase 'male chauvinist pig' – was it unquestionably a woman?

... THE *MAN ON THE CLAPHAM OMNIBUS*?
i.e. the ordinary or average man, the man-in-the-street, particularly when his point of view is instanced by the Courts, newspaper editorials, etc. He was first evoked in 1903 by Lord Bowen when hearing a case of negligence: 'We must ask ourselves what the man on the Clapham omnibus would think.'

Quite why he chose that particular route we shall never know. It sounds suitably prosaic, of course, and the present 77A to Clapham Junction (1987) does pass through Whitehall and Westminster, thus providing a link between governors and governed.

There is evidence to suggest that the 'Clapham omnibus' had already become a figure of speech by the mid-nineteenth century.

... *MARIJUANA*?
See *gone to pot*.

... TELL IT TO THE *MARINES*?
See *tell*.

... *MARMALADE*?
Marmelo is the Portuguese word for quince: quince jam is *marmelada*. *Marmelade* is the French form. In Europe, this is still a word used for jams in general, but, in English, it has for a long time been applied to preserve of orange, lemon or grapefruit jam.

The most fanciful etymology of the word is that it was a favourite food of Mary Queen of Scots (1542–87) when she was ill – hence its being dubbed *Marie Malade* ('sick Mary'). As the word has been known since at least 1480 this is quite clearly fictitious.

... ALL MY EYE AND BETTY *MARTIN*?
See *all*.

... A STRICT PERSON IS A *MARTINET*?
Jean Martinet (*d*.1672) was a French colonel, general or even marquis, who served under Louis XIV and helped remodel the king's army. He was known as an especially severe, almost fanatical, disciplinarian, relying heavily upon drill and punishment using a whip (which also became known as *martinet*).

... WE DRINK A *MARTINI*?
Take a deep breath, because no two people seem capable of agreeing on what a martini, or a dry martini, or a dry martini cocktail consists of. Let us start from the term 'dry martini'. Why is it so called? If we listen to John Doxat, author of *Stirred – Not Shaken*, we learn that it evolved around 1910 in the Knicker-

bocker Hotel, New York City, and was named after its originator, the head bartender, Martini di Armi di Taggia, who later retired to his native Italy and was buried in Genoa.

His invention, if such it was, consisted of one third French vermouth and two thirds dry gin. This recipe was also listed in the *Savoy Cocktail Book* of the 1920s, using either French or Italian vermouth (or a mixture of same) and it is significant that vermouth is stipulated and not any vermouth with the brand name 'Martini'. In the US, there is usually more gin included.

However, there has been an Italian firm, Martini and Rossi, makers of Italian vermouth, around since 1894.

So where does this leave us? Is it that the word 'martini' is derived from Martini and Rossi and '*dry* martini' from the Signor Martini who devised the cocktail? An unlikely coincidence, surely.

But, to muddy the path further, according to Flexner 2, people were drinking something called a *martinez* in the 1860s (half gin, half dry vermouth). This may have taken its name from one of several hotels, restaurants or bars with that name. Or it may have been given it by 'Professor' Jerry Thomas who claimed to have invented the cocktail at San Francisco's Occidental Hotel while tending the bar there in 1860–2, 'first making it for a thirsty traveller on the way to Martinez, California'.

The British term 'gin and it' is short for 'gin and Italian (vermouth)'.

... A PERSON IS A *MASOCHIST*?

Leopold von Sacher-Masoch (1836–95) was an Austrian novelist who specialized in writing about a sexual abnormality wherein one takes pleasure from humiliation and pain inflicted by oneself or other people. He submitted to various women who would gratify his wishes in this way, but ended up in an asylum. The German psychiatrist Krafft-Ebing immortalized his name by introducing the word 'masochism' to describe the condition.

More recently the meaning of the word has been broadened to describe more general forms of enjoying humiliation and pain, without a necessarily overt sexual connotation.

129

... A PERSON IS A *MAVERICK*?
i.e. an individualist, unorthodox, independent-minded. Samuel
A. Maverick (1803–70) was a Texas cattle-owner who left the
calves of his herd unbranded. The word 'maverick' was applied to
such yearlings and then to any calf which could be separated from
its mother cow. Maverick claimed not to want to brand his calves
because it was cruel. But it also enabled him to claim any unbranded calves he found on the range.

In time, the word took on a wider meaning and was particularly
used in American politics. There it described a man who would
not affiliate with a particular party.

... *MAYDAY*?
See *SOS*.

... PEACH *MELBA*?
See *peach*.

... *MERDE*?
See *mot de Cambronne*.

... SOMETHING IS *MESMERIZING*?
Dr Franz or Friedrich Anton Mesmer (1734–1815) was a German
physician who practised a form of hypnotism in Vienna as a way
of treating certain ailments. Operating in Paris, his theory of
'animal magnetism' was discredited in his lifetime but his reputation was rescued by a pupil who identified what Mesmer had
done and gave it the name 'mesmerism'.

'Mesmerizing' now means simply 'fascinating, spell-binding'.

... TAKE THE *MICKEY*?
See *taking*.

... SOMEONE HAS BEEN SLIPPED A *MICKEY FINN*?
i.e. a draught or powder has been put into his drink to knock him
out or give him diarrhoea. The idea behind this action (known
since *c.*1930) is to drive away an unwelcome customer from a bar
or simply to play a joke on him.

130

DOAS claims that originally the term meant a laxative for horses.

The original Mickey Finn may have been a notorious bartender in Chicago (*c*.1896–1906) who proceeded to rob his unconscious victims.

Also, occasionally, the term is rendered as 'Mickey Flynn' or simply 'Mickey'.

'... MIND HIS PS AND QS'?

i.e. be careful. Various explanations have been advanced for this:

It was a warning to printers to make sure they did not mix up the similar-looking letters 'p' and 'q'.

It was a warning to public-house customers to insist on accuracy when their *p*ints and *q*uarts were being chalked up on a black-board for future payment.

In the days of wigs, it was a warning to Frenchmen not to get their *pieds* (feet) mixed up with their *queues* (tails of wigs) when bowing and scraping.

It was a warning to men not to soil their navy pea-jackets with their 'queues' or pigtails.

SOED renders Ps and Qs as 'peas and cues'. Although it translates 'cues' as 'queues', one almost feels like pursuing a line to do with 'peas and cucumbers'.

Burman 2 would sternly squash almost every theory in sight and states: 'The fact is that no one knows how the expression originated. The most obvious explanation (and thus, one is tempted to say, the least likely to be accepted) is that the letters "p" and "q" look so much alike that a child learning to write might well be admonished to mind his or her "p's and q's"'.

... A SECRETARY KEEPS THE *MINUTES* OF A MEETING?

This has nothing to do with the minutes of time that might pass during a meeting, though the term comes from the same Latin word, *minutus*. No, in this context, the meaning is as in 'minute' (pronounced 'my newt'). The original minutes were taken down in minute or small writing so that they could be 'engrossed' or put into larger writing later.

... *MOANING MINNIES*?

On 11 September 1985, Mrs Margaret Thatcher, the British Prime Minister, made a visit to Tyneside and was reported as accusing those who complained about the effects of unemployment of being 'Moaning Minnies'. In the ensuing uproar, a Downing Street spokesman had to point out that it was the reporters attempting to question her, rather than the unemployed, on whom Mrs Thatcher bestowed the title.

As a nickname, it was not an original alliterative coinage. Anyone who complains is a 'moaner' and a 'minnie' can mean a lost lamb which finds itself a mother. But the original 'Moaning Minnies' were something quite different. In the First World War, a 'Minnie' was the slang word for a German *minenwerfer*, a trench-mortar or the shell that came from it, making a distinctive moaning noise. In the Second World War, the name was also applied to air-raid sirens which were also that way inclined.

... A PERSON IS A *MOD*?

The word 'mod' or 'Mod' had emerged by 1960 in Britain to denote tidy, clean-cut, slightly effete and clothes-conscious teen-agers who rode around on motor-scooters. This was in contrast with the rougher, hairier Rockers with their leather jackets and motorbikes who had developed out of the 1950s Teddy Boys and rock'n'roll enthusiasts.

I suppose it is obvious, but the name 'mod' derives not so much from 'modern' as from 'modernist'. A somewhat more effete source?

... 'GOT YOUR *MOJO* WORKING'?

In 1960, Muddy Waters, the American blues singer (*b.*1915) was singing a song with the refrain, 'Got my mojo workin', but it just don't work on you.' He knew what he was singing about because he had written the song under his real name, McKinley Morganfield.

DOAS simply defines a 'mojo' as 'any narcotic' but a sleeve note to an album entitled *Got My Mojo Workin'* by the jazz organist Jimmy Smith (1966) is perhaps nearer to the meaning in the song. It describes 'mojo' as 'magic – a spell or charm guaranteed to make the user irresistible to the opposite sex'.

It seems to me that 'mojo' may well be a form of the word 'magic', corrupted through Negro pronunciation, though the *OED Supp.* finds an African word meaning 'magic, witchcraft' that is similar. The *OED Supp.* derives the narcotic meaning of the word from the Spanish word *mojar*, 'to celebrate by drinking'.

... AN INFILTRATOR IS A *MOLE*?
In the late 1970s and early 1980s, a number of espionage scandals in Britain, e.g. the exposing of Sir Anthony Blunt as the 'Fourth Man' in the Burgess-Maclean spy case of the 1950s, ran parallel with fictional spy frolics contained in the novels of 'John le Carré' (ex-spook, David Cornwell). The word 'mole' had a particular vogue and was used eventually in a very general way to describe anyone who infiltrated a large organisation (not necessarily for spying).

In Le Carré's world, a mole is an operative placed in another country's intelligence network, often years before he is needed. The CIA term for this is 'penetration' and former CIA chief Richard Helms told Safire he had never encountered the use of the word 'mole'.

Did Le Carré invent the term or did he acquire it in his days with British intelligence? Jonathon Green in his *Newspeak* summarizes thus: 'While Francis Bacon uses the word in his *History of the Reign of King Henry VII* (1622), it was otherwise to be found in the works of John le Carré, notably *Tinker Tailor Soldier Spy* (1974). In a BBC-TV interview in 1976, Le Carré claimed that *mole* was a genuine KGB term.'

... A TYPE OF BOMB IS A *MOLOTOV COCKTAIL*?
This is a very simple kind of incendiary device, like a petrol bomb, and acquired its nickname in Finland during the early days of the Second World War. Quite why it was named after Vyacheslav Mikhailovich Molotov (1890–1986) is another matter. He had become Soviet Minister for Foreign Affairs in 1939. The Russians invaded Finland and these cheap grenades proved an effective way for the Finns to oppose their tanks. Perhaps the idea was that throwing the burning liquid in a container at the Russians was like delivering a fiery cocktail to the Soviet Foreign Minister.

. . . 'THIS IS THE *MOMENT OF TRUTH*'?

i.e. a crucial point. This is a direct lift from bull-fighting where *el momento de la verdad* is that when the final sword-thrust finishes off the animal.

. . . WE MIGHT THROW A *MONKEY WRENCH* INTO THE MACHINERY?

Because this spanner, or wrench with an adjustable jaw, is a notable tool that any engineer might possess. But why a *monkey* wrench? It is said that it was invented by Charles Moncke, a London blacksmith, or by a Mr Monk, who was an American (*c.*1856).

. . . A RICH MAN HAS LOTS OF *MOOLA*?

i.e. money. Sometimes 'moolah' or 'moo'. US slang. For once, nobody has the slightest idea where this word comes from.

. . . OVER THE *MOON*?

See *over*.

. . . ILLICIT LIQUOR IS *MOONSHINE*?

As we have it today, this word has reached us via the US where it was used to describe whisky, illegally *made* by moonlight, i.e. at night. However, even before this, in the eighteenth century, the word had been used in England to denote brandy illegally *smuggled* in by moonlight.

. . . *MORTON'S FORK* IS A KIND OF TEST?

This is a historical term dating from England in the fifteenth century. John Morton (*c.*1420–1500) was Archbishop of Canterbury and a minister of Henry VII. As a way of raising forced loans he would apply his 'fork' – the argument that if people were obviously rich, then they could afford to pay, and if people looked poor, then they were obviously holding something back and so could also afford to pay. An early form of Catch-22, indeed.

. . . LE *MOT DE CAMBRONNE*?

The French word in question is *merde*, meaning shit. At the Battle of Waterloo, the commander of Napoleon's Old or Imperial Guard is *supposed* to have declined a British request for him to surrender with the words, *La garde meurt mais ne se rend jamais/ pas* ('The guard dies but never surrenders/ does not surrender').

However, it is more likely that what he said was, *Merde! La garde ne se rend jamais* ('Shit! etc.).

The man in question was Pierre Jacques Etienne, Count Cambronne. Hence, in France, *merde* is sometimes known as *le mot de Cambronne* – a useful euphemism when needed.

At a banquet in 1835, Cambronne denied saying the more polite version. That may have been invented for him by Rougemont in a newspaper, *L'Indépendent*.

... FOOD IS JUST LIKE *MOTHER/GRANDMA USED TO MAKE/BAKE?*

i.e. it is home cooking and very acceptable. This expression seems to have acquired figurative quotation marks around it by the early years of this century, though presumably people used it beforehand. As such, it is of American origin and was soon seized upon by advertisers as a form of slogan.

Vance Packard in *The Hidden Persuaders* (1957) records an example of its effectiveness in this respect:

When the Mogen David wine people were seeking some way to add magic to their wine's sales appeal (while it was still an obscure brand), they turned to motivation research via [their] ad agency. Psychiatrists and other probers listening to people talk at random about wine found that many related it to old family-centred or festive occasions. The campaign tied home and mother into the selling themes. One line was: 'the good old days – the home sweet home wine – the wine that grandma used to make.' As a result of these carefully 'motivated' slogans, the sales of Mogen David doubled within a year.

Which reminds me of the joke advertisement which proclaimed:

BUCK WHEAT CAKES
Like mother used to bake – $1.25.
Like mother thought she made – $2.25.

... A MAN IS *MR CLEAN?*

i.e. an honourable or incorruptible person (usually said of a politician). 'Mr Clean' is the brand name of an American household cleanser. Examples of the application of this phrase as a nickname include:

Pat Boone (*b.*1934), the US pop singer and film actor, noted for his clean image – he was also known as 'Mr Toothpaste' – and habits (he would never agree to kiss girls in films).

John Lindsay (*b.*1921), Mayor of New York City (1965–73).

Elliot Richardson (*b.*1920), US Attorney-General who resigned in 1973 rather than agree to the restrictions President Nixon was then placing on investigations into the Watergate affair.

... MRS WHITEHOUSE?
See *Mrs Grundy.*

... MS TO DENOTE A WOMAN?
'Ms' (pronounced *miz*) is 'a title substituted for Mrs or Miss before a woman's name to avoid making a distinction between married and unmarried women', according to the *Collins Dictionary of the English Language* (1979). Thus, it is a compromise designed to solve an age-old problem, and, frankly, it sounds like one.

It became popular with feminists in about 1970 at the start of the modern thrust by the Women's Movement. The New York Commission on Human Rights adopted it for use in correspondence at about that time. By 1972, a feminist magazine called *Ms* was being launched.

The idea had been around for quite some time before it became (in the words of the *OED Supp.*) 'an increasingly common, but not universally accepted, use'. In 1952, the National Office Management Association of Philadelphia was recommending, 'Use the abbreviation Ms. for *all women* addressees. This modern style solves an age-old problem.'

... But it created new ones. In August 1984, Geraldine Ferraro was the first woman to be selected as an American vice-presidential candidate. In what is known as 'private life', she was in fact, Mrs John Zaccaro. In public she declined to be known as 'Miss Ferraro', feeling this was inapposite for a woman who was the mother of three children. She asked that she be called either Ms or Mrs Ferraro. The *New York Times*, in its traditional way, found this very hard to swallow.

The paper liked to attach honorifics to names but did not permit the use of Ms in its columns and had to call her 'Mrs Ferraro' – despite pleadings from its own 'word' expert, William

Safire, who protested that 'Mrs Ferraro' is 'a person she is not ...
It is unacceptable for journalists to dictate to a candidate that she
call herself Miss or else use her married name'.

In the end, in 1986, the *New York Times* gave way. But one can
understand its reluctance. Not for opposing the motives behind
the coinage, but on the grounds that it is not an elegant or happy
coinage.

... MY NAME IS *MUD(D)*?
See *name*.

'... MUM'S THE WORD'?
i.e. we are keeping silent on this matter. No mother is invoked
here. 'Mum' is just a somewhat misleading representation of
'Mmmm', the noise made when lips are sealed.

It is neatly explained in a line from Shakespeare's *King Henry
VI, Part II*: 'Seal up your lips, and give no words but – mum.'

(The word 'mumble' obviously derives from the same source.)

... MURPHY'S LAW?
Most commonly known as Murphy's Law (and indistinguishable
from Sod's Law or Spode's Law) the saying, 'If anything can go
wrong, it will' dates back to the 1940s. Macquarie suggests that it
was named after a character who always made mistakes in a series
of educational cartoons published by the US Navy.

The *Concise Oxford Dictionary of Proverbs* suggests that it was
invented by George Nichols, a project manager for Northrop, the
Californian aviation firm, in 1949. He developed the idea from a
remark by a colleague, Captain E. Murphy of the Wright Field-
Aircraft Laboratory.

The most notable demonstration of Murphy's Law is that a
piece of bread when dropped on the floor always fall with its
buttered side facing down (otherwise known as the Law of Uni-
versal Cussedness). The idea, however, pre-dated the promul-
gation of the Law. In 1867, A.D. Richardson wrote in *Beyond
Mississippi*: 'His bread never fell on the buttered side.' In 1884,
James Payn composed the lines:

> I never had a piece of toast
> Particularly long and wide,
> But fell upon the sanded floor,
> And always on the buttered side.

The corollary of this aspect of the Law is that bread always falls buttered-side down *except* when demonstrating the Law.

Some would argue that Murphy's Law was originally designed to be constructive rather than defeatist – that it was a prescription for avoiding mistakes in the design of a valve for an aircraft's hydraulic system. If the valve could be fitted in more than one way, then sooner or later someone would fit it the wrong way. The idea was to design it so that the valve could only be fitted the right way.

'... MY GIDDY AUNT!'?

This is one of those trivial exclamations – others include 'My sainted aunt!', 'My sacred aunt!', 'My Aunt Fanny!', or simply, 'My aunt!' – which seem to have arisen in the mid-nineteenth century. They appear to have been especially popular among schoolboys. 'My sainted aunt!' pops up quite frequently in the Billy Bunter of Greyfriars stories by Frank Richards (e.g. in *The Magnet*, No. 401, 16 October 1915).

In a wry note in Partridge, Paul Beale wonders whether 'My aunt!' was originally a euphemism for *my arse*. I'm sure he is quite right, though he adds, '... or have I been working on this Dictionary too long?'

... IT'S *NAFF*?

Largely restricted to British use, the word 'naff' had been bubbling underground for many a year before it suddenly took off and became firmly established as a slang adjective in 1982. (However, by 1986, it was already out of fashion.)

In the summer of 1982, I made a note of it, not being entirely sure what it meant. A friend of my mine who had been stopped by the police for speeding in his new car, reported the policeman remarking of the vehicle, 'It's a bit naff, isn't it?'

Did he mean, 'It's a bit nasty and flashy', or what?

Before I had had time to brood on this, the word was suddenly on everybody's lips.

Earlier, on 17 April 1982, Princess Anne had used the word in a particular way. Riding at Badminton horse trials – according to a report in the *Daily Mirror* next day – she had told a group of photographers, '"Why don't you naff off" ... Just to make her meaning clear, the 31-year-old Princess added: "Shove off. Why don't you grow up".'

Helpfully, the paper said: 'The phrase – coined by Ronnie Barker in the TV series *Porridge* – took onlookers by surprise.' A little later when Anne produced what the *Mirror* considered a churlish response to the birth of an heir to her brother Charles, the paper came up with the headline: 'NAFF OFF, ANNE'.

Clearly, here, 'naff off' was no more than a euphemistic way of saying 'fuck off'. Perhaps Her Royal Highness would have hesitated over using it if she had been aware that 'naff' is an old slang word for the vagina. Or perhaps she would not. Who can say?

But what of the earlier adjectival use? Words like these can quite often flourish concurrently in different sections of society. A 'Roller' for a Rolls Royce is just as likely to be heard on the lips of a cockney bruiser as on those of a Hooray Henry. Another such word is 'brill', short for 'brilliant'. So it may be with 'naff'.

The *Official Sloane Ranger Handbook* (published in late 1982 but presumably written prior to Princess Anne's outburst) lists the word in its 'Sloane Dictionary':

Naff *adj.* What old SRs call 'poll'. They don't know what naff means exactly but they use it of clothes etc. that look wrong, unfashionable, drear.

This seems to me to put it rather well – 'worthless, not worth bothering with', said from a position of superiority.

But attempts have been made to derive the word from NAAFI – the familiar acronym for the Navy, Army and Air Force Institutes which has been the butt of pejorative remarks from the ranks more or less since its inception in 1921.

On the other hand, if 'naff' does come to us this way, it could equally have come from superiority towards the NAAFI by those of higher rank. So, perhaps there is no point in looking for a precise class colouring to the expression.

A derivation from the French *rien à faire* is the sort of thing etymologists come up with who have never been in a pub or watched TV.

I have equal doubts about it being 'back slang', i.e. 'fanny' backwards. Rhyming slang teaches us that people go through incredible contortions to invent slang expressions, but back slang has always struck me as most contrived.

So, where does that leave us? As a euphemistic expletive, the use by Ronnie Barker in *Porridge* has been traced back to the novel *Billy Liar* by Keith Waterhouse (1959), the writers of the TV series having also adapted the novel. Waterhouse became familiar with it during his RAF service (*c.*1950).

As for the adjectival use, it seems to have found its way into 'society' use (though Nigel Dempster was writing in March 1979 that it was even then an 'out' expression) from theatrical slang. The camp 'parlare' which has its roots in Romany/gypsy or fairground/circus/theatre language was brought to a wider public by its use in the BBC Radio show *Round the Horne* (1964–9). In the scripts of the show (published in 1974) we find in the glossary, the simple entry:

Naph = Bad.

I still feel, however, that the proper meaning of the word is more akin to the Sloane Ranger definition. It was regrettable that the pseudonymous author of two popular paperbacks, *The Complete Naff Guide* (July 1983) and *The Naff Sex Guide* (Autumn 1984), sought just to list those things (and people) he disliked. This seemed to weaken the meaning of the word and destroy what little subtlety there was in it. In fact, the books were not good enough. In the true meaning of the word, they were naff themselves.

... THE *NAKED TRUTH*?
i.e. the absolute truth. An old fable states that Truth and Falsehood went swimming and Falsehood stole the clothes that Truth had left upon the river bank. Truth declined to wear Falsehood's clothes and went naked. In Latin, as in the works of Horace, the phrase was *nuda veritas*.

... A PERSON IS *NAMBY-PAMBY*?
i.e. insipid, wishy-washy, soft. Ambrose Philips (1675–1749) was a writer and politician whom the dramatist Henry Carey ridiculed with this nickname (obviously derived from *Am*brose). The occasion was when Philips addressed some insipid verses to Lord Carteret's children. Carey, Pope and Swift thought his work received more attention than it deserved. Philips edited a Whig magazine, was an MP and a judge in Ireland. The nickname was taken into the language to describe an insipid, pampered and childishly sentimental person.

... 'MY *NAME IS MUD(D)*?
i.e. I am held in the lowest esteem.

It so happens that when John Wilkes Booth, the actor who assassinated President Lincoln in 1865, was escaping from the theatre in which he had committed the deed, he fell and broke his leg. A country doctor called Dr Samuel Mudd tended Booth's wound without realizing the circumstances under which it had been received. When he *did* realize, he informed the authorities, was charged with being a co-conspirator, and sentenced to life imprisonment.

Mudd was pardoned by Andrew Johnson, Lincoln's successor, after he helped stop an outbreak of fever at the prison in which he was incarcerated. A hundred years later, in the 1970s, Mudd's descendants were still trying to clear his name.

The question is, though, how we came by the expression 'My/his name is mud'? Is it not sufficient to believe that by saying someone's name is mud is, quite simply, to liken it to the dark, murky substance?

As the Morrises point out, 'mud', in the sense of scandalous and defamatory charges, goes back to a time well before the American Civil War. There had been an expression 'the mud press', to describe mud-slinging newspapers in the US, before 1846. 'So it seems most likely that the expression was well established before Dr Mudd met his unhappy fate.'

Partridge found an 1823 citation for: 'And his name is mud', which seems to be conclusive.

... NO *NAMES, NO PACK DRILL*?
See *no*.

... SEE *NAPLES AND DIE*?
See *see*.

... *NEITHER FISH, FLESH, FOWL, NOR GOOD RED HERRING*?
i.e. suitable to no class of people, neither one thing nor another. There are various ways in which this expression has been expressed, e.g. either 'neither fish, flesh, nor fowl' or 'neither fish, flesh, nor good red herring'. But the basic meaning (from the Middle Ages) is that whatever it is is unsuitable food for a monk (fish), for people generally (flesh), or for the poor (red herring).

In Shakespeare's *King Henry IV, Part I* (III.iii.128), Falstaff says of an otter: 'Why? she's neither fish nor flesh; a man knows not where to have her.' The *Oxford Dictionary of English Proverbs* finds its earliest citation – 'We know not ... whether they be fish or flesh, for they do nought for us' – in 1535.

... THE *NELSON TOUCH*?

i.e. any action which bears the mark of Lord Nelson or which he might have been proud to be associated with. It was coined by Nelson himself before the battle of Trafalgar (1805). In a letter, he wrote: 'I am anxious to join the fleet, for it would add to my grief if any other man was to give them the Nelson touch, which *we* say is warranted never to fail.' Of telling his plan of attack to his captains, he said: 'When I came to explain to them the "Nelson touch", it was like an electric shock. Some shed tears, all approved ...'

The *Oxford Companion to Ships and the Sea* provides this gloss:

Elsewhere he described the 'Nelson touch' as the fact that his order of sailing was his order of battle, i.e. that no time need be wasted in bringing the enemy fleet to battle. The phrase is indeterminate, it could also have been his favourite battle tactic of concentrating his whole force on part of the enemy's line of battle, to annihilate it before the rest of the line could tack or 'wear' to come to its assistance, or equally, it could have meant the magic of his name among officers and seamen of his fleet, which was always enough to inspire them to great deeds of heroism and endurance.

This last seems to be how the phrase would now be understood.

... *NETTY* FOR LAVATORY?

This term – to be heard in certain parts of northern Britain and recorded in the *English Dialect Dictionary* (1898) – is short for *gabinetti*, the Italian word for closets, small rooms, lavatories. Presumably, it must have been picked up from Italian immigrants at some stage.

Compare the equally cosy Australian term 'dunny', for an outside lavatory. This, however, comes from the same root as 'dung'.

... ON THE *NEVER-NEVER*?

See *on*.

... BRAND-*NEW*?

See *brand-new*.

... 'IN THE *NEWS*'?

One of my earliest memories is of reading in a little book – possibly dating from the 1920s or 1930s – that the word 'news' was an acronym made from all the points of the compass, north, east, west, south, where good or bad tidings may come from.

It seemed such a neat explanation that I later was disappointed to learn that 'news' was no more than the plural of 'new'. Meaning 'tidings', the word was current by the sixteenth century and came to us from French where the equivalent expression is *les nouvelles*.

Nowadays, we treat the word as singular – 'Here is the news' say broadcasters, rather than 'Here are the news'. In Shakespeare's *King Henry VI, Part II* (III.ii.378), however, Queen Margaret exclaims: 'Ay me! What is this world! What news are these!' And, last century, Queen Victoria stuck to the plural use, as in this letter from 1865 reacting to the assassination of President Lincoln: 'These American news are most dreadful and awful! One never heard of such a thing! I only hope it will not be catching elsewhere.'

... PISSED AS A *NEWT*?
See *pissed*.

... A *NINE DAY('S) WONDER*?
i.e. short-lived in appeal and soon forgotten. Brewer cites an old proverb: 'A wonder lasts nine days, and then the puppy's eyes are open' – alluding to dogs which (like cats) are born blind. After nine days, in other words, their eyes are open to see clearly.

Another etymologist finds a link with the old religious practice of selling indulgences, one of which – guaranteeing the purchaser nine day's worth of prayers – was called a *novem*. Like this explanation, the indulgence in question was held to be a bit suspect.

Chaucer expressed the old proverb thus: 'For wonder last but nine night nevere in toune.' Surely we do not need to look further for an expression of which the truth is self-evident: wonder dies in time.

... DRESSED UP TO THE *NINES*?
See *dressed*.

... TALKING *NINETEEN TO THE DOZEN*?
i.e. very quickly. A very literal derivation comes from Cornish tin mines of the eighteenth century. When pumps were introduced to

get rid of flooding, they were said to pump out 19,000 gallons of water for every 12 bushels of coal needed to operate the engines.

But, surely, one can be even more basic than that: to speak nineteen words where only twelve are needed gets across the idea very nicely. Nineteen is a surprising number to choose. Oddly it sounds right and better than any other number. 'Twenty to the dozen', for example, sounds rather flat.

... *NIPPLE COUNT*?
See *Page 3 girl*.

... 'LET'S GET DOWN TO THE *NITTY-GRITTY*'?
i.e. to the real basics of a problem or situation (like getting down to brass tacks). Sheilah Graham, the Hollywood columnist, in her book *Scratch an Actor* (1969) says of Steve McQueen: 'Without a formal education – Steve left school when he was fifteen – he has invented his own vocabulary to express what he means ... His "Let's get down to the nitty-gritty" has gone into the American language.'

All she meant, I feel, is that McQueen popularized the term, for it is generally held to be a Negro phrase and was talked about before the film star came on the scene. It seems to have had a particular vogue among Black Power campaigners (*c*.1963). Flexner 2 comments: 'It may have originally referred to the gritlike nits or small lice that are hard to get out of one's hair or scalp or to a black English term for the anus.'

... A GRAND PERSON IS A *NOB*?
The word is simply short for *nabob* (from the Hindustani *navah* or *nawab*) which described a governor or ruler of a district under the old Mogul regime in India. Subsequently, the word was applied to Britons (and others) who had been to India and acquired great wealth.

Consequently, in San Francisco, many of the merchants who had made their fortunes by trading with the Far East lived in splendour in an area called Nabob Hill. This is now known as Nob Hill.

References to 'his nibs' (someone grander than yourself) probably derive from the same source.

'...NO COMMENT'?

This useful phrase, when people in the news are being hounded by journalists, has not quite been condemned as a cliché. After all, why should people in such a position have to find something original to say? Nevertheless, it has come to be used as a consciously inadequate form of evasion, often in an obviously jokey way (cf., 'We are just good friends' when evading questions on the degree of intimacy between two people).

I suspect that it arose by way of reaction to the ferretings of Hollywood gossip columnists in the 1920s and 1930s, though perhaps it was simply a general reaction to the rise of the popular press in the first half of the century.

Winston Churchill appears not to have known of it until 1946, so perhaps it was not generally known before then, at least not outside the USA. After a meeting with President Truman, Churchill said: 'I think "No comment" is a splendid expression. I got it from Sumner Welles.'

Martha 'The Mouth' Mitchell, the blabber who helped get the Watergate investigations under way and who was the wife of President Nixon's disgraced Attorney-General, once declared: 'I don't believe in that "no comment" business. I always have a comment.'

'...NO NAMES, NO PACK-DRILL'?

i.e. we're not going to betray any confidences by mentioning any names. Somehow this alludes to a one-time British army punishment when soldiers were made to march up and down carrying a heavy pack. It is probably a short form of saying, 'As long as I don't give away any names, I won't get punished for it – that's why I'm not telling you.'

...NOOKIE WHEN WE MEAN 'A BIT OF THE OTHER'?

DOAS has this established in the US by the 1920s and states that 'nookie' (or 'nookey') means something else in addition to 'sexual activity'. It is not too hard to make a connection with 'nook', meaning a sheltered place, and the other meaning: the vagina.

In the light of this, it is odd how inoffensive the term 'nookie' is. In Britain from the 1970s onwards, a ventriloquist called Roger de Courcy has made great play with the catchphrase, 'I like Nookie'. It refers to his doll, in the form of a bear.

... PAY THROUGH THE *NOSE*?
See *pay*.

... AN INTERFERING PERSON IS A *NOSEY PARKER*?
A person with a prominent or unusual nose is often nicknamed 'Nosey' or 'Old Nosey' (as, for example, was the first Duke of Wellington). The nose has long been associated with an inquisitive nature. But why the connection with Parker?

Traditionally, a link has been suggested with Matthew Parker, Queen Elizabeth I's Archbishop of Canterbury.

'To pauk' is a dialect verb meaning 'to be inquisitive'.

At the turn of the century (1907) there was a comic character on postcards called 'Nosey Parker'.

Partridge gets excited about the 'park' aspect, wondering whether nosey people would enjoy spying on lovemaking couples in London's Hyde Park. (A 'parker' has been a name for a park-keeper since the fourteenth century.)

The modern expression may be a running together of any of these elements, but it looks as if there is no hard and fast origin.

... THAT SOMETHING IS *NOT* SOMETHING?
Television programme titles have a way of establishing format-phrases which then crop up, to an extent, in conversation and are irresistible to journalists and headline-writers. Examples from Britain include *That Was the Week That Was* (1962–3) – said to have been modelled on the 'That's Shell That Was' slogan of the early 1930s – and *Not So Much a Programme, More a Way of Life* (1964). In the US, *The Name of the Game* (1968–71) – originally *Fame is the Name of the Game* (1966) – is perhaps the most insidious of such phrases.

But what of the comedy show *Not the Nine O'Clock News* (1979–82)? This was broadcast on BBC2 opposite the *Nine O'Clock News* on BBC1. Accordingly, there were any number of derivatives, e.g. *Not Private Eye* (1986), a spoof of the satirical fort-nightly magazine brought out by some of its supposed victims, and *Not Yet the Times* (when the actual newspaper *The Times* was not being published in 1978–9.)

In fact, the model for all these titles was not *Not the Nine O'Clock News* but *Not the New York Times*, a spoof on the newspaper, published in 1978.

... TO THE *NTH DEGREE*?
i.e. to any extent. This derives from the mathematical use of 'n' to denote an indefinite number.

... FEELING ONE'S/SOWING ONE'S WILD *OATS*?
See *sows*.

... *OGGI-OGGI-OGGI/OI, OI, OI*?
I first encountered this as a chant at Rugby Union matches in the
late 1970s. It was also featured in the routines of the Welsh
comedian (and rugby enthusiast) Max Boyce about the same time.

Its use may be much broader than this, especially among
children. In 1986 I heard of a Thames River police inspector who
believed that the shout (as used by children) was similar to that
used by watermen to warn their thieving mates of approaching
police.

A correspondent suggests that it comes from Cornwall where an
'oggy' or 'oggie' or 'tiddy-oggie' is the nickname for a Cornish
pasty. Partridge has the same nickname and adds that 'Oggy-land'
is a name for Cornwall itself. Another correspondent, also from
Cornwall, states that 'oggi-oggi-oggi' was long a rallying cry in
those parts before being taken up in Wales and elsewhere.

... *'OH! CALCUTTA!'*?
Kenneth Tynan's famous, sexually explicit (and rather boring)
stage revue, first presented on Broadway in 1969, took its title
from a curious piece of word-play. It is the equivalent of the
French *oh, quel cul t'as*, meaning, broadly speaking, 'Oh, what a
lovely bum you have'. French *cul* is derived from Latin *culus*,
meaning buttocks, but, according to context, may be applied to
the female vagina or male anus. This, a professor of French
hazards a guess, may have originated in the France of the Belle
Epoque (*SOTC*).

149

... *O.K.?*

i.e. yes. The origin of this expression has occasioned more speculation (and acrimonious debate) than any other in the language.
Some of the suggestions put forward:

President Andrew Jackson, when a court clerk in Tennessee,
would mark 'O.K.' on legal documents as an abbreviation for the
illiterate 'Orl Kerrect'. (I have not seen any evidence adduced for
this proposal.)

It was first used by US President Martin van Buren as an election
slogan in 1840. The initials stood for 'Old Kinderhook', his nickname, which derived from his birthplace in New York State.

The previous year, 1839, had witnessed the first recorded use in
the US of the jocular 'O.K.' for 'oll korrect'.

Inspectors who weighed and graded bales of cotton as they were
delivered to Mississippi river ports for shipment would write *aux
quais* on any found faulty. This meant they had to be sent back to
the jetty.

It comes from Aux Cayes, a port in Haiti famous for its rum.

It is an Anglicization of the word for 'good' in Ewe or Wolof, the
West African language spoken by many of the slaves taken to the
southern US.

The letters O.K. derive from the Greek words *ola kala* meaning 'all
is fine, everything is good'.

In the First World War, each night soldiers would report the
number of deaths in their group. 'O.K.' stood for 'O killed'.

A railroad freight agent Obadiah Kelly used his initials on bills of
lading.

An Indian chief, Old Keokuk, used his initials on treaties.

It stood for 'outer keel' when shipbuilders chalked it on timbers.

Teachers used it instead of *omnes korrectes* on perfect exam
papers.

From boxes of Orrins-Kendall crackers, popular with Union
troops in the American Civil War.

From an English word 'hoacky', meaning the last load of a harvest.

From a 'Finnish word *oikea* meaning 'correct'.

From a Choctaw word *okeh* ('it is') or *hoke*.

One need look no further than the second and third explanations above (with help from Flexner). I feel sure the jocular initials started it, in Boston. Van Buren set the seal on the use of the formula.

. . . ICE CREAM IS *OKEY-POKEY*?
This is the same as 'hokey-pokey' which was the name given to a form of imitation ice-cream made from shaved ice mixed with syrup. It may have arisen from a feeling that the imitation was a form of hocus-pocus or trickery. Or else it may have been a corruption of *ecce, ecce* ('look, look'), the cry with which Italian street vendors would call attention to their wares. Either way, the name was established by the turn of the century.

A children's rhyme is remembered (in England) that goes: 'Okey-pokey penny a lump,/ The more you eat the more you jump.' Iona and Peter Opie in *The Lore and Language of School-children* (1959) wonder whether this could derive from Italian *O che poco*! ('O how little!') – though why vendors would shout that, they do not explain.

. . . *OLD BILL* FOR THE POLICE?
(Properly, the Metropolitan Police, in London, but generally applied to all police.) The best suggestion for this name is that as so many policemen wore walrus moustaches after the First World War, they reminded people of Bruce Bairnsfather's cartoon character 'Old Bill'. He was the one who said, 'Well, if you knows of a better 'ole, go to it'.

Partridge, who provides this explanation, also wonders whether there might be a connection through the song *Won't You Come Home, Bill Bailey*? and the Old Bailey.

'The Bill', meaning 'the police' is an alternative expression.

. . . THE *OLD CONTEMPTIBLES*?
i.e. First World War veterans, in particular rank and file survivors of the British Expeditionary Force. The BEF crossed the English

Channel in 1914 to join the French and Belgians against the German advance. It was alleged that Kaiser Wilhelm II had described the force as 'a contemptibly little army' (referring to its size rather than its quality). The British press was then said to have mistranslated this so that it made him appear to have called the BEF a 'contemptible little army'.

After the war, BEF veterans who had happily adopted the name kept contact and paraded annually until 1974 when too few remained.

The truth is that the whole episode was a propaganda ploy master-minded by the British. A fake order from the German Emperor, using the phrase, had been issued by the War Office. No evidence of any similar order was ever found in German archives. The ex-Kaiser himself later denied having said any such thing (*WWNN*).

... OMELETTE ARNOLD BENNETT?

Not created *by* but *for* the novelist (1867–1931). It is an omelette of haddock, grated cheese and cream, put under the grill. Bennett was a great frequenter of the Savoy Hotel in London where the recipe was concocted. The hotel also features in a number of his novels.

... A PERSON IS *ONE OVER THE EIGHT*?

i.e. drunk. For some reason, eight beers was considered to be a reasonable and safe amount for an average man to drink. One more and you were incapable. From services' slang.

... A LONELY PERSON IS *ON HIS TOD*?

This is rhyming slang. On one's tod = Tod Sloan = own. But who was Tod Sloan? A famous American jockey (1874–1933).

... WE PAY *ON THE NEVER-NEVER*?

i.e. on a hire purchase scheme (making payments by instalments over a lengthy period of time). The *OED Supp.* finds its first example of this phrase in 1925. It also lists 'never-never' as an adjective meaning 'unrealistic, unrealizable, imaginary'.

What one would like to know is whether there is a link between these and the Never-Never Land, the ideal and imaginary country as featured by J.M. Barrie in his play *Peter Pan* (1904). The phrase

was not original to him, but perhaps it was made sufficiently so by
Barrie for it to have led to these other uses?

At very much the same time there appeared Mrs Aeneas Gunn's
Australian classic *We of the Never-Never* (1908). In this context,
the never-never country or lands were those unexplored in the
north of Australia.

'... OPEN SESAME!'?

Sometimes used as a catchphrase, meaning 'open up (the door)!' or
as a mock password, this comes from the tale of 'The Forty
Thieves' in the ancient oriental *Tales of the Arabian Nights*.

Sesame seed is also famous for its other opening qualities – as a
laxative.

... AN OSCAR?

See *Emmy*.

... WE ARE *OVER THE MOON*?

In about 1978, in Britain, two alternative cliché expressions
became notorious if you wished to show pleasure or dismay at the
outcome of anything, but especially a football match. You were
either 'over the moon' or 'sick as a parrot'.

It probably all began because of remorseless post-game analysis
by TV football commentators and the consequent need for players
and managers to provide pithy comments. Liverpool footballer
Phil Thompson said he felt 'sick as a parrot' after his team's defeat
in the 1978 Cup Final.

Private Eye fuelled the cliché by constant mockery, to such an
extent that by 1980 an 'instant' BBC radio play about the European Cup Final (written on the spot and developed according to
the outcome) was given the alternative titles *Over the Moon/Sick
as a Parrot*. The writer was Neville Smith.

Some failed to note the cliché. *The Times* (21 January 1982)
reported the reaction of M. Albert Roux, the London restaurateur,
on gaining three stars in the *Michelin Guide*: '"I am over the
moon", M. Roux said yesterday ... he quickly denied, however,
that his brother [another celebrated restaurateur] would be "sick
as a parrot".'

'Over the moon' is probably the older of the two phrases.
Indeed, in the diaries of May, Lady Cavendish (published 1927)

there is an entry for 7 February 1857 saying how she broke the news of her youngest brother's birth to the rest of her siblings: 'I had told the little ones who were first utterly incredulous and then over the moon.' The family of Catherine Gladstone (née Gwynne), wife of the prime minister, is said to have had its own idomatic language and originated the phrase. The nursery rhyme 'Hey diddle diddle/ The cat and the fiddle,/ The cow jumped over the moon' dates back to at least 1765, however.

The specific application to football was already in evidence in 1962, when Alf Ramsey (a manager) was quoted as saying, on one occasion, 'I feel like jumping over the moon'.

What may be an early version of 'sick as a parrot' appears in Robert Southey's Cumbrian dialect poem *The Terrible Knitters e' Dent* (1834). There, 'Sick as a peeate' (pronounced pee-at') means a feeling akin to a heavy lump of peat in the stomach (the equivalent of having a heart feeling as heavy as lead, perhaps).

A more likely origin is in psittacosis or parrot disease/fever. In about 1973 there were a number of cases of people dying of this in West Africa. It is basically a viral disease of parrots (and other birds) but can be transmitted to man. Even here, there may be an older source. In the eighteenth century there was an expression, 'melancholy as a parrot'. And Morris claims that the original expression was, 'as sick as a parrot with a rubber beak' – like 'no more chance than a cat in hell without claws' referring to an animal incapacitated without a sharp weapon.

... A PERSON IS *OVER THE TOP*?

i.e. exaggerated in manner or performance, 'too much'. The expression 'over the top' originated in the trenches of the First World War. It was used to describe the method of charging over the parapet and out of the trenches on the attack.

In a curious transition, the phrase was later adopted by show business people when describing a performance that goes beyond the bounds of restraint. In 1982, a near-the-bone British television series reflected this by calling itself *O.T.T.* Then you heard people saying that someone was 'a bit O.T.T.' instead of the full expression.

... DON'T EAT *OYSTERS*?

See *don't*

P

... *PAGE 3 GIRL*?

This euphemistic term for a topless model arose when Larry Lamb, editor of the *Sun* newspaper, decided to put scantily clad females as a regular feature on page three. This was within a year of the paper's re-launch on 17 November 1969, following its acquisition by Rupert Murdoch, the Australian-born newspaper emperor.

I think it would be true to say that the term has tended to be applied to almost any nude photographic model whether or not she has actually appeared in the *Sun*. The phrase 'nipple count' came into use when the *Sun* and other British newspapers began a 'war' in which the number of nipples shown per issue was of importance (compare 'body count' in the Vietnam war).

An American drive-in movie critic, Joe Bob, who wrote for the *Dallas Times Herald*, literally counted the nipples he saw and rated the films accordingly. His column was dropped in April 1985.

... SOMEONE OR SOMETHING IS A *PAPER TIGER*?

i.e. appears outwardly strong but is, in fact, weak. The use of the expression is entirely due to the Chinese leader, Chairman Mao Tse-tung (1893–1976). Speaking to an American interviewer in 1946, he said: 'All reactionaries are paper tigers. In appearance, the reactionaries are terrifying, but in reality they are not so powerful. From a long-term point of view, it is not the reactionaries but the people who are really powerful.'

Taken from Mao's *Selected Works*, this is how the saying appears in his famous *Quotations* – the little red book brandished

155

during the Cultural Revolution (1966–9). However, the actual saying probably pre-dates Mao himself.

... BEYOND THE *PALE*?
See *beyond*.

... THE WEATHER IS *PARKY*?
i.e. nippingly cold, as in 'It's a bit parky, isn't it?'. The *Concise Oxford English Dictionary* has 'nineteenth century, origin unknown'. *SOED* wonders whether it has something to do with 'park', i.e. the weather you might expect in a park. Partridge wonders about Parkin Cake which you would eat in such weather.

No one knows for sure.

... SICK AS A *PARROT*?
See *over the moon*.

... *PASS THE BUCK*?
i.e. shift responsibility onto someone else. In some card games, a marker called a 'buck' is put in front of the dealer to remind players who *is* the dealer. When the turn is someone else's, the card is put in front of them – thus, the 'buck' is 'passed'.

The original 'buck' may have been a buckthorn knife. Or, in the Old West, a silver dollar – hence the modern use of the word 'buck' to denote a dollar.

The expression, 'The buck stops here' – famously invented by President Harry S Truman and inscribed on a plaque which he kept on his desk – follows on from all this. Truman was a keen poker-player.

...WE EAT A *PAVLOVA*?
The most important element in this dessert or cake, especially popular in Australia and New Zealand, is meringue. But there must also be whipped cream and fruit (quite often strawberry). Created as a sort of compliment to the Russian-born ballerina, Anna Pavlova (1885–1931), during or after one of her visits to the Antipodes, the concoction may be said to bear a resemblance to the spreading out skirts on a ballerina's tutu. The word was

established in New Zealand by 1927 (*OED Supp.*) which conflicts with the information given by Macquarie: 'Invented in 1935 by Herbert Sachse, 1898–1974, Australian chef, and named by Harry Nairn of the Esplanade Hotel, Perth.'

... *PAYOLA* IS A CRIME?

More recently (in the 1950s) used in the sense of a bribe to persuade radio disc jockeys to play particular records, the idea goes back to the 1930s at least, to describe various forms of inducement in the record and music publishing business. The word is formed, clearly, from 'pay' as in 'pay-off' plus '-ola', a suffix familiar in the music business from such terms as 'pianola' and 'Victrola'.

Jonathon Green in *Newspeak* lists the variants 'plugola' (purchased plugging of specific records on radio) and 'royola' (extra royalties available for corrupt disc jockeys who plug certain records).

'Payola' has also progressed to refer to bribing outside the record and music businesses.

The word 'plug' in this context seems to derive from an association with trickery that began when counterfeit coins were 'plugged' or filled up with base metal.

... WE *PAY THROUGH THE NOSE*?

i.e. pay heavily. A possible explanation for this lies in the 'nose tax' levied upon the Irish by the Danes in the ninth century. Those who did not pay had their noses slit.

The Morrises, however, come up with something completely different. 'In British slang the word *rhino* means "money". *Rhinos* is the Greek word for "nose", as we see in rhinoceros.' The Morrises go on to speculate about being 'bled' of money having to do with nosebleeds.

... WE EAT A *PEACH MELBA*?

Dame Nellie Melba (1861–1931), the Australian opera singer, was staying at the Savoy Hotel in London in 1892 when the *chef de cuisine*, the famous Auguste Escoffier, created the pudding to which he attached her name. She had sent him two tickets for a Covent Garden performance of *Lohengrin* in which she was appearing. Next day, he insisted on her trying a newly invented dessert which he served between the wings of a swan (alluding to *Lohengrin*) made of ice. The dish of peaches in vanilla-flavoured syrup on top of ice-cream and coated with raspberry sauce became publicly famous five years later when he took over the kitchen at the Carlton.

In 1897, Escoffier also invented Melba Toast (made with extremely thin bread), though the name was applied by M.L. Ritz.

Oddly, in the light of various other foods and objects being named after her, 'Melba' was not her real name. She was born Helen Mitchell. In a bid to acquire the more exotic name thought necessary for an opera singer, she adopted and adapted a portion of Melbourne, her home town.

... TAKE DOWN A *PEG*?
See *taken*.

... PEOPLE SPEAK *PIDGIN ENGLISH*?
i.e. a jargon made up of mainly English words but arranged according to Chinese methods (and pronounced in a Chinese way). This arose to facilitate communication between Chinese and Europeans at seaports and has nothing to do with 'pigeon', the bird. It is no more than a Chinese corruption of the English word 'business'. So, in essence, it is 'business English', a *lingua franca*, which allows people of two different languages to converse by recourse to a third.

Nor is pidgin (or 'pidjin') restricted any more to China (or even, for that matter, to English plus another language – there could be a form of it involving any two languages).

Cameroonian pidgin can be understood as far away as Gambia, Nigeria, Benin, Ghana and Sierra Leone. Nowadays, it is not thought right that pidgin should be allowed to perish as a relic of colonialism. When Prince Charles opened a new parliament house in Papua New Guinea in August 1984, he said: *'Em I bigpela haus na yupela mas givim ologeta tingting na laik bilong yupela I go long en.'* ('This is a big house and you must give all your support to it.') The Prince's name in pidgin is *'Namba wan pikinini bilong Misis Kwin'* ('first child of the Queen').

The Pope has recited the Lord's prayer in pidgin, beginning

thus: *'Papu bilong mipela yu stap long heuven, ol I santium nem bilong yu ...'*

The expression, 'That's your pigeon', meaning 'that's your look-out/ responsibility' is derived from a reverse process. It means, 'that's your business', but uses the Chinese pronunciation of 'business', i.e. 'pidgin'.

... WE'VE BOUGHT A *PIG IN A POKE*?
See *let the cat out of the bag*.

... SHOCKING *PINK*?
See *shocking*.

... *PISSED AS A NEWT*?
i.e. very drunk. Partridge gives various metaphors for drunkenness from the animal kingdom – 'pissed as a coot/ rat/ parrot', among them. None seems particularly apposite. So why newt? Could it be that the newt, being an amphibious reptile, can submerge itself in liquid as a drunk might do? Or is it because its tight-fitting skin has anything to do with being 'tight'.

We shall never know, though the alternative (and, according to Partridge, original) espression 'tight as a newt' has a pleasing sound to it. Such folk expressions have been coined with less reason.

... A PERSON IS *PLAYING FAST AND LOOSE*?
i.e. messing one about, resorting to deceit. 'Pricking the Belt' was an old fairground trick, akin to 'Find the Lady' (the so-called Three Card Trick). The victim was invited to pin a folded belt to the table. The operator would then show that the belt was not (held) 'fast' but 'loose'. So the victim would lose the bet (Radford).

... WE DRINK *PLONK*?
i.e. very cheap wine. There is little doubt that this expression started in Australia (it is so listed in *Digger Dialects*, 1919). But why? There have been various etymologies suggested, including that 'plonk' is like the sound of a cork being pulled from a bottle. The *OED Supp.* plumps for a derivation from *'vin blanc'*, although it admits that plonk is usually applied to *red* wine.

... WE EAT A *PLOUGHMAN'S LUNCH*?

It sounds very redolent of olden days – a meal of bread, cheese and pickle, just the sort of thing you might imagine a ploughman taking to work, all wrapped up in a spotted handkerchief, to consume with a tankard of beer. Although the *OED Supp.* finds an example of 'ploughman's luncheon' being written in 1837, the use of the term in British pubs is, in fact, a marketing ploy dating from the early 1970s. Radford credits the coinage to Richard Trehane, chairman of the English Country Cheese Council.

A British film with the title *The Ploughman's Lunch* (1983) revealed this curious information to a wider audience. The film was, in part, about how history gets rewritten.

... *PLUG*?
See *payola*.

... SOMEONE IS A *POISONED DWARF*?

Terry Wogan, when a BBC Radio 2 disc-jockey, was credited with having ensured the success in Britain of the imported American TV series *Dallas* (*c.*1979). He poked fun at it. In particular, he drew attention to the diminutive proportions of the actress Charlene Titton who played the character 'Lucy Ewing'.

She was in unenviable company. Joseph Goebbels (1897–1945), Hitler's propaganda chief, was popularly known by this epithet – in Germany itself – from the late 1930s onwards.

... PIG IN A *POKE*?
See *let the cat*.

... AN ENGLISHMAN IS A *POM*?

(or pommy or pommie) in Australian usage (especially in the expressions 'pommy bastard' and 'whingeing poms'). There are various suggestions:

It is due to a melding of 'pomegranate' and 'immigrant'. Was it that the white complexion of the new arrivals caught the sun and resembled the skin of a pomegranate (golden with red patches)? Or was it, as Partridge quotes, simply because 'colonial boys and girls, ready to find a nickname, were fond of rhyming "immigrant", "Jimmygrant", "pommygrant".'

It has something to do with the French *pomme* ('apple') (compare
the origin of 'limey') or Breton *pomme* ('downright, out and
out').

It is from an acronym stamped on shirts of convict settlers –
POHMS (Prisoners of Her Majesty).

Convict settlers called themselves POMES (Prisoners of Mother
England).

The *Australian National Dictionary* accepts the 'pomegranate'
explanation, surfacing in 1912, while the Australian Macquarie
settles for 'Orig. uncert.'

... A WOMANISER IS A *POODLEFAKER*?
This term crept back into limited use in certain British newspaper
gossip columns in the early 1980s. Partridge defines it as 'a man,
especially a Service officer, who, for the time being rather than
habitually, cultivates the society of women'.

In origin it is an Anglo-Indian term. It describes a type of man
to be found in the hill stations and alludes to lap-dogs. As such, it
refers to a fairly mild sort of liaison. One wonders, though,
whether its revival might have something to do with a link
between '-faker' and 'fucker'?

... *POOR LITTLE RICH GIRL*?
i.e. a woman whose wealth has not brought her happiness.
Although Noel Coward's song with the title *Poor Little Rich Girl*,
written in 1925, probably encouraged many people to use the
term, it had been used earlier as the title of a film starring Mary
Pickford (1917).

... A PRISONER DOES *PORRIDGE*?
The *OED Supp.* ducks giving the origin of this slang expression, as
well it might. Current since at least the 1950s, and made known to
a wider audience by its use as *Porridge*, the title of a BBC TV
comedy series about prison life (1974–7), the term is said by some
to derive from a very odd piece of rhyming slang. At least, that is
how it appears in *A Load of Cockney Cobblers, London's Rhyming
Slang Interpreted*, Bob Aylwin, 1973. According to him, it is
borage and thyme (the plants) = time, i.e. the time served, as in
'doing time'. Peculiar, but there it is ... There is no mention of this

in Julian Franklyn's more substantial *Dictionary of Rhyming Slang* (1961).

The porridge-stirring connection with the (more American) expressions 'stir', meaning prison, 'in stir', meaning in prison, 'stir-crazy', meaning insane as a result of long imprisonment, may be no more than a coincidence. *These* terms are said to derive from the Anglo-Saxon word *styr*, meaning punishment, reinforced by the Romany *steripen*, meaning prison (*DOAS*). Partridge seems to prefer this etymology.

On the other hand, if porridge was once the prisoner's basic food – and it was known as 'stirabout' – perhaps there could be more than coincidence at work here.

... A PERSON IS *POSH*?

First, the popular myth – as demonstrated by Shook: 'When a ship travelled from England to India, the port side of the ship was shady, and therefore the most desirable and expensive. On the homeward journey the starboard side was shady. Thus the most desirable staterooms were *P*ort *O*ut, *S*tarboard *H*ome.'

It is an ingenious theory but there is quite a lot to be said against it. The P&O Line, which was the principal carrier to and from British India in the nineteenth century, has no evidence of a single POSH booking. Nor was there any differentiation in cabin price according to which side of the ship it was on. Nor would it have made much difference to the heat of the cabin which side you were on. It would be interesting to know who first came up with this theory.

On the other hand, it is not at all clear how else this familiar word arose. The *OED* has no citations for it (in this sense) earlier than the twentieth century. However, posh, meaning a 'dandy' or 'money', was nineteenth-century (especially Romany) slang. It is not too hard to see either of these meanings, or both combined, contributing to what we now mean by posh.

In 1981, the *Daily Mail* reported a joke about the latest smart way to travel from London to New York and back again – COSH (standing for *C*oncorde *O*ut, *S*kytrain *H*ome). It meant that export- and cash-conscious executives could do a whole day's work on arrival, yet did not break the bank getting there. (Skytrain, a cheapo airline, folded shortly afterwards.)

... *POSSE*?
See *lynch*.

'... *POSSESSION IS NINE POINTS OF THE LAW*'?
i.e. out of a possible ten points, meaning: in a dispute over ownership of property, the present owner is in the strongest position. An alternative: 'Possession is nine-tenths of the law'. An earlier version: 'Possession is eleven points of the law' (i.e. out of a possible twelve).

The original nine points of the law were said to be: 1) a lot of money; 2) a lot of patience; 3) a good cause; 4) a good lawyer; 5) a good counsel; 6) good witnesses; 7) a good jury; 8) a good judge; 9) good luck.

This proverbial expression dates at least from the seventeenth century.

... GONE TO *POT*?
See *gone to*.

... *PRESTIGIOUS*?
If you look up this word in the *SOED* you find the warning 'now rare' and the definition: 'practising juggling or legerdemain; cheating; deceptive; illusory'.

So, what has happened, as 'prestigious' is now much used to denote something carrying prestige, having status? This apparent reversal of meaning can just about be explained by an evident need for an adjective linked to prestige ('prestigeful' being rejected for good reason). But it is also true that the 'cheating, deceptive, illusory' original meaning easily slips into the idea of 'dazzling'. From that it is not too big a jump to bring us to the modern meaning.

... A DETECTIVE IS A *PRIVATE EYE*?
Although, it is true, a private detective's job often consists of keeping an eye on people, there may be more to it than that. The term could derive from 'private *in*vestigator' or from the wide-open 'eye' symbol of the Pinkerton detective agency, founded in Chicago (1850). It went with the slogan 'We never sleep'. The agency came to be referred to as the 'Eye' by criminals and others.

The full term 'private eye' seems to have emerged in the 1930s and 1940s, particularly through the fiction of Raymond Chandler and others.

... A JUDGE *PRONOUNCED THE DEATH SENTENCE*?

Well, it really was a sentence and quite a long one. Here, for example, is what Lord Chief Baron said when William Corder was found guilty of the murder, on 18 May 1827, of Maria Marten at a place known as the Red Barn, Polstead, Suffolk:

... That sentence is, that you be taken back to the prison from which you came, and that you be taken thence, on Monday next, to the place of execution, and there be hanged by the neck till you are dead, and that your body shall afterwards be dissected and anatomized, and the Lord God Almighty have mercy on your soul!

After getting through this, according to *The Times* (9 August 1828), 'the Lord Chief Baron, who was evidently much affected, then retired from the Court'.

By the time Dr Harvey Crippen was being sentenced to death for the murder of his wife by poisoning, the Lord Chief Justice (Lord Alverstone), having assumed the black cap, was solemnly saying this:

The sentence of the Law is that you be taken from this place to a lawful prison, and thence to a place of execution, that you be there hanged by the neck until you are dead, and that your body be buried within the precincts of the prison in which you shall be confined before your execution. And may the Lord have mercy on your soul!

The origins of the death sentence are lost in the mists of time. The last execution in Britain was in 1964. The death penalty was suspended in 1965 and abolished in 1970. However, on the Isle of Man in 1982, Stephen Moore, a nineteen-year-old was convicted of murder and sentenced by Deemster Jack Corrin, the senior island judge:

You will be taken from this place to the Isle of Man prison and thence to a place of lawful execution where you will be hanged by the neck until you are dead.

However, he was not. His sentence was commuted to life imprisonment.

... MIND YOUR *PS AND QS*?
See *mind*.

... A PERSON IS A *PSEUD*?

There have been suggestions that this word was an original coinage by the editors of *Private Eye*, the British satirical magazine. According to *The Private Eye Story* by Patrick Marnham (1982) it was an old Salopian word (i.e. one from Shrewsbury School where a number of the magazine's founders were educated) and was short for 'pseudo-intellectual'.

Certainly, the term was popularized by its use in the title of the magazine's feature 'Pseud's Corner' (from 1968 onwards). Suggested by the first editor, Christopher Booker, this column reprints statements, culled from the press and books, thought to be of a pseudo-intellectual nature.

However, the *OED Supp.* lists a number of citations from 1962 which are apparently unrelated to *Private Eye*. There seems to have been a good deal of playing with the word 'pseudo' at about this time (it comes from the Greek for 'false'). In 1962, Daniel J. Boorstin, the American author, in his book *The Image*, coined the term 'pseudo-event' to describe 'the new kind of synthetic novelty', an event whose sole *raison d'être* was to attract news coverage by the media.

... WE'RE GOING TO *PULL THE WOOL OVER A PERSON'S EYES*?

i.e. hoodwink him. When wigs were commonly worn, they were sometimes referred to as wool (because of the resemblance, particularly the curls). Thus to pull the wool over someone's eyes was to pull their wig over their eyes and render them incapable of seeing.

... WE EAT *PUMPERNICKEL*?

– the coarse German rye bread. *SOED* settles for 'orig. unknown' and offers a first use in 1756. Other, braver or more foolhardy souls suggest it was so named by Napoleon Buonaparte. He did not like the bread, saying it was only fit for his horse, Nicole – *pain pour Nicole*.

The Morrises weigh in with the information that the word is made up of *pumper* – the sound made by a person falling – and *nickel*, a dwarf or goblin. 'Thus the original *Pumpernickel* was an object of derision ... why the name was later applied to loaves of dark rye bread is a matter of speculation.'

This is not quite how the *COD* sees things. Although linking it to the earlier German meaning of 'lout' or 'stinker', it says that *pumpe(r)n* meant 'break wind' and *Nickel* was Nicholas.

... A JOKE ENDS WITH A *PUNCHLINE*?

– the term is also applied to the last line or key line of a sketch, play, or song. Bob Monkhouse, the British comedian and student of humour, was quoted in *Radio Times* (August 1983) as believing 'it was Fred Allen who invented the word "punchline". He called it the gag that got you right in the belly.' Lesser varieties, he said, included the low joint-laugh, which provides a squeal rather than a laugh.

'We once used "pay-off" as a British synonym, but this became associated with bribery and corruption, and so was discreetly dropped from the comic vocabulary.'

This could well be the case and I am sure the word is of American origin but I am slightly suspicious about the attribution to Allen (1894–1956). The *OED Supp.* provides a citation from *Variety* in 1921 (by which time Allen can hardly have got going as a comedian – and certainly not in American radio where he made his name). Perhaps it was one of *Variety*'s own famous coinages – though I suspect it came from within vaudeville rather than from the reporters of it.

... A NOISY PERSON SHOULD *PUT A SOCK IN IT*?

– in his mouth, to stop talking. Ewart confidently asserts that this dates from the days of wind-up, 'acoustic' gramophones from which the sound would emerge from a horn. With no electronic controls to raise or lower the volume, the only way to regulate the sound was to put in or take out an article of clothing which deadened it.

The *OED Supp.* has a citation from 1919 (an explanation of the phrase from the *Athenaeum* journal – which suggests it was not widely known even then).

I am not totally confident of the gramophone derivation. Partridge compares the earlier expression 'put a bung in it' (as in a bath or leak). So I reserve judgement. Why shouldn't a sock inserted in the mouth do the trick? After all, a sock in the jaw would be the next best thing.

... WE *PUT A SPOKE IN SOMEONE'S WHEEL?*

– meaning, prevent him from doing something. This may strike you as odd if you know, for example, that bicycle wheels *already have* lots of spokes in them (i.e. thin slats connecting the hub to the rim of the wheel).

Or, the mental picture conjured up by the phrase might be that of a stick being stuck between the spokes already on a wheel in order to bring the vehicle to a halt.

In fact, we are referring here to the days when carts had solid wheels and no spokes in the modern sense. The spoke then was a pin which could be inserted into a hole on the wheel to act as a brake.

... WE *PUT THE SCREWS ON SOMEBODY?*

i.e. apply pressure to make someone do something. Clearly, 'screws' here is short for 'thumbscrews', the ancient and medieval method of torturing prisoners.

This could be why prison guards have been nicknamed 'screws', although another explanation is from screw meaning key. It is not too hard to see how this slang expression arose from the turning motion involved in locking or unlocking something. The gaolers were sometimes known as 'turnkeys' as this would appear to be their most significant function.

... WE'RE *PUTTING ON THE DOG?*

i.e. putting on airs, fine clothes, and so on. This appears to be an American expression dating from the 1870s – perhaps among college students (especially at Yale) who had to wear stiff, high collars (jokily known as dog-collars) on formal occasions. In the previous decade – according to the *OED Supp.* – the nickname 'dog-collar' for the clerical collar had been established in England. I would be prepared to believe that these two usages, though based on a common idea, developed in isolation.

Incidentally, the *OED Supp.* has it as simply 'to put on dog' (excluding the definite article).

167

... WE SET SAIL ON THE *QE2*?

The Cunard liner which made its maiden voyage in May 1969 is known universally as 'the QE2', which is rather odd when you come to think about it. It was the successor to the liner known as the *Queen Elizabeth* named after the wife of King George VI and launched by her in 1938.

It seems that the idea was *not* to call the ship the *Queen Elizabeth II* or the *Queen Elizabeth the Second* (i.e. after Her Majesty Queen Elizabeth II). There was a tradition that only capital ships in the Royal Navy were named after sovereigns. Cunard apparently thought that another *Queen Elizabeth* would do, leaving the queen referred to obscure. This was akin to the practice (later widespread in the cinema) of slapping on a numeral '2' (or more) for a sequel (as in *Jaws 2, Death Wish II,* etc.) The idea was to evoke a second *Queen Elizabeth* liner like the first.

While she was being built, the vessel was known as 'Q3' (for the third of the queens', the other having been the *Queen Mary*) or simply as 'No. 736'. Nevertheless, when the (reigning) Queen launched the ship in 1967 she distinctly named her the 'Queen Elizabeth the Second', as though after herself.

But so common is the short name, *QE2*, that you might expect it to be written on the bow and stern of the vessel. Not so. It simply says *Queen Elizabeth 2* which should make the intention of the owners clear, even if this is claimed to be what the Queen said rendered 'in modern style' and even if it is not exactly what you would call a proper name for a fine ship.

... AN ORGANIZATION IS A *QUANGO*?
This odd-sounding word is an acronym standing for 'QUasi-Autonomous-Non-Governmental-Organization', though some-times 'National' has been substituted for 'Non-Governmental'. It describes a type of statutory public body set up outside the Civil Service but appointed by and financed by central government.

The name seems to have originated in the US, where it was first used in the 1960s. It became popular in the UK from the 1970s.

The Australian Macquarie sources it from Britain, though this is probably wrong.

... *QUEEN FOR A DAY*?
This is a catchphrase – not very widely used now, I should think – for a woman who is given a special treat. It derives from an American radio programme of the *c.*1940s. According to my informant, 'Being a queen for a day didn't mean they gave you a country; you only got your wish, that's what. No one complained.'

I notice that when Radio Luxembourg adopted the format they changed the title to *Princess for a Day*. Was this because the wishes fulfilled were more modest, the participants younger, or was the word 'queen' already too tainted by its double-meaning by that time?

... A HOMOSEXUAL MAN IS (A) *QUEER*?
See *gay*.

... WE TAKE PART IN A *QUIZ*?
Another classic of etymological myth, this one. It is said that the word came into use in the 1780s when Mr Daly, a Dublin theatre manager, had a bet that he could introduce a new word into the language within twenty-four hours. Somehow he came up with the word 'quiz', had it chalked on walls all over Dublin, arousing the curiosity of the populace, and thus 'quiz' for 'to question' duly passed into the language. (The story was first related in 1836.)

It is true that the *SOED* dates the word at 1782 with the now rare meaning of 'an odd or eccentric person, in character or appearance'; that a 'practical joke, hoax' was being so termed by

1807; and that the element of 'questioning, interrogating' was established in the US by 1886. But the dictionary cautiously notes 'origin obsc.'.

As Burnam 2 points out, however, quiz is not a very big step from the Latin interrogative pronoun *quis* ('who?' or 'what?') and it also bears a remarkable resemblance in sound to the second syllable of the word 'inquisitive' (from the Latin *inquisitere*, meaning to inquire) which was current by the sixteenth century.

R

... *R IN THE MONTH*?
See *don't eat*.

... WE NAVIGATE BY *RADAR*?
So familiar is this word now that it is worth remembering it has a down-to-earth derivation. It is made up of the first part of the word '*ra*dio' and the initial letters of '*d*irection *a*nd *r*anging'. The word was established – along with the invention – during the first two years of the Second World War. The device was the brainchild of Sir Robert Watson-Watt who had developed it in 1933–5.

... CHEW THE *RAG*?
See *chew*.

... TAKE A *RAIN-CHECK*?
See *take*.

... IT'S *RAINING CATS AND DOGS*?
i.e. extremely hard. Morris likes to think that this expression comes from the days when towns and cities had such poor street drainage that a heavy rain storm would easily drown cats and dogs. After the storm people would see the number of dead cats and dogs and assume they had fallen out of the sky.

Brewer suggests that in northern mythology cats were supposed to have great influence on the weather and dogs were a signal of wind, 'thus cat may be taken as a symbol of the downpouring rain, and the dog of the strong gusts of wind accompanying a rain-storm'.

The other explanation, that the phrase derives from the Greek *catadupa*, meaning waterfall, is hardly more convincing, so perhaps Morris will have to do.

... *RAISING CAIN*?
i.e. making trouble, a fuss, a disturbance. The allusion in this phrase is to the biblical Cain ('the first murderer') who killed his brother Abel (Genesis 4:2–8). Thus, a person who does this, 'raises the spirit of' Cain by behaving in a similar (though not necessarily so violent) way. In fact, the name 'Cain' came to be used to evoke the Devil – rather than the specific murderer – hence the alternative expression, 'to raise the Devil'.

The phrase apparently originated in the US where it was recorded in 1840.

... A PERSON (USUALLY FEMALE) IS *RAUNCHY*?
There are two meanings to this word, both from the US. One is 'disreputable, dirty, grubby' (and may come from the word 'ranchy', as from 'ranch'). The other, more common, describes an aspect of sexuality which it is a little hard to pinpoint. It evokes elements of earthiness and suggestiveness, though it can be used to describe anything that excites sexual feelings. It was first used in this sense in the early 1960s.

... WE'LL *READ THE RIOT ACT*?
i.e. make strong representations about something, express forcibly that a situation must cease. This derives from an actual Riot Act that was passed by the British Parliament in 1714 (and repealed in 1973). It provided for the dispersal of crowds (defined as being of more than twelve people) by persons in authority. The method was, literally, to stand up and read out the terms of the Act so that the rioters knew what law they were breaking: 'Our Sovereign Lord the King chargeth and commandeth all persons assembled immediately to disperse themselves and peacefully to depart to their habitations or to their lawful business.'

One wonders how often they actually listened to – or even heard – the words?

... THE *REAL MCCOY*?
– meaning, 'the real thing, the genuine article'. Inevitably, there have been many attempts at establishing which Mr McCoy in particular gave his name to the language in this way.

The answer usually given is that 'Kid' McCoy was an American welterweight boxing champion in the late 1890s. When challenged by a man in a bar to prove that he was who he said he was, McCoy flattened him. When the man came round, he declared that this was indeed the 'real' McCoy. As Burnam 2 notes, 'Kid' McCoy promoted this story about himself.

However, Messrs G. Mackay, the Scottish whisky distillers, were apparently promoting their product as 'the real *Mackay*' in 1870, as though alluding to an established expression. This could have derived from the Mackays of Reay in Sutherland claiming to be the principal branch of the Mackay clan.

The association with booze endured. During Prohibition it was common practice to say that first-rate booze was 'the real McCoy' or simply 'the McCoy'.

The Morrises suggest that as boxers used to take the names of famous predecessors, 'Kid' McCoy may have had to bill himself as 'Kid "The Real" McCoy' to distinguish himself from his imitators. This seems a touch elaborate.

There are a number of other candidates for the original: a cattle-baron (Joseph McCoy of Abilene, Texas), an Irishman, a character in an Irish ballad, and a Prohibition rum-runner (Bill McCoy) – not to mention 'the real Macao' used to denote uncut heroin from Macao. Which, of all these, is the real McCoy is anybody's guess.

... WE CELEBRATE A *RED LETTER DAY*?
In almanacs and on old calendars feast days and saints' days were often printed in red rather than black ink. Thus a special day was one you would find in red letters.

... *REDS UNDER THE BED*?
A red flag was used in the 1789 French Revolution and the colour had come to be associated with various revolutionary movements during the nineteenth century before being adopted by Communists (and their sympathisers). It was said that originally the flag had been dipped in the blood of the victims of oppression.

That watchword of anti-Bolshevik scares – that there were 'reds under the bed' – was current within a few years of the 1917 October Revolution in Russia. Obviously, the rhyme 'red/bed' has a lot to do with the origin of the phrase. If they'd been greens, would they have been 'in the tureens'?

. . . BUREAUCRACY PRODUCES *RED TAPE*?

. . . and thereby causes delay in decision-making. The allusion here – dating from the eighteenth century – is to the ribbons that lawyers and other public officials still use to bind up their papers. In fact, they look more pink than red. The phrase existed before Charles Dickens (whom Ewart suggests as its originator). Washington Irving used it in the early 1800s.

. . . ACTORS IN CROWD SCENES MUMBLE *RHUBARB-RHUBARB*?

– to give the impression of speech, as a background noise, without actually producing coherent sentences. I suppose some unwise actors might think they could actually get away with saying 'rhubarb' but the idea is to repeat a word which, uttered by various voices, adds together to sound like the noise a crowd makes. I am not sure that it dates from much before this century but it is a well-known concept now, as demonstrated by the use of the verb 'to rhubarb' meaning to talk nonsense in a general sense.

Another phrase said to have been repeated by actors is 'My fiddle, my fiddle, my fiddle' and, I am assured, there is a phrase used by Russian actors in similar situations (meaning, literally, 'I speak – and I don't speak').

One wonders whether the adoption of the word 'rhubarb' in the English version has anything to do with its slang use to denote the male (and occasionally female) genitals. Or could there have been some rhyming slang phrase, i.e. rhubarb (tart) as fart, akin to raspberry (tart) = fart? The rhyming-slang books I have consulted do not support me in this, however.

. . . POOR LITTLE *RICH GIRL*?
See *poor*.

'... *RIGHT ON!*?
– to signify enthusiastic agreement. Flexner notes: ' "Tell it like it is!" [was] a 1965 Civil Rights shout of encouragement and approval to speakers at demonstrations. It was replaced by "Right on!" in 1967, which then became a general term meaning "you're absolutely right, you tell 'em".'

As such it became a fad expression, by no means restricted to Blacks, among whom, nevertheless, the saying originated. The notion of calling out agreement to a speaker or preacher – sometimes regularly, rhythmically, in response to his statements – is deeply rooted in Black speech. In *The Negro and His Songs* by Odum and Johnson (1925), we find: 'Railroad Bill was a mighty sport./ Shot all button of the high sheriff's coat./ Den hollered, "Right on, Desperado Bill!".'

... BANG TO *RIGHTS*?
See *bang*.

'... WHAT A *RIGMAROLE!*'?
i.e. fuss, palaver, lengthy procedure.

At the Public Record Office in London you will still find the 'Ragman Roll', a sequence of documents joined together to form a sheet some 40 feet long and dating from 1296. Each document was a pledge of loyalty by Scottish noblemen to King Edward I (1272–1307). This use of 'ragman roll' conveys the idea of a catalogue. The term was also used to describe the Hundred Rolls submitted to Edward in 1274–5. Because of the many seals hanging from them, they had a ragged appearance.

Since the eighteenth century a 'rigmarole' has been used to describe a rambling tale or yarn. Could it be derived from the earlier phrase? Nobody is too sure.

... DEAD *RINGER*?
See *dead*.

... *RITZY*?
i.e. smart, stylish, elegant, glamorous, ostentatiously rich. In 1980, the following advertisement appeared in a British magazine: '74 years ago, the language acquired a new word to indicate the

ultimate in luxury and elegance. It remains the last word to this day.'

The word comes from the surname of César Ritz, the Swiss-born hotelier (1850–1918) who established luxury hotels in Paris, London, New York and elsewhere at the turn of the century.

Colloquialisms employing the name were establishing themselves in the 1910s and 1920s – 'putting on the Ritz', a *Diamond as Big as the Ritz* – but not always in a complimentary way. The word could also denote things that were flashy and pretentious. There were also Ritz biscuits, watches, magazines, and other unrelated Ritz hotels.

'It is the strength of its image and the style of its clientele which has propelled its name into use as a common adjective in less than a century,' commented a writer in the *Observer* in October 1980. 'Like any sort of style, I suppose some words have it and some just don't. I never heard of anyone described as "so Savoy" or "heavily Hilton" or "terribly Inn-on-the-Parkish".'

Quite so. Indeed, it may have been more the style and sound of the word 'ritz' itself, rather than its associations that ensured its adoption.

... SOLD DOWN THE *RIVER*?
See *sold*.

... THE *ROARING 20s/ THE ROARING 40s*?
The urge to label decades usually owes more to alliteration than accurate description – 'Naughty Nineties', 'Swinging Sixties' – so where does this leave the 'Roaring Twenties' (i.e. the 1920s)?

The idea was to reflect the heady, buoyant atmosphere in certain sections of society following the horrors of the First World War. The adjective 'roaring', meaning boisterous, riotous, noisy had previously been applied to the 1850s and, in Australia, to the 'roaring days' of the gold-rush. The same meaning occurs in the expression 'roaring drunk'.

The expression 'Roaring Twenties' was known by 1939. F. Scott Fitzgerald provided his own (perhaps better) label, 'the Jazz Age', when he entitled a book, *Tales of the Jazz Age*, as early as 1922.

By the time the 1940s came along, together with another world war, there was no calling the decade the Roaring Forties – in fact, I am not aware of any label applied to that period.

Besides, the 'roaring forties' had already been applied to parts of the oceans between 40 degrees and 50 degrees south where strong westerly winds blow. This use had been established by the mid-nineteenth century.

By extension, it has been applied to the fifth decade in people's lives and, I believe, to the streets numbered 40–49, east and west of Fifth Avenue on Manhattan's grid system.

... RULE THE *ROAST*/*ROOST*?
See *rule*.

... ROUND *ROBIN*?
See *round*.

... *ROCK 'N' ROLL*?
As applied to a type of popular music, this term was first popularized by Alan Freed, an American disc jockey (1922–65). He is generally credited with first discovering and promoting the music. He acted as an impresario for rock 'n' roll performers in concerts and on radio and TV programmes. In 1951, for example, he was hosting *Moondog's Rock 'n' Roll Party* on a radio station in Cleveland. It was not until he moved to New York City in 1954, however, that the term 'took off'.

But he did not invent the term 'rock 'n' roll'. The combination of 'rock' and 'roll' (attractive because of the alliteration) had been used in the title of a 1934 song, *Rock and Roll*. I have also been told that it was originally a piece of Black slang for the sexual act. As 'jazz' meant the same thing, it is interesting that the twentieth century's two most significant inventions in popular music both derive from the same Black sexual source.

... WE SEND A *ROUND ROBIN*?
i.e. a letter where the responsibility for sending it is shared by all the signatories. In eighteenth-century France, petitioners would sign their names on a ribbon that was joined up. This was to prevent a situation where the first signatory on a list could be

singled out for punishment. A similar procedure operated in the British Navy where names were signed like the spokes of a wheel.

Nowadays, the term is often applied to a letter of protest with signatures not arranged in any special way, except perhaps alphabetically.

A 'round robin' is also a tournament in which every player or team competes with each of the others.

In neither sense does the term have anything to do with a bird. 'Round' is from French *rond* and 'Robin' is a corruption of French *ruban*, meaning ribbon.

... A MONARCH USES THE *ROYAL 'WE'*?
The first English sovereign to say 'we' instead of 'I' in an official or constitutional capacity was Richard I (the Lionheart) – and he actually 'said' it in Latin. The reasoning behind it was that the king spoke for his subjects as well as himself.

Before this, when Roman consuls *shared* power, it was appropriate for each of them to speak in this collective manner.

Some monarchs seem to have been more prone to using it than others. As is obvious from her alleged expression, 'We are not amused', Queen Victoria was one who did, but nevertheless her letters and journals are full of the first person singular. Elizabeth II has allowed herself a little joke about it – referring to her husband on one occasion, she began, 'We – and by that I mean both of us ...'.

... WE USE A *RULE OF THUMB*?
i.e. a rule taken from experience, not theory. This refers either to the use of a thumb's width as a rough and ready means of measurement or to the use of a thumb for dipping into liquids to test them.

... RULE THE *ROAST/ROOST*?
Well, which is it? These days, I think it would be true to say that most people would say 'rule the roost', meaning to 'lord it over'. The image they probably think they are evoking is of a cock strutting his stuff before the insubordinate hens on the roost, meaning perch.

That suits very well, but, as the existence of the (probably) earlier expression, 'to rule the roast', shows, that is not where the saying comes from.

In Shakespeare's *King Henry VI, Part II* (I.i.108), the Duke of Suffolk is 'the new-made Duke that rules the roast', i.e. presides at the head of the dinner table. I feel sure that this form is the original of the phrase, but it is just possible that both forms developed side by side.

... A PERSON *RUNS THE GAUNTLET*?

– meaning, endures something of a prolonged nature, attacked on all sides. There is no connection between this use of the word and 'gauntlet' meaning glove (from the medieval French *gantelet*). The origin here is from the Swedish *gatlop* or *gatloppe* which means 'lane run'. It conveys the idea of someone having to run as a punishment (in military circles) between two lines of people who torment him.

In turn, this expression should not be confused with 'run the gamut' which means to have wide experience, to cover the whole range of something. This comes from the use of 'gamut' in connection with musical scales.

... GETS GIVEN THE *SACK*?
See *gets given*.

'... *SAFETY FIRST*'?
According to the 1926 *Encyclopedia Britannica*, the slogan 'Safety First' was first used in the US in connection with railroad safety. In the UK of the 1890s, this was also the first use when a railway slogan declared, 'The Safety of the Passengers is our First Concern'.

In 1916, the London General Bus Company formed a London Safety First Council. The 1922 General Election saw the phrase in use as a political slogan for the Conservatives. Again, in 1929, it was the Tory slogan under which Stanley Baldwin fought for re-election. Posters showed the 'wise and honest face' of the prime minister who, inevitably, was smoking a pipe, and the further words: 'Stanley Baldwin, the Man You Can Trust'. Conservative Central office had thought that the General Strike of not long before (1926) called for this reassuring tone but, with growing unemployment and the Depression on the way, the slogan proved a loser.

In 1934, the National Safety First Association was formed, concerned with road and industrial safety, and it is in this connection that the slogan has endured.

... A SWEET TEA-CAKE IS A *SALLY LUNN*?
because it was 'sold by Sally Lunn, a pastry-cook, in the streets of Bath around 1800', announces Vernon Noble, confidently, in his book *Nicknames Past and Present* (1976).

Step forward Elizabeth David in her *English Bread and Yeast Cookery* (1977):

As for the name, Miss Dorothy Hartley's explanation that Sally Lunn and solimemne, as [Eliza] Acton calls it, are both corruptions of the French *soleil lune*, or sun and moon cake, sounds reasonable enough, and disposes of the picturesque legend that one Sally Lunn, a West Country Molly Malone, cried the cakes in the streets of eighteenth-century Bath, and that a baker and musician called Dalmer bought her business *and* composed a song in her honour. In his *Up-to-Date Breadmaking* (1968), however, Mr W.J. France asserts that Sally Lunn in fact had a pastry-cooks' shop in Lilliput Alley in Bath.

The 'picturesque legend' appeared in *The Gentleman's Magazine* in 1827 and was quoted by the *OED* with a citation from 1789. The *OED Supp.* found an earlier reference in P. Thicknesse's 1780 *Valetudinarian's Good Bath Guide*: 'I had the misfortune to lose a beloved brother ... who dropt down dead ... after drinking a large quantity of Bath Waters, and eating a hearty breakfast of spungy hot rolls, or *Sally Luns*'.

Now, who are we to believe?

... WITH A GRAIN OF *SALT*?
See *grain*.

... HAPPY AS A *SANDBOY*?
See *happy*.

... WE EAT A *SANDWICH*?
John Montagu, fourth Earl of Sandwich (1718–92) was a Hell-Fire Club rake in his youth. A committed gambler, he disliked having to stray from the gambling table for such small matters as eating. Hence, he would call for a piece of beef between two slices of bread to sustain him and once played for twenty-four hours non-stop. That was how the sandwich was born *c*.1762. The Sandwich Islands in the Pacific (later part of Hawaii) were named after him (rather than the food) by Captain Cook.

... PORTABLE ADVERTISEMENTS ARE CARRIED BY *SANDWICH MEN*?
Obviously, there is a resemblance – the men are sandwiched between the boards – but I am told that Charles Dickens invented the phrase. The earliest citation in the *OED Supp.* is 1890.

'... SAPRISTI!'?

In the BBC radio *Goon Show* of the 1950s, the character 'Count Jim Moriarty' had a way of exclaiming, 'Sapristi!' or 'Sapristi nuckoes!' Others may remember it being said by 'Corporal Trenet', friend of 'Luck of the Legion' in the boys' paper *Eagle*, also in the 1950s. The *OED Supp*. has citations going back to Thackeray in 1839.

It is not just a nonsense word for surprise, as might be expected. *Sapristi!* is a Fench interjection, meaning 'Dear me!', 'Hang it!', 'By jove!'. Other forms are *saperlotte!*, *saperlipopette!* and *sacristi!* (from which last religious-sounding oath it most probably derives).

... SAVVY TO FOREIGNERS?

– meaning, 'do you understand?' (also to people who may not be very bright). One's first reaction is that this is a contraction of French *savoir-faire* (knowing how to do) and, indeed, another meaning of 'savvy' is 'knowingness, understanding, nous, gumption'.

There is a common root, but in fact the word in this form comes to us – probably via the US (where it was established by the mid-nineteenth century) – from the Spanish *sabe usted* ('you know'). In Spanish, *b* and *v* sound very similar.

'Savvy' as we have it is from a Negro- and Pidgin-English version of this Spanish.

... A PERSON IS A 'GENTLEMAN AND A *SCHOLAR*'?

Once, when I was walking down a street in Oxford (*c*.1964), I was approached by an Irish 'gentleman of the road' who asked, 'May I shake the hand of a scholar and a gentleman?'. In fact, what he was after was 'sixpence for a cup of tea' but I was intrigued by his complimentary combination of 'gentleman' and 'scholar' (usually with the words in this order).

Paul Beale notes in Eric Partridge's *A Dictionary of Catchphrases* (2nd edition) that he was familiar (in *c*.1960) with the use of the phrase 'Sir, you are a Christian, a scholar and a gentleman' in the British Army. It was 'often used as jocular, fulsome, though quite genuine, thanks for services rendered'.

Partridge, earlier, had been tracking down a longer version – 'A gentleman, a scholar, and a fine judge of whiskey' – but had only been able to track down the 'gentleman and scholar' bit in Robert Burns (1786):

> His locked, lettered, braw brass collar
> Shew'd him the gentleman an' the scholar.

It looks, however, as though the conjunction goes back even further. *SOED* has a citation from 1621 – 'As becommed a Gentleman and a Scholer'. I suspect the phrase was born originally out of a very real respect for anyone who could claim to have both these highest of attributes.

'...SCOTTISH PLAY'?
See *break a leg.*

...PUT THE SCREWS ON?
See *put.*

'...SEE NAPLES AND DIE'?
This well-known saying is little explained in British reference books. Brewer, however, states that it is an Old Italian saying, implying that 'nothing more beautiful remains to be seen on earth'. The meaning is ambivalent in that Naples was once known as a centre of typhoid and cholera.

'...SEE YOU ON THE GREEN'?
This is a theatrical slang expression meaning 'I'll see you on the stage'.

Has it something to do with the 'Green Room' to which actors and actresses retire when they are not appearing or in their dressing rooms – and which is said to get its name from being painted green to rest the eyes of those who have been in the glare of harsh lighting?

Apparently not. It is rhyming slang: 'greengage' = stage.

...SEGUE?
(pronounced 'segway'). In broadcasting jargon this word is used to mean that you will go from one piece of music to another, or from one record to another, without a spoken link. A producer

might say, 'We'll *segue* from the Sinatra to the "Nuns' Chorus"
...'.

DOAS provides a rare use in another context, with the meaning
simply 'to go': 'When I sagway [sic] up to the roadside abattoir,
and order the concentric waffle', (Arthur Baer, newspaper column, 1947).

It comes from the Italian word meaning 'follows' and has been
used as a written instruction in music since at least the eighteenth
century. Clearly broadcasters have adopted the musicians' use.
Variety, the American showbiz paper, also uses it to mean that one
thing leads on to another.

... A PERSON GETS *SENT TO COVENTRY*?

i.e. ignored when people refuse to speak to him. As far as one can
tell, this originated with an old story that soldiers stationed at
Coventry were so unwelcome that the citizens carried on as if they
did not exist. Or that if women talked to the soldiers, they were
ostracized.

Another version comes from the English Civil War in the
seventeenth century. When captured Royalists were sent to
Coventry, a strongly Roundhead (Parliamentary) town, they were
bound to be ignored. This would appear to be supported by a
passage in Clarendon's *History of the Rebellion* (vi. 83) (1702–4):
'[Birmingham] a town so wicked that it had risen upon small
parties of the the King's [men], and killed or taken them prisoners
and sent them to Coventry.'

... A WOMAN *SETS HER CAP* AT A MAN?

i.e. tries to make a man notice her with a view to matrimony. This
expression dates from the eighteenth century when women did
wear caps for social occasions, and was later used by Thackeray in
Vanity Fair (1847–8).

... A MAN HAS THE *SEVEN YEAR ITCH*?

i.e. to be unfaithful to a spouse after a certain period of matrimony. The *OED Supp.* provides various examples of this phrase
going back from the mid-twentieth to the mid-nineteenth century, but without the specific matrimonial context. For example,
in one, the 'seven year itch' describes a rash from poison ivy

which was believed to recur every year for a seven-year period. Then one has to recall that since biblical days seven-year periods (of lean or fat) have had special significance, and there has also been the army saying, 'Cheer up – the first seven years are the worst!' Seven, in any case, is a mystical number.

But the specific matrimonial use did not arise until popularized and possibly invented by the title of George Axelrod's play (1952) and then film (1955). 'Itch' had long been used for the sexual urge but, as Axelrod commented on my *Quote ... Unquote* programme (BBC Radio 4, 1979), 'There was a phrase which referred to a somewhat unpleasant disease but nobody had used it in a sexual context before. I do believe I invented it in that sense.' Oddly, I can find no mention in any reference book I have consulted of 'itch' being used in connection with venereal diseases.

Nevertheless, I was interested to come across the following remark quoted in *W.C. Fields: His Follies and Fortunes* (Robert Lewis Taylor, published *1950*): 'Bill changed women every seven years, as some people get rid of the itch.'

... WE ARE IN FOR *SEVEN YEARS OF BAD LUCK*?

– if we break a mirror. According to Shook, this superstition began with the Romans who believed life renewed itself every seven years (one is also told that the skin on the human body renews itself every seven years). 'Since a mirror held a person's image, when it was broken, the health of the breaker – the last person to look into it – was also broken.'

... *SEXUAL CHEMISTRY*?

In the period prior to the start of TV-am, the British commercial station devoted solely to producing breakfast-time programmes, David Frost, one of the founders, talked frequently to newspaper journalists about hoped-for new approaches to presentation. According to Michael Leapman in his book *Treachery? The Power Struggle at TV-am* (1984), 'It was during one of these sessions that David invented – or had put into his mouth – the phrase "sexual chemistry" to describe the mood the presenters would try to create on screen.'

It became a catchphrase, like the station having 'a mission to explain' (the motto of another founder, Peter Jay), which became

more than risible when TV-am got off to a memorably cata-
strophic start.

Had the phrase been used before? Obviously the importance of
'chemistry' between personalities must have been noted before,
but beyond that ...?

'... SHAKE A LEG!'? AND 'SHOW A LEG!'?
Not quite the same phrase ...

To 'shake a leg' means no more than to dance, but 'show a leg'
(meaning to get up out of bed in the morning or get a move on) is
rather more interesting. It dates from the days when women were
allowed to spend the night on board naval ships when they were
in port. Next morning, at the cry, 'Show a leg!', if a woman's leg
was stuck out of a hammock, she was allowed to sleep on. If it was
a man's, he had to get up and get on with his duties.

Radford adds that the full expression was: 'Show a leg or a
purser's stocking.'

... THREE *SHEETS* TO THE WIND?
See *three*.

'... SHINE ON, HARVEST MOON'?
Well, that was the title of a song written in 1908, but what is so
special about the *harvest* moon? It seems particularly bright
between 15 and 20 September, thus enabling farmers to harvest
by moonlight, should they need to. The next full moon is sometimes called the 'hunter's moon'.

... SOMEONE/SOMETHING IS A *SHIRTLIFTER*?
Now what does this word mean? I first encountered it in the late
1970s when it was being used to refer to a meal made up of lentils
and beans and other currently fashionable fibre-full ingredients.
The net result would be a good deal of farting on the part of the
diners, lifting the shirts of those who happened to be wearing
them (though here the explanation gets a little pedantic).

However, I then heard 'shirtlifter' used to describe a homosexual male, i.e. one who lifts the shirt of another man in the
course of obtaining his pleasure (though Partridge, curiously,
hears it as rhyming slang for 'poofter'). The *OED Supp.* labels this
as Australian slang, although it is commonly used elsewhere.

I also vaguely remember hearing the expression used to describe something (a pornographic book, film or whatever) that would cause a man to have an erection.

... A COLOUR IS A *SHOCKING PINK*?
This coinage comes from the Italian fashion designer Elsa Schiaparelli (1896–1973). She used it in 1938 to describe a lurid pink she had created. As such it made a pleasant change from alliterative coinages and has undoubtedly stuck. In her autobiography, entitled, understandably, *Shocking Life* (Chapter ix) she notes that her friends and executives warned her off creating a 'nigger pink' but 'the colour "shocking" established itself for ever as a classic. Even Dali dyed an enormous stuffed bear in shocking pink.'

... CHIP ON THE *SHOULDER*?
See *chip*.

... *SHOW A LEG*?
See *shake*.

... THE *SHOW MUST GO ON*?
'Why Must the Show Go On?' asked Noel Coward in a 1950s song which neatly questioned the most famous of showbiz maxims.

But how did the maxim arise? The Morrises quote Abel Green, editor of *Variety*, writing in the paper's 60th anniversary issue:

Despite the early Warner Brothers film musicals, wherein Dick Powell conned and charmed Ruby Keeler that 'the show must go on' – because it was backstage tradition – it was fundamentally a circus phrase. It was meant to save lives, property and animals, and the ringmaster told the band to keep playing; the show must go on with all the available acts (except any injured) to divert the audience and to curb any possibility of panic as a result of whatever was a mishap.

Other sources agree that it is primarily a circus slogan, though no one seems to be able to turn up a written reference much before the 1930s.

... *SICK AS A PARROT*?
See *over the moon*.

... A MAN HAS *SIDEBURNS*?

i.e. long sidewhiskers or side*boards* (as I used to call them when I first started going to the hairdresser, or barber as he was then still called). Originally, the word was 'burnsides' and derived from General Ambrose E. Burnside (1824–81) who fought in the American Civil War and was famous for having a generous pair himself (meeting up with his moustache but with the chin clean shaven). I suppose the syllables were transposed (by 1887) because 'sideburns' was a fraction easier to say than 'burnsides' and related more to the form of the word 'sidewhiskers'.

... AN OUTLINE IS A *SILHOUETTE*?

Etienne de Silhouette (1709–67) was the Controller-General (finance minister) to Louis XV of France. A 'silhouette' is an outline of a person, originally sold as a portrait. What is the connection?

One suggestion I have heard is that his tenure of office was extremely short – only eight months – and that it seemed to pass 'as a fleeting shadow – like a silhouette'. Another is that he was 'associated with policies of retrenchment, and these cheap cut-out portraits gained their name by association with ideas of cheapness and economy' (Radford). The second explanation seems the more likely.

Whether de Silhouette practised the art of making silhouettes himself is not clear.

... SOMETIMES I JUST *SITS*?

See *sometimes*.

... A MUSICIAN PLAYS *SKIFFLE*?

According to Chris Barber, the musician, quoted in *Radio Times* (11 February 1984), 'The term "skiffle" occurs only twice on old records – a 1929 sampler on the Paramount label, featuring various blues artists and made to sound like a party, called "Home Town Skiffle", and there's a record made in the 1940s by Dan Burley's Skiffle Boys ... So we assume that "skiffle" must have been part of the jazz terminology of the time.'

The *OED Supp*. concurs with the American jazz origin of the phrase and finds a 1926 jazz title, *Chicago Skiffle*.

In Britain, the skiffle craze occurred in the 1950s. It was do-it-yourself music, often played on improvised instruments like tea-chest double basses and washboards.

But the word itself remains a mystery. In Black American usage, a 'skiffle' was a rent party where guests contributed to the host's rent bill. These were popular at the time of the Depression and perhaps such makeshift music was played at them. All one can say for certain is that the word sounds like something impro-vised – a skiffling, shuffling thing.

... SLOANE RANGER?
This term (echoing a Western character, the Lone Ranger) was popularized in 1975 and cultivated by Peter York in the magazine *Harpers and Queen* to describe a type of posh, country girl of good family, on the look-out for a husband. She lives in a flat around Sloane Square in London, probably sharing, and has an artistic job, does social service work, or teaches in a nursery school.

When the Princess of Wales ('Supersloane') entered public life in 1981, the phenomenon became much more generally under-stood, was the subject of several books by Peter York with Ann Barr, and gave rise to a whole Sloane industry. All this broadened the term to include other members of the British upper classes beyond the original idea. Martina Margetts, a sub-editor on the magazine is now credited with championing the phrase (York had wanted to call the girls 'Connaught Rangers').

... A PERSON HAS SLUNG HIS HOOK?
i.e. gone/run away. This British slang expression dates from the nineteenth century but no one seems too sure where it comes from. One reasonable explanation is that hook means anchor, so it means the equivalent of 'slipping anchor'.

... A POLITICIAN OPERATES A SLUSH FUND?
– meaning, a (probably) illegal stash of money for paying off people. Safire says the word is probably 'derived from the Swed-ish *slask*, meaning wet, or filth. Naval vessels would sell the slush and other refuse on board; the proceeds went into a fund to purchase sundries for the crew. Later this practice was extended to war-damaged equipment as well.'

Shook specifically defines the slush as grease from the cook's galley which was used to lubricate the masts. 'Whatever was left over was sold, and the money put into a fund for the enlisted men.' Both meanings were established by the end of the nineteenth century – the political one via the US.

... COCK A *SNOOK*? AND ... *SNOOKER*?
See *cock*.

... ABOMINABLE *SNOWMAN*?
See *abominable*.

... A BROADCAST IS A *SOAP OPERA*?
This type of seemingly endless melodramatic serial was first broadcast on radio, then on TV, in the US. By the late 1930s they were being referred to as 'soap operas' or 'soaps' or 'soapers' because the original sponsors were soap manufacturers. A critic writing in 1938 makes this clear – although he chooses a variation on the term: 'These fifteen-minute tragedies ... I call them "soap tragedies" because it is by the grace of soap that I am allowed to shed tears for these characters who suffer so much from life.'

The word 'opera' is used in this expression following the example set by 'horse opera', meaning cowboy film, a term in use by 1927.

... PUT A *SOCK IN IT*?
See *put*.

... *SOLD DOWN THE RIVER*?
i.e. betrayed. In the American south, after 1808, it was illegal to import slaves, so they were (according to Shook) purchased in the 'exhausted tobacco belt area of the upper south and brought down the Mississippi to the slave markets of Natchez and New Orleans'. Hence, if a slave was 'sold down the river', it meant he had lost his home and family.

The *OED Supp.* provides a slightly different gloss, defining the term as selling 'a troublesome slave to the owner of a sugar-cane plantation on the lower Mississippi where conditions were harsher than in the northern slave states'.

'... *SOMETIMES I JUST SITS AND THINKS – AND SOMETIMES I JUST SITS*'?

You may know this folksy saying. You may even use it from time to time. But even if you do not, it is probable that your parents or grandparents did. Yet, surprisingly, it did not feature in any dictionary of quotations until recently. So where did it originate?

On first being asked about it, people I approached would invariably say, 'Oh, that's what my father used to say.' Pressed as to its possible origin, they would come up with a bewildering variety of suggestions – Lewis Carroll, Laurel and Hardy, Winnie-the-Pooh, Uncle Remus (it certainly could be made to sound southern American), Mark Twain ...

Driven to desperation by an increasingly obsessive desire to have more positive proof, I mentioned my plight on the radio, knowing full well that what was puzzling to me would be as plain as a pikestaff to someone else. I did, however, request not wild surmises but chapter and verse.

This did not prevent some listeners providing me with *wrong* chapters and *wrong* verses. For example, one thought I would find it in 'Chapter 8, probably' of *Pickwick Papers* by Charles Dickens. But if he could find it, I could not.

Several others were absolutely positive I would find it in that little American book *The Specialist* by Charles Sales, the one about a man who specializes in the building of outside privies and which was published in 1930. The connection with sitting and thinking seemed highly likely but, no, it does not even rate a mention.

A woman, aged 50, remembered seeing, as a child, a china ornament made to look like a wooden shed. When you looked in the door, you saw a little curly-headed black boy sitting on the lavatory with his trousers round his knees. And 'Sometimes I just sits ...' was written underneath.

Even more correspondents knew for certain that the saying had been used as the caption for a picture postcard drawn by Mabel Lucie Atwell in the 1930s. I am sure they may be right, but no one was able to turn up the picture in question. One had 'thrown it out last week, as it happens'.

From the same decade came further memories of advertising slogans along the lines of 'Sometimes I just sits . . . and sometimes I sits and drinks a cup of Mazawattee Tea', and 'Sometimes I just sits . . . and listens to my Philco [radio]'.

I am sure these memories are correct but still I had no hard evidence. Then I was referred to the novel *Anne of the Island* by L.M. Montgomery, the Canadian writer who also gave us *Anne of Green Gables*. At one point in the book, an old woman who drives a mail-cart remarks: 'O' course it's tejus [tedious]. Part of the time I sits and thinks and the rest I jest sits.' Pretty close. And, as the book was published in 1925, was this the first outing for what was clearly to become a much used and popular saying?

Well, no, it was not. And if you thought you knew the answer all along, such evidence-sifting probably seems a shade preposterous . . . not least because the answer (when you know it) is a very obvious one.

On 24 October 1906, *Punch* carried a cartoon which shows a vicar's wife talking to an old, somewhat rustic, gentleman who has been laid up with an injured foot. She is sympathising with him and saying: 'Now that you can't get about, and are not able to read, how do you manage to occupy the time?'

He replies: 'Well, mum, sometimes I sits and thinks and then again I just sits.'

The cartoonist's name was Gunning-King and, unless someone can provide an even earlier use of the saying, I shall look upon his mild little joke as the end of my quest.

. . . A MAN IS A *SON OF A GUN*?
– nowadays, an inoffensively jocular name to describe someone, though originally less so.

If a pregnant woman somehow found herself upon an old-time warship and was ready to go into labour, the place traditionally made available to her – the only space affording a woman on board any privacy and without blocking a gangway – was between two guns. If the father was unknown, the child could be described as 'the son of a gun'. That sounds a bit pat but it will have to do, *faute de mieux*.

Partidge quotes an 1823 source as defining the term as a

'*soldier*'s bastard'. This makes one wonder even more whether the naval explanation is really the correct one.

... A STUDENT IS A *SOPHOMORE*?
i.e. in his or her second year at an American university (after being a freshman). The Greek *sophos* means 'wise' and *moros* means 'foolish'. So a second-year student is half-way between ignorance and wisdom. Well, that is more or less the idea. The *SOED* clings to an obscure definition relating the word to 'sophism' plus 'or'.

Sophomoric means 'pretentious, bombastic, foolish'.

... *SOS* WHEN WE ARE IN TROUBLE?
The original international Morse Code distress signal was 'C.Q.D.'. Although this had been abandoned by 1908, it indicates that we should not be looking upon SOS as an acronym. The letters do not stand for 'Save Our Souls' or 'Save Our Ship' or anything else. The letters S.O.S. were chosen because they were the simplest to be transmitted and recognised – dot, dot, dot, dash, dash, dash, dot, dot, dot.

It is true, however, that, in other fields, the letters S.O.S. *are* initials. For instance, in medical circles, they can stand for 'Si Opus Sit', meaning 'give relief where necessary' (i.e. administer a drug when the occasion arises, in such continuous conditions as cancer).

The initials have been used in any number of jokey ways and have been said to mean: 'Slip On Show' (schoolgirls), 'Same Old Slush' (school dinners), 'Short of Sugar' (wartime), and so on.

'Mayday' is the *spoken* distress call and comes from the French *venez m'aider* which means 'come to my assistance'.

... AN EXPLANATION FOR A PERSON'S BEHAVIOUR IS *SOUR GRAPES*?
– meaning, he affects to despise something because he knows he cannot have it. This derives from Aesop's fable of 'The Fox and the Grapes' in which a fox tries very hard to reach some grapes but, when he is unable to do so, says they looked sour anyway.

... A YOUNG MAN *SOWS HIS WILD OATS*?

A wild oat is a common weed, so for anyone to sow it means that he is doing something useless or worthless. Hence, the expression is employed to describe behaviour, usually by a man, prior to his 'settling down'. Quite how much sense there is of him wasting his semen in unfruitful couplings is hard to judge, though the expression often has reference to sexual dissipation. Perhaps this connotation has increased with the popularity of such nudging expressions as 'getting one's oats' (for having sex).

'Feeling one's oats', however, has nothing to do with this. It means to act in an important way as though pleased with oneself, and seems to have originated in the US. It refers to the way a horse was thought to feel friskier and more energetic after it had eaten its oats.

... OLD *SPANISH CUSTOMS*?

i.e. a long-standing practice which is unauthorised or irregular. In the mid-1980s, as Fleet Street struggled to embrace the 'new technology' of newspaper production, it had to throw off the 'old Spanish customs' first. But what was meant by this? In Tom Baistow's *Fourth-Rate Estate* (1985) we read:

The combination of high incomes and a very short working week enables many print workers in Fleet Street both to set themselves up as proprietors in their own right, owning newsagents' and other shops, launderettes and taxis, and to take time off to run them ... The high degree of casual working offers almost unlimited scope for bunce [profit] and the 'old Spanish customs', as the more unorthodox work practices are known.

In David Goodhart and Patrick Wintour's *Eddie Shah and the Newspaper Revolution* (1986), it is stated that,

Fleet Street production workers are by a long way the best-paid group of manual workers in Britain ... [despite] the decline of the standard working week ... To the long-established work-hopping tricks ... were added the celebrated Mr Mickey Mouse and others – names scribbled on attendance registers to ensure that the wage-packets of nonexistent workers were collected and shared round ...

Such was an example of an 'old Spanish custom'. It is hard to say quite why the Spanish have to carry the responsibility for this sort of thing, unless it be that they tend to attract the pejorative (see *spic* below), especially with regard to working practices (cf.

the *mañana* approach). In fact, the term has been around for some considerable time. *OED Supp.* cites a 1932 inquiry as to its origin to the journal *Notes and Queries*. Unfortunately, answer came there none.

... A SPANISH-SPEAKING LATIN-AMERICAN IS A *SPIC*?
During Britain's 1982 clash with Argentina over the Falklands Islands, the inevitable pejorative names for the 'enemy' were trotted out, including 'Argies' (which is understandable enough) and 'spics' or 'spiks'.

This last word puzzled me – was it something to do with their '*S*panish-speaking' habits. Or had the word come to us from the adjective 'hispanic'? The answer appears to be even more curious.

'Spic' comes from 'spiggoty' (various spellings) which has been the US abusive term for Spanish-speaking people from Central and South America since very early this century. As for the origin of the word, it was suggested in the journal *American English* that it came from Panama during the time the canal was being constructed (1904–14). Panamanians would say, 'No spikee de English'. The 'spikee de' element in this became 'spiggoty'.

DOAS adds that, in the US, 'spic' has also been applied to Italians or Italian-Americans. The dictionary derives it from 'spaghetti ... reinforced by the traditional phrase "No spika da English"'.

... DIVULGING SOMETHING IS *SPILLING THE BEANS*?
Shook traces this back to the ancient Greeks who held secret ballots for membership of clubs by using beans. A white bean was a 'yes' vote, a brown bean a 'no' vote. 'The beans were counted in strict secrecy so that a prospective member would never know how many people voted against him.' If the jar containing the beans was knocked over, the secret would' get out.

This is very grand, but the phrase only entered American speech (from whence it passed into English generally) early this century. Why did it take so long? Perhaps there is a less high-falutin explanation.

... ONE PERSON IS ANOTHER'S *SPITTING IMAGE*?
A popular British television series of the mid-1980s, called *Spitting Image*, may, because of its venomous use of grotesque puppets

to mock contemporary figures, have encouraged viewers to think that the 'spitting' here has to do with saliva. Indeed, one suggestion for the phrase is that, if one person so resembles another, it is as though one person were to spit out of another's mouth.

Joel Chandler Harris Jr (presumably son of the 'Uncle Remus' author), wrote to *Time* magazine in 1937 and attempted to set the record straight: 'It originated, I believe, among the darkies of the South and the correct phrasing – without dialect – is "spirit and image". It was originally used in speaking of someone whose father had passed on – and the colored folks would say – "the very spi't an' image of his daddy".'

This sounds quite convincing, although other theories are that the phrase is a corruption of 'speaking image', or 'splitting image' (a country saying derived from the two split halves of the same tree which provide an exact likeness).

'. . . *SPLICE THE MAIN BRACE!*' BEFORE HAVING A DRINK?

The attempted comparison here is between the reviving effect of strong alcoholic drink and the repairing or strengthening of the mainbrace – the rope used for holding or turning one of the sails on a ship.

As used in the navy itself, the term denotes an extra tot of grog all round – 'a very rare occurrence', according to Brewer, which suggests the term comes 'possibly from the issue of an extra rum ration to those who performed the hard and difficult task of splicing the mainbrace'.

The Oxford Companion to Ships and the Sea adds:

In sailing ship days the main brace was spliced (in terms of drink) in very bad weather or after a period of severe exertion by the crew, more as a pick-me-up for the crew than any other purpose. But with the introduction of steamships, with machines to take most of the harder labour out of seagoing, the main brace was spliced only on occasions of celebration or, occasionally, after battle. Now that, since 1970, rum is no longer issued in the British Navy, it is no longer possible to splice the main brace.

. . . PUT A *SPOKE IN?*
See *put.*

. . . BACK TO *SQUARE ONE?*
See *back.*

... ONE SIDE OF A SHIP IS *STARBOARD*?

i.e. the right-hand side as you face forward. The Anglo-Saxon words *steor* and *bord* meant 'rudder' and 'side', respectively. So, the *steorbord* was the side of the ship on which the rudder was positioned. The other side was probably called the 'port' side because it was the side that was put against the harbour (which the starboard side could not be because of the rudder).

... WE *STEAL A MARCH* ON SOMEONE?

i.e. gain an advantage by acting earlier than expected. If one army wished to gain advantage over another, it could march while the other one slept, hence it would 'steal a march' on its opponent.

... A COWBOY HAT IS A *STETSON*?

John B. Stetson (1830–1906) was the man who originally created the characteristic broad-brimmed, high-crowned cowboy hat. His hat-producing company was founded in Philadephia in 1865. Sometimes the hat is referred to by the nickname 'John B.'

As for the phrase 'ten-gallon hat' – this refers not to its literal capacity but to its usefulness, when necessary, as a means of carrying water.

... A PRISONER IS IN *STIR*?

See *porridge*.

... WE MUST *STIR OUR STUMPS*?

i.e. walk or dance briskly. 'Stump' here means leg, as it has done since at least the fifteenth century.

... A PERSON HAS *STOLEN ANOTHER'S THUNDER*?

i.e. has got in first and done whatever the other wanted to make a big impression with. This saying is said to derive from an incident involving the dramatist John Dennis (1657–1734). He had invented a device for making the sound of thunder in theatrical productions and had used it in one of his plays, *Appius and Virginia*, at the Drury Lane Theatre, London. The play was not a success and the management withdrew it. Subsequently, at the same theatre, Dennis saw a performance of *Macbeth* and noted that the thunder was being produced in his special way. He remarked: 'That is *my* thunder, by God; the villains will play my thunder, but not my play.'

Clearly the phrase is derived from the incident, rather than from what Dennis actually said.

. . . A HARD-UP MAN IS *STONE BROKE*?
(sometimes 'stony-broke'.) This expression refers to the custom of breaking up a craftsman's stone bench when he failed to pay his debts (Shook).

. . . WE HAVE INFORMATION *STRAIGHT FROM THE HORSE'S MOUTH*?
It is not that the horse is doing the speaking, of course. A horse's age can more accurately be judged by looking at its teeth (which grow according to a strict system). So, if you were buying the horse, you would do better to look at its teeth than rely on any information about its age that the vendor might give you.

. . . IN BIG CITIES THERE ARE *STREETS PAVED WITH GOLD*?
When Hollywood was in its heyday, many writers were reluctant to go there fearing how badly they would be treated. According to Arthur Marx in *Son of Groucho* (1973), his father tried very hard to persuade the dramatist George S. Kaufman to join him out on the west coast.

'No, no,' said Kaufman. 'I don't care how much they pay me. I hate it out there.'

'But, George,' pleaded Groucho, 'the streets out here are paved with gold.'

There was a moment's pause, and then Kaufman said, 'You mean, you have to bend over and pick it up?'

Where did this cliché originate? In the story of Dick Whittington, he makes his way to London from Gloucestershire because he hears the streets are paved with gold and silver. The actual Dick Whittington was thrice Lord Mayor of London in the late fourteenth and early fifteenth century. The popular legend does not appear to have been narrated before 1605.

. . . *STRICT TEMPO*?
There is nothing new about the idea of *a* strict tempo in music. The *OED Supp.* finds the term *tempo giusto* in 1740. But used,

especially from the 1950s onwards, to mean a type of ballroom dancing to such a strict beat, the coinage is that of Victor Sylvester (1902–78). This ballroom dance instructor and orchestra leader was notable for his distinctive enunciation of the strict foxtrot tempo: 'slow, slow, quick, quick, slow'.

... TEACH YOUR GRANDMOTHER TO *SUCK EGGS*?
See *grandmother*.

... *SUNRISE INDUSTRIES*?
These were much talked about in the early 1980s in comparison with 'sunset industries'. The image is a simple one. Sunrise industries are on the way up, sunset industries are on the way down. The term 'sunrise' does not mean that people have to get up early to go to work in them.

President Reagan, in his January 1984 State of the Union message, paid tribute to the 'entrepreneurs and risk-takers in the "sunrise industries" of high tech'. The quotation marks in the *Washington Post* report indicate that it must still have been a newish phrase. The *Economist* was, however, using it in February 1982.

... *SURE AS EGGS IS EGGS*?
Meaning absolutely certain. There is no very obvious reason why eggs should be 'sure', unless the saying is a corruption of the mathematician or logician's 'x is x'.

... A FAREWELL APPEARANCE IS A *SWAN SONG*?
The legend has it that swans 'sing' once only in their lives – just before they die. In fact, they never sing at all. The phrase is now broadly applied to anyone's last appearance or act before retiring from almost any activity.

... WE *SWEAR TO TELL THE TRUTH, THE WHOLE TRUTH AND NOTHING BUT THE TRUTH*?
There are various forms of oath in British and American courts but they all contain the basic line about telling 'the truth, the whole truth, and nothing but the truth'. I have been unable to ascertain how and when this crept in, but I shall keep on trying.

A modern form would be (taking the *New Testament* in one

hand): 'I swear by Almighty God that the evidence I shall give is the truth, the whole truth, and nothing but the truth.'

In British courts, it is not permitted to add: 'So help me, God', as many might be tempted to do from observing American procedure in countless films.

Here is the line again in a different legal system, that of Jersey, in a charge to a witness: 'You swear to tell the truth, the whole truth, and nothing but the truth in the prosecution against (. . . . .) by Her Majesty's Attorney-General which you will do without hatred, favour or partiality, as you are answerable to Almighty God at your peril.'

Since the Oaths Act of 1978, in British courts all witnesses have been able to refuse the *New Testament* and instead 'affirm' or demand their own holy book. (Chinese witnesses may ask to crack a saucer to express the hope that their soul shall be so cracked if they tell a lie.) Before the Act, only those without religion were allowed to affirm, save for Quakers and Moravians.

... SWEET FANNY ADAMS?
i.e. nothing at all (sometimes abbreviated to 'sweet F.A.', from which derives the alternative 'sweet fuck-all').

There actually was a person called Fanny Adams. Her gravestone is in the cemetery at Alton in Hampshire and records: 'Sacred to the memory of Fanny Adams, aged 8 years and 4 months, who was cruelly murdered on Saturday, August 21, 1867'. She was the victim of Frederick Booth, a 29-year-old solicitor's clerk, who grotesquely mutilated the body. His diary entry for the day read, 'Killed a young girl – it was fine and hot'. He was executed on Christmas Eve, 1867.

At about the same time, tinned meat was introduced to the Royal Navy and sailors, unimpressed, said it was probably made up from the remains of 'Fanny Adams'. 'Fanny Adams' became the naval slang term for mutton or stew and then, by extension, for anything that was worthless. More recently 'sweet Fanny Adams' has become a euphemistic way of saying 'sweet fuck-all' (if 'Sweet F.A.' is not resorted to).

... NO ROOM TO SWING A CAT?
i.e. a confined space. As is well known, the 'cat' was the name given on old sailing vessels to a whip used in discipline. It left

scars on the back reminiscent of a cat's scratches. A sailor condemned to be so punished had to be taken up on deck because below deck there literally was no room to swing the whip.

... SWINGING LONDON?

(to describe London during the 'Swinging Sixties'). 'Swinging' had been a musician's commendation for many years before it was adopted to describe the free-wheeling, uninhibited atmosphere said to have existed during the 1960s. By extension, 'swinging' came to denote sexual promiscuity. A 'swinger' was one who indulged in such activity.

How the word caught on is not totally clear. In the early 1960s, a Liverpool-born comedian, Norman Vaughan (*b.*1927) used to say, 'Swingin'!' or 'Dodgy!' (when conferring or withdrawing approval) and would accompany his words with a thumbs up or thumbs down gesture. In 1962, these verbal and visual catchphrases became well known through his compering of the ITV show, *Sunday Night at the London Palladium*.

According to *The Making of the Prime Minister 1964* by Anthony Howard and Richard West, the Labour Party considered using the word 'swinging' with a visual of an upraised thumb as the basis of its advertising campaign prior to the 1964 general election. However, doubts were expressed as to whether everyone would get the allusion and only the thumb was used.

It might be mentioned that 'swinging', in any case, was a much used concept in show business at the time. Frank Sinatra had an album entitled *Songs for Swinging Lovers*, Peter Sellers, *Songs for Swinging Sellers* and Diana Dors, *Swinging Dors*.

The coming together of 'swinging' and 'London' may first have occurred in an edition of the *Weekend Telegraph* magazine of 30 April 1965 in which the words of the American fashion journalist Diana Vreeland were quoted: 'I love London. It is the most swinging city in the world at the moment'. In addition, a picture caption declared, 'London is a swinging city'. Almost exactly one year later, *Time* magazine picked up the angle and devoted a cover-story to the concept of 'London: The Swinging City' (edition dated 15 April 1966).

... *FITS ONE TO A T*?
See *fits*.

... A NEWSPAPER IS A *TABLOID*?
i.e. has smaller pages than a 'broadsheet' newspaper and is written in a particular downmarket, popular style. The word 'tabloid' was coined by the chemist Sir Henry Wellcome in the 1880s to describe a new small tablet he had invented. Until then, medicine had either been taken in liquid or powder form, or in the shape of large tablets. 'Tabloid' was registered as a trademark. In a short space of time, however, it came to be applied to anything miniature. Newspaper magnates Alfred Harmsworth and Lord Northcliffe both used the word to describe new, small, popular papers at the start of this century, and the name stuck.

... THE *TAFFIA*?
i.e. a group of Welshmen who look after their own interests. For example, in the media, one might have said that the founders of Harlech TV in 1968 were members of the Taffia – including Richard Burton, Lord Harlech, Sir Geraint Evans, John Morgan and Wynford Vaughan-Thomas. The word is an obvious combination of 'Taffy' (the traditional nickname for a Welshman, from the supposed Welsh pronunciation of Davy = David) and *mafia*, the Sicilian-Italian word meaning 'bragging', applied to the organized body of criminals among Italian immigrants in the US.

A similar light-hearted coinage is 'the Murphia' (from Murphy, the typical Irish name and nickname for a potato), applied to the apparent media-group of Irish broadcasters in the UK, Terry

Wogan, Henry Kelly, Frank Delaney and Dr Anthony Clare. This
second group (from the mid-1980s) only exists in the minds of
others as it is not a cohesive force like the first.

... WE HAVE TO *TAKE A RAIN-CHECK*?
Originally, in the US, a rain-check (or -cheque) was a ticket for
re-admission to a sporting event when the event had to be post-
poned because of rain. The person to whom it was given would be
able to produce it at a later date and claim free admission.

According to Philip Howard in *The Times* (19 April 1984),
people in Britain misunderstand this term and think that the
'check' is on the weather. Hence, they mean 'let us test whether it
is raining, or will rain' and, by extension, 'let us check out
whether a future event of almost any kind is likely to occur'.

I am not sure that the confusion is total. The *OED Supp.* gives
two meanings – first, the 'ticket' one, and second, 'to reserve
the right not to take up a specified offer until such time as it
should prove convenient'. I have not encountered the phrase
used, as Howard claims, in the sense of 'I don't want to (e.g.)
have lunch with you'. I think that, although it could be used
in a calculatedly delaying way, it still must contain some sort
of commitment to 'renegotiate' a 'date' or appointment at a later
time.

... A PERSON OUGHT TO BE *TAKEN DOWN A PEG*?
– meaning, humbled, reduced in self-esteem. The phrase comes
from its nautical use in connection with flags, which were raised
and lowered with pegs. A flag flying high would carry more
honour than one lower down.

... A GULLIBLE PERSON HAS BEEN *TAKEN FOR A RIDE*?
i.e. deceived, tricked. Perhaps the original meaning of this US
slang expression was a euphemism for 'killed'. Those who fell foul
of gangsters were invited to 'take a ride' with the boss in his car.
Flattered they might have been, but it was possible they might not
return (another form of the phrase is 'taken for a *one-way* ride').
From this, probably, came the meaning to be tricked, conned.
Twentieth-century and no earlier, anyway.

... WE ARE *TAKING THE MICKEY* OUT OF SOMEONE?
i.e. poking fun at him, deflating him. This could be rhyming slang for taking the Mickey Bliss = taking the piss. Mike/Mickey Bliss is definitely rhyming slang for 'piss'. But could it be helped by the echo of the word 'mockery' it contains? Radford suggests that it has something to do with the fact that Irishmen are often called 'Mick' and are renowned for their scattiness.

... WE *TALK TURKEY*?
i.e. get down to business, talk seriously. Although a widely known expression, this originated in the US and was known by the mid-nineteenth century. Shook says it first appeared in American colonial days when the Pilgrim Fathers always seemed to want turkeys when they traded with the Indians. So familiar did their requests become that the Indians would greet them with the words, 'You come to talk turkey?'

This seems rather more to the point than the tale (recounted by the Morrises and others) usually given as the origin of the phrase: in colonial days, a white hunter and an Indian made a pact that they would share equally between them anything they caught. However, at the end of the day, when they came to share out what they had bagged – three crows and two turkeys – the white man first handed a crow to the Indian and a turkey to himself, then another crow to the Indian and a second turkey to himself. At which point the Indian is said to have remarked, 'You talk all turkey for you. Only talk crow for Indian.'

... *TASK FORCE*?
A 1949 US film called *Task Force* was a 'flag-waver' (according to *Halliwell's Film Guide*) portraying 'an admiral about to retire recalling his struggle to promote the cause of aircraft carriers'. In the early 1970s (according to *Halliwell's Television Companion*, there was a TV series 'rather clumsily' entitled *Softly, Softly: Task Force*. Then, finally, in 1982, the Falkland islands were liberated from the Argentinians by what was widely referred to as the British Task Force.

So what precisely is a 'task force'? The *OED Supp.* agrees with the American origin of the phrase and defines it as, 'an armed force organized for a special operation under a unified command, hence ... any group of persons organized for a special task.'

It offers no citations prior to the Second World War.

... THE WEATHER IS *TATERS*?

i.e. cold. Another of the more obscure rhyming slang derivations. 'Taters' or 'taties' as potatoes. The rhyming phrase is 'potatoes in the mould'. But what is that supposed to mean? One of the meanings of 'mould' is easily broken-up surface soil. Perhaps this conveys the idea of earth which is liable to be colder than that deep down.

... SOMETHING IS *TAWDRY*?

i.e. cheap and trashy. If I tell you straight away that this word comes from St Audrey (otherwise Etheldreda, Abbess of Ely, in the seventh century AD), you may wonder how it is that a saint could be associated with anything despicable. Well, St Audrey developed a breast tumour which she blamed on wearing rich necklaces of jewels as a child. She died of it in 679. After this, and especially much later in the sixteenth and early seventeenth century, women wore rich necklaces of *silk* which they called St Audrey's lace.

At one time also, in Cambridgeshire, there used to be an annual fair on the Isle of Ely in honour of the said St Audrey at which the lace was sold.

Alas, poor imitations of the lace drove out the good and, by an unfortunate process, the good lady's name came to be given to anything of a gaudy nature.

... *TAXI*?

A chauvinistic Englishman once tried, in my presence, to pour scorn on the French because they did not have their own word for 'taxi'. Poor fool, if he had only known, quite the reverse was true. The *taximetre* (i.e. *taxe*, meaning tarriff plus *metre*, meaning meter) was a French word for the device invented (c.1898) for clocking up the cost of hiring a cab. The abbreviation 'taxi' for the vehicle itself was soon applied (by 1907) and English-speakers adopted it, *from* the French.

... ONE WHO ABSTAINS FROM ALCOHOL IS *TEETOTAL*?

He may drink a lot of 'tea' instead but this is not where the name comes from. Rather, it is an emphasis of the initial 't' of 'total', just as we might say, 'Total with a capital T'. The totality of abstaining became important when the American Temperance Union extended its ban beyond hard liquor to include beer, wine and cider, too. This was in 1836. However, three years before, the word 'teetotal' had been used in this context by Richard Turner of Preston, England. Ewart repeats the unlikely story that it was because of Turner's stutter that the word took its present form, the speaker having said, 'Nothing but t-t-t-t-total abstinence will do.' (Would not the result have sounded more like 'tut-tut-tut-total' rather than 'tee-tee-tee-total'?) Brewer considers the word to have arisen in Britain and America independently.

According to Flexner, the word 'teetotally' had been used in America as early 1807 by Parson Mason Locke Weems in the 'T-totally' rather than abstinence sense.

... PRESIDENT REAGAN HAD A *TEFLON PRESIDENCY*?

'Teflon' is the proprietary name for Polytetrafluoroethylene (first produced 1938, US patent 1945), a heat-resistant plastic chiefly known as the name given to a range of cookware coated with it that 'won't scratch, scar or mar' (1965).

Hence, when President Reagan exhibited an ability during his first term (1981–5) to brush off any kind of 'dirt' or scandal that was thrown at him (chiefly through the power of his personality) this was the obvious epithet to apply to him. *Time* magazine wrote (7 July 1986), 'Critics say that he is coated with Teflon, that no mess that he makes ever sticks to him. That is perfectly true.'

As his second term wore on, however, as happens with an old non-stick frying pan, the story was a little different.

The original coinage was by Representative Patricia Schroeder (Democrat, Colorado) in a House speech in August 1983, saying that Reagan was 'perfecting the Teflon-coated presidency', because nothing stuck to him.

'... TELL IT TO THE MARINES'?

i.e. 'don't expect us to believe that!' This apparently dates from the days, in Britain, when Marines were looked down upon by ordinary sailors. Working on land and sea, the Marines were clearly neither one thing nor the other, and thus stupid. So perhaps they would believe a piece of unbelievable information.

Brewer derives it from an occasion when Samuel Pepys, no less, was regaling Charles I with stories from the navy. An officer of the Maritime Regiment of Foot (the precursors of the Marines) gave his support to Pepys when doubt was cast on the existence of flying fish. Said the king, 'Henceforward ere ever we cast doubts upon a tale that lacks likelihood we will first "Tell it to the Marines".'

The phrase is also well-known in the US. Sometimes it takes the form, 'Tell *that* to the marines', sometimes, 'Tell that to the *horse-*marines'.

... THINK-TANK?
See *brains trust*.

... A DRUNK HAS THREE SHEETS TO THE WIND?
The 'sheets' in question are not, as you might expect, sails but the ropes or chains attached to sails to trim them with. If the sheet is free, the sail is unrestrained. As Shook puts it, 'if these sheets are loose, the ship will be as unstable on the water as a thoroughly drunk man is on his feet'.

... TO STEAL ONE'S THUNDER?
See *stolen*.

... TICH?
See *titch*.

... A PERSON WHO IS PLEASANTLY DRUNK IS TIDDLY?
It is rhyming slang: tiddlywink = drink. And rather a pleasant euphemism.

... WE DON'T GIVE A TINKER'S CUSS?
(or, a 'tinker's dam(n)' or, simply, a 'tinker's'.) The simplest explanation is that because tinkers swore so much, one of their cusses would not be worth very much. Or, because tinkers were not exactly outstanding figures, to be damned by one would not

bother you. However, there was a thing called a tinker's 'dam' – a piece of bread used to plug a leak in a pot until solder had been poured in. This was not worth anything and was useless afterwards.

Given the existence of the 'cuss' version, I think the expression must involve the idea of swearing and I would thus discount the second.

... AN OLD MOTOR CAR IS A *TIN LIZZIE*?

The name was first applied to Henry Ford's Model T, introduced in 1908. The nickname was not given to the car by the manufacturer. One story has it that the car was named after Ford's wife, but her name was Clara Bryant. The Morrises suggest that 'lizzie' is a corruption of 'limousine', which I am not sure about, and Shook pins his faith on a comparison between the usefulness of the car and domestic servants, many of whom were called Lizzie. I am not sure about that either. The citations in the *OED Supp*. indicate that 'Lizzie', on its own, somehow emerged as an affectionate name for a car.

Later, the name was applied to any old jaloppy (and no one knows where *that* name came from ...)

... MUSIC PUBLISHERS WORK IN *TIN PAN ALLEY*?

(both in New York and London). The New York use was the original and it applied to the area variously described as having been 'near 14th street', 'around 28th street and Broadway', later shifting up to '42nd and Broadway' or 'between 48th and 52nd streets on 7th Avenue' – all in Manhattan. In time, the phrase was used generically to describe the business of popular music.

Ian Whitcomb in *After the Ball* says:

Many and conflicting stories [are adduced] – a British folk-song researcher told me that the phrase was coined in Georgian times to describe the flourishing 'broadside ballad' trade ... The most plausible (and most colourful) explanation of the phrase is this one: Monroe Rosenfeld, a tear-jerker specialist and journalist, wrote a series of comic articles about the new business for the *New York Herald*, and thought up the collective title 'Tin Pan Alley'. The publishing houses were clustered on top of each other. Every window was open. Almost every room had an upright piano being played. The Babel of different embryonic tunes all playing at once in the song factory must have struck Rosenfeld as being reminiscent of tin pans being clashed. That's one story.

The Morrises supply the information that, around 1900, the term 'tin pan' was used to describe a cheap, tinny piano. As these were the type you would hear being pounded in music publishers' offices, it was natural so to describe the area. This sounds very likely. In London, Tin Pan Alley was centred in Denmark Street, off the Charing Cross Road.

Apparently, the first US use of the term was in 1908, in the UK, 1934.

... A DRUNK IS *TIRED AND EMOTIONAL*?

A pleasant euphemism, ideally suited to British newspapers which have to operate under libel laws effectively preventing any direct statement of a person's fondness for the bottle. The expression 't and e' (to which it is sometimes contracted) is said to have arisen when *Private Eye* printed a spoof Foreign Office memo suggesting it was a useful way to describe the antics of George Brown, Foreign Secretary, 1966–8. Ironically, there was never any question that Brown *did* get drunk.

I am not convinced that *P.E.* actually coined the phrase, though it undoubtedly popularized it.

... A CONFUSED PERSON IS 'ALL OF A *TISWAS*'?

Partridge suggests that this might be an elaboration of 'tizz' or 'tizzy' and I suspect there is a hint of 'dizziness' trying to get out somewhere. But no one really knows. The acronym, meaning 'Today Is Saturday, Wear A Smile' seems not to have anything to do with the meaning of the word and to have been imposed later. The acronym-slogan was the apparent reason for the title *Tiswas* being used for a British children's TV show of the 1970s, famous for its bucket-of-water-throwing and general mayhem. Broadcast on a Saturday morning, its atmosphere was certainly noisy and confused.

... A SMALL PERSON IS A *TITCH* OR *TICH*?

As an example of the strange ways in which words can evolve, this one is hard to beat. In the middle of the last century, there was a famous court case featuring Arthur Orton, known as the Tichborne Claimant, who sought to inherit the baronetcy of a man lost a sea. Orton was discredited and gaoled. He was a huge, fat man and so when Harry Relph (1868–1928), a very small person, was looking for a stage name he called himself 'Little Tichborne'. In time, this was shortened to 'Little Tich' and it was under this name that the famous comic impressed himself upon his audiences. To speak of a 'little ti(t)ch' now is to speak tautologically, so firmly has the meaning of the word been fixed.

... A PERSON IS A *TOADY*?
i.e. a creepy sycophant. This is short for 'toad-eater'. A charlatan or quack-doctor would employ a toad-eater to appear to eat a 'poisonous' toad so that he could be 'cured' with the medicines the quack had for sale.

... WE DRINK A *TOAST*?
(rather than eat it ...) At one time a piece of toast would be put in a glass of wine in order either to improve the flavour or to collect the sediment. The word 'toast' thus became identified with the drink.

... ON HIS *TOD*?
See *on*.

... A MALE CAT IS A *TOM*?
Simple: in 1760 there was published an anonymous story called *The Life and Adventures of a Cat* which was very popular. The male cat was called Tom and soon every male cat was so called (Morris).

... A SHOW BUSINESS AWARD IS A *TONY*?
This is the name given to the annual awards presented by the American Theatre Wing (New York) for excellence in the theatrical arts. From their inception, the awards have been called Tonys, after the nickname of Antoinette Perry (1888–1946), the actress and manager. She died the year before the first awards were made.

The word may gain something from the fact that 'tony' is also an informal American adjective, derived from 'tone', for 'stylish, distinctive, classy'.

'... TOODELOO!' WHEN WE PART?
The *OED Supp.* offers a connection with 'toot', as though, perhaps, one were to go 'toot, toot', like a horn, on parting. I incline
more to something to do with 'toddling off' or 'tootling off'. 'I
must tootle-o', perhaps led to it?

A much better idea is that it derives from the French *à tout à
l'heure* ('see you soon').

... LONG IN THE *TOOTH*?
See *long*.

... *OVER THE TOP*?
See *over*.

'... *TOP HOLE!*'
i.e. excellent. Probably referring to holes or notches cut in a board
to record the points scored in some games. The top hole represents
the highest, best score. Particularly popular towards the start of
the century.

**... WE WOULDN'T *TOUCH SOMEONE/SOMETHING WITH
A BARGE-POLE*?**
i.e. we would keep our distance. From the *length* of a barge-pole.

... *TRILLIONS*?
See *billions*.

... *ECONOMICAL WITH THE TRUTH*?
See *economical*.

... MOMENT OF *TRUTH*?
See *moment*.

... THE NAKED *TRUTH*?
See *naked*.

... A *T-SHIRT* IS AN ARTICLE OF CLOTHING?
Because this simplest of garments is, if you think about it, shaped
like a letter T. Originally from the US, the word describes a form of
cotton shirt, simple to cut out and make.

... SWEAR TO TELL THE *TRUTH*?
See *swear*.

... WE TALK *TURKEY*?
See *talk*.

... WE *TURN THE TABLES* ON SOMEONE?
i.e. gain an advantage over them. This derives from playing games
(like chess or draughts) which require the use of marked boards or
moving pieces about on table-tops. If one player is not doing well,
then were he to 'turn the table' on his opponent, he would be in
the winning position.

'... WHAT A *TURN UP FOR THE BOOKS!*'?
i.e. what an unexpected outcome, what a surprise! The 'books'
here are those kept by bookies to maintain a record of bets placed
on a race. Does he have to turn up the corner of a page if a race has
an unexpected outcome, or something? No, the phrase merely
means that something unexpected has 'turned up'.

... A BALLERINA WEARS A *TUTU*?
You mean you've never wondered? Well, you will be amazed by
the explanation, which is attested to by all the dictionaries you
may care to consult. 'Tutu' is a corruption of *cucu* which is French
baby-talk for *cul-cul* which is the equivalent of English 'botty-
wotty' (*cul* is French slang for 'arse' or 'bum' and derives from the
Latin *culus*, buttocks).

... AN EVENING JACKET IS A *TUXEDO*?
Made of light-weight wool, the tuxedo was introduced to the US
from Europe by one Griswold Lorillard. He did so at an Autumn
Ball held on 10 October 1886 at the Tuxedo Club, Tuxedo Park, a
fashionable country club in Orange County, New York State. So
much more convenient to wear than tails, the garment obviously
took its name from the scene of its first appearance.

There are other claimants to the introduction, but there is no
mistaking why Tuxedo (the place) gave its name.

... A TWIT IS A *TWERP* (OR *TWIRP*)?

i.e. foolish fellow. The *OED Supp.* has unearthed the fact that there was a man called T.W. Earp who matriculated at Exeter College, Oxford, in 1911. The dictionary produces a couple of citations to demonstrate that it was believed this man was the original 'twerp'. (One of the citations, let it be noted, is from a 1944 letter by J.R.R. Tolkien, no slouch in the linguistic stakes.)

Quite what Mr Earp did to make his unfortunate gift to posterity, is not very clear. He became President of the Oxford Union after the First World War and was perhaps the opposite of a rugger-hearty.

I remember, when I was at school, hunting through the dictionary (vainly in those days) for interesting four-letter words and, instead coming across the fascinating information that a 'twirp' was a name for a pregnant fish. This information seems to be ignored by the dictionaries I possess nowadays.

... A BIRDWATCHER IS A *TWITCHER*?

This term became popular during the late 1970s and onwards and is said to derive from the nervous tics or twitches such enthusiasts have when they get to hear of rare birds arriving or when they do not manage to sight them. I should have thought some combination of 'watcher' and 'twitch' was more likely.

Some birdwatchers, however, hate being given the name as they feel it denotes a mindless enthusiasm for spotting birds (just as a trainspotter pursues trains). They prefer to be thought of as serious ornithologists.

As the Reverend W.A. Spooner once accurately observed, 'I am not a word-botcher.'

... DISCUSSING *UGANDAN AFFAIRS*?
– a euphemism for sexual intercourse, popular among readers of
the satirical magazine, *Private Eye*. Other forms: 'talking about
Uganda', 'Ugandan practices', 'Ugandan discussions', etc.

These all stem from a gossip item in *Eye* no. 293 (9 March 1973):

> I can reveal that the expression 'talking about Uganda' has acquired a new
> meaning. I first heard it myself at a fashionable party given recently by media-
> people Neal and Corinna Ascherson. As I was sipping my Campari on the ground
> floor I was informed by my charming hostess that I was missing out on a
> meaningful confrontation upstairs where a former cabinet colleague of President
> Obote was 'talking about Uganda'.
>
> Eager, as ever, to learn the latest news from the Dark Continent I rushed
> upstairs to discover the dusky statesman 'talking about Uganda' in a highly
> compromising manner to vivacious former features editor Mary Kenny ... I
> understand that 'Long John' and Miss Kenny both rang up later to ascertain each
> other's names.

In a letter to *The Times* (13 September 1983), Corinna Ascherson
(now Adam) identified the coiner of the phrase as the poet and
critic James Fenton.

... THE LATE *UNPLEASANTNESS*?
See *late*.

... WE'RE *UP A GUM TREE*?
i.e. stuck, isolated, in a difficult position. Presumably because not
only could a person (or animal) be trapped by pursuers if he went
up a tree, but his position would be made doubly difficult if the
tree was of the type he would stick to.

... U-TURN?

Originally, this term was used (possibly for the first time in the US) to describe the turn a motor car makes when the driver wishes to proceed in the opposite direction to the one he has been travelling in. The *OED Supp.* finds an American example in 1937.

The figurative, political use of the term to denote a reversal of policy was established in America by 1961, according to *Webster's Dictionary*. In British politics, I seem to recall it being used particularly at the time of the Heath government (1970–4). In a speech to the 1980 Conservative Party Conference, Mrs Margaret Thatcher responded to critics who had accused her of making (or wanting to make) U-turns, by saying: 'To those waiting with bated breath for that favourite media catchphrase, the U-turn, I have only one thing to say. You turn if you want to. The lady's not for turning.'

... A FLIRTATIOUS, PREDATORY WOMAN IS A *VAMP*?

Much in vogue in the early silent film days, the 'vamp' character reached her apogee in the peformances of Theda Bara. In the film *A Fool There Was* (US 1914), she played a *femme fatale* who lures a European financier. He forsakes all for her and dies in her arms. It was this film which put the word into the language – it is short, of course, for 'vampire' – but the film was based on a play by Porter Emerson Brown which was based in turn on the poem *The Vampire* (1897) by Rudyard Kipling (which begins 'A fool there was ...'). So, understandably, the idea of a woman who behaves towards men as a vampire behaves towards his victims pre-dates the coining of 'vamp'.

. . . A WASTEPAPER BASKET IS A *WAGGER*?

This is an example of the (now rather dated) slang popular in
Oxford in the early years of the century. A whole range of words
was transformed into different words ending in '-agger'. For
example, a wastepaper basket was, in full, a 'wagger-pagger-
bagger'. The Prince of Wales was the 'Pragger Wagger'. Jesus
College was known as 'Jaggers'. And a curious working-class
character who used to hang around Oxford and was known as the
British Workman came, inevitably, to be called the 'Bragger
Wagger'.

The whole scheme is a variant upon the old English Public
School custom of adding '-er' to everything: rugby becoming
'rugger', football becoming 'footer', and so on.

Silly, but rather fun. The slang survives in small pockets. There
are still people who call a wastepaper basket a 'wagger'. I'm
married to one.

. . . WE'RE *WAGING A BATTLE ROYAL*?

i.e. a keenly fought contest. This term originated in cockfighting.
In the first round, sixteen birds would be 'pitted' (put into a pit)
against each other, until only half the number was left. The
knock-out competition would then continue until there was only
one survivor.

. . . A FOOLISH, INEPT OR INEFFECTUAL PERSON IS A *WALLY*?

Well now . . ! This became a vogue word in Britain *c.*1983, and
many and various were the attempts at explaining its origin. Here
are some of them:

An Arab is born either a *walad* (boy) or *bint* (girl). The 'd' in *walad* often gets swallowed and so, when a bazaar tout is offering his brother's rather than his sister's sexual services, he may speak of a 'wali'. (I've taken this from a letter in the *Guardian* of 1 July 1983.)

A 'wolly' or 'wally' was the name given to pickled cucumber on sale in fish and chip shops – not least to the last, shrivelled-up, unwanted one left in the jar.

It is a slang word for 'breast' (cf., 'tit' and its use as a pejorative name for a person).

'Wallies' are teeth, especially 'false teeth', especially in Scotland and said to derive from Wally Close, a Glasgow tenement where the walls are covered with white, shiny tiles.

It is Sloane Ranger shorthand for a 'wall-flower' (i.e. one who stays by the wall and does not come onto the floor at a dance).

It is a variation of the well-known word 'willy', meaning penis.

Rhyming slang for Scottish 'wally-dug', meaning mug, 'and so for a po-faced china dog that graces many a Scottish hearth' (this, via Godfrey Smith in his *Sunday Times* column of 20 July 1986).

Short for 'wally-draigle', Scots slang for the youngest daughter, a sloven or wastrel.

At a 1971 pop festival at Weeley, near Colchester, a fan called Wally wandered off to the loo and got lost. His friends started chanting his name and it became associated with a forlorn twit. (This explanation seemed to win Godfrey Smith's vote but, as I know for sure that people were using the term in the 1960s, it does not cut much ice with me.)

At a pop festival near Stonehenge (*c*.1974) when several fans were arrested by the police, they all gave their names as Wally Smith, Wally Jones, Wally Bloggs.

I would venture towards the conclusion that the coinage had *something* to do with Scotland. I expect it all began with a particular 'Walter' who was 'that way inclined'. There is great appeal in the sound of the word. A similar expression I also first noted in 1983 is 'woolly-pully' to describe a bad 'Sunday driver'. Why so called? Because such people tend to wear woollen pullovers.

... *WALTER PLINGE* IS APPEARING IN A PLAY?

Traditionally, in British theatre, when an actor plays two parts he uses the name 'Walter Plinge' as a stage-name in one of them. One theory is that Walter Plinge was the name of a stage-struck pub landlord from near the Theatre Royal, Drury Lane, London, in the nineteenth century. Having his name used like this was the nearest he ever got to appearing on stage.

The equivalent American expression is 'George Spelvin'.

... ROYAL 'WE'?

See *Royal*.

... SOMETHING IS A *WELLINGTON*?

The first Duke of Wellington (1769–1852) most famously gave his name to Wellington boots – which is what we now call waterproof (usually rubber) boots that come up to the knee. Originally it referred to a military boot that came over the knee but was cut-away behind or to a short boot worn under the trousers. The name had stuck within a year or two of the Battle of Waterloo in 1815.

So great was the duke's fame that his name has also been bestowed upon: a coat, a hat, trousers, a cooking apple, a bomber, a chest of drawers, a term in card-playing, a public school, and, as 'Wellingtonia', a coniferous tree.

... *WELSH RAREBIT*?

... when the dish should really be called 'Welsh rabbit'?

Firstly, what is the dish? It is melted cheese and butter mixed with seasoning and poured over buttered toast. The *SOED* finds it being called 'Welsh rabbit' by 1725, but 'rarebit' by 1785. It describes this process as 'etymologizing', i.e. someone too learned for his own good, finding that the dish had nothing literal to do with rabbit, had turned its name into something more sensible.

But why 'Welsh rabbit' in the first place? Well, Bombay duck is a fish and mock-turtle soup has nothing to do with turtles (it is made from calf's head), so why not?

... *WENDY* AS A GIRL'S NAME?

The name was invented by J.M. Barrie and given to a character in his play *Peter Pan* (1904). A friend of Barrie's was the poet, W.E.

Henley who, indeed, used to call him 'Friend'. Henley's daughter, four-year-old Margaret, echoed this but, unable to pronounce her r's, distorted it to 'My Fwiendy' or 'Fwendy-Wendy'. Margaret died at the age of six, but her name lives on through the play, and the subsequent novel, and all the 'Wendy' houses that followed.

... GONE *WEST*?
See *gone*.

... COULDN'T RUN A *WHELK-STALL*?
See *couldn't*.

... *WHISTLE DOWN THE WIND*?
Encountering the author Mary Hayley Bell in 1980, I asked her about the title of her story *Whistle Down the Wind* from which the 1961 film was made. She said that it was not consciously a quotation but that Len Deighton had told her the line occurred in Shakespeare's *Othello*. Indeed, it does, at III.iii.266: 'I'd whistle her off and let her down the wind' – a metaphor from falconry. Indeed, in falconry you release a hawk down or with the wind when turning it loose, whereas you send it into or against the wind when it is pursuing prey. From this use, comes the figurative expression meaning 'to cast off lightly'.

I have since discovered that 'to whistle down the wind' was something to be avoided on board ship. The superstition was that whistling, because it sounded like the wind, could raise the wind, as if by magic. (Whistling backstage at the theatre is also said to bring bad luck.)

... A GREAT HOPE IS A *WHITE HOPE*?
Jack Johnson (1908–15) was the first Black to be World Heavyweight Boxing Champion. A 'white hope' was, originally, a white boxer who might have been able to beat Johnson. From there, the phrase came to refer to anyone who might be able to bring about a much-desired end and upon whom hopes were centred.

... GRASS *WIDOW*?
See *grass*.

... SOW ONE'S *WILD OATS*?
See *sows*.

... *I WILL*?
See *I do*.

... SOMETHING GIVES US THE *WILLIES*?
i.e. frightens us, makes us nervous. The *Concise Oxford* has '19th century, origin unknown'; the *OED Supp.* suggests that the expression comes from the US. My only small offering is to point out that in *Giselle*, the ballet with music by Adam (Paris, 1841) there are spirits called *Wilis*. In fact, the ballet's full title is *Giselle, ou les Wilis* (... or the Wilis.) The Wilis are spirits of maidens who die before their marriage. If there is no connection, it seems an odd coincidence.

... A WEAK PERSON IS A *WIMP*?
Like 'wally' (q.v.), this word had a vogue in the early 1980s. Jilly Cooper defined it thus in the *Mail on Sunday* (9 May 1982): 'Wimp is US slang for men who have become increasingly wet, indecisive and lacking in male virility, because their confidence has been shattered by the feminist.'

But, of course, the word had existed for a while before this connotation accrued. The *OED Supp.* states that 'wimp' is of American origin, finds an example in 1920, and suggests an origin derived from 'whimper' (which sounds plausible). Partridge claimed a Cambridge, England use *c*.1909.

In 1981, in Aberdeen, I observed a football graffito which declared, 'Spurs OK – ye wimps', making me wonder whether 'wimp' like 'wally' was another Scottish coinage. But the American explanation holds, I think.

'... *WOMEN AND CHILDREN FIRST!*'?
HMS *Birkenhead* was one of the first warships to have a hull of iron. In 1852 she was taking 476 British soldiers to the eighth 'Kaffir War' in the Eastern Cape of South Africa when she ran aground 50 miles off the Cape of Good Hope. It was clear that the ship would go under but only three of the eight lifeboats could be used and these were rapidly filled with the twenty women and

children on board. According to tradition, the soldiers remained calm and did not even break ranks when the funnel and mast crashed down on to the deck. 445 lives were lost but the tradition of 'women and children' first was born. In naval circles, this is still known as the Birkenhead Drill.

... PULL THE *WOOL OVER ONE'S EYES*?
See *pull*.

... *WORLD WAR I AND II*?
It was known at first as 'The European War', then quite rapidly it became known as 'The Great War'. By 10 September 1918, Lieut.-Colonel C.A. Court Repington was describing it in his diary as the 'First World War':

I saw Major Johnstone, the Harvard Professor who is here to lay the bases of an American History. We discussed the right name for the war. I said that we called it now *The* War, but that this could not last. The Napoleonic War was *The Great War*. To call it *The German War* was too much flattery for the Boche. I suggested *The World War* as a shade better title, and finally we mutually agreed to call it *The First World War* in order to prevent the millenium folk from forgetting that the history of the world was the history of war.

Repington's book entitled *The First World War 1914–18* was published in 1920, ominously suggesting that the Great War had been merely the first of what might turn into a series.

They did not call it 'the Second World War' straightaway for the simple reason that it was, like the First, initially confined to Europe. Even so, *Time* mentioned the prospect of 'World War II' as early as June 1939 and, in its edition dated 11 September 1939, stated confidently: 'World War II began last week at 5.20 a.m. (Polish time) Friday September 1, when a German bombing plane dropped a projectile on Puck, fishing village and air base in the armpit of the Hel Peninsula.'

When the conflagration quite clearly *was* a world war, in 1942, President Roosevelt tried to find an alternative name for it. After rejecting 'Teutonic Plague' and 'Tyrants' War' he settled for 'The War of Survival'. But it did not catch on. Finally, in 1945, the American *Federal Register* announced that, with the approval of President Truman, the late unpleasantness was to be known as 'World War II'.

Y

... *YE OLDE TEA SHOPPE*?

The form 'ye olde' (pronounced 'yee oldee') has become the conventional way of evoking and reproducing the speech and writing of English earlier than, say, 1600.

It is, however, based on a misconception that the letter 'þ' that appears on old manuscripts is the equivalent of the modern 'y'. In fact, 'þ' – known to philologists as the letter 'thorn' in Old English and Icelandic – is pronounced with a 'th' sound. Thus, even in Anglo-Saxon times, however peculiar some pronunciations might have been, 'þ' would still have been pronounced like modern 'the'. 'Ye' did, of course, exist as the second person pronoun.

... SOLDIERS GO *YOMPING*?

This word became general knowledge from its use by Royal Marines during the 1982 Falklands campaign. It means to march over difficult terrain carrying heavy equipment. Clearly, it is akin to the word 'stomp' which means much the same thing. But one explanation is that it is like 'yump', a Scandinavian pronunciation of 'jump', familiar in motor rallying where Scandinavian drivers predominate. It is used to describe the action of a car that takes a corner at high speed and leaves the ground.

... 'I HAVEN'T SEEN HIM FOR *YONKS*'?

See *donkey's years*.

... A MAN IS A *YOUNG FOGEY*?

– meaning he is below the age of 40 but dresses and behaves as if he were prematurely middle-aged. The species was fashionable

223

from 1984 onwards, although observed and commented on as early as the 1920s.

In *The Young Fogey Handbook* (edited by Suzanne Lowry, 1985), the turning-point in the observation of the species is said to have been an article by Alan Watkins in the *Spectator* in May 1984. The Young Fogey, he wrote, 'is libertarian but not liberal. He is a conservative but hasn't time for Mrs Thatcher ... He is a scholar of Evelyn Waugh. He tends to be coolly religious ... He makes a great deal of fuss about the old prayer book, grammar, syntax and punctuation ... he enjoys walking, and travelling by train.'

Earlier uses of the term appear in John Wain's autobiography *Sprightly Running* (1958) and a Dornford Yates novel, *Maiden Stakes* (1929). The *OED Supp.* even manages to turn up a use in 1909.

... YUPPIES?

i.e. young urban professional. In the late 1970s and the 1980s there seemed to be a never-ending stream of journalistic coinages designed to identify select groups – 'Sloane Rangers' and 'Young Fogeys' in the UK, 'Preppies' in the US, and so on. Sometimes the names endured, sometimes they did not. Each group had to have a 'handbook' published about it as soon as it came up. It seemed that people actively *needed* such labels to stick on others.

'Yuppie' came up in 1984 and, at this distance, three years later, it seems to have stuck. It came originally from the US and was first noticed in the UK because of Piesman & Hartley's *The Yuppie Handbook*. Whether the authors coined the word, I am not sure. It featured prominently in reports of Senator Gary Hart's bid for the Democratic nomination in the 1984 presidential race. He and his supporters seemed to belong to the Yuppie tendency. The launch of the word was slightly confused by the similar-sounding 'yumpie', standing for 'young upwardly-mobile people', which arose at the same time. At this distance one can say that 'yuppie' is winning out over 'yumpie'.